the

Beneficiary

the

Beneficiary

Fortune, Misfortune, and the Story of My Father

Janny Scott

RIVERHEAD BOOKS
New York
2019

RIVERHEAD BOOKS
An imprint of Penguin Random House LLC
penguinrandomhouse.com

Photograph credits appear on pages 269–70.

Library of Congress Cataloging-in-Publication Data
Names: Scott, Janny, author.
Title: The beneficiary : fortune, misfortune, and the story of my father / Janny Scott.
Description: New York : Riverhead Books, 2019. | Includes bibliographical references.
Identifiers: LCCN 2018029516 (print) | LCCN 2018052501 (ebook) |
ISBN 9780698195752 (E-book) | ISBN 9781594634192 (hardcover)
Subjects: LCSH: Scott, Robert Montgomery, 1929–2005. |
Scott, Janny—Family. | Philadelphia (Pa.)—Biography.
Classification: LCC F158.54.S36 (ebook) | LCC F158.54.S36 S36 2019 (print) |
DDC 974.8/11043092 [B] —dc23
LC record available at https://lccn.loc.gov/2018029516

Printed in the United States of America
1   3   5   7   9   10   8   6   4   2

Book design by Cassandra Garruzzo

For Mia and Owen

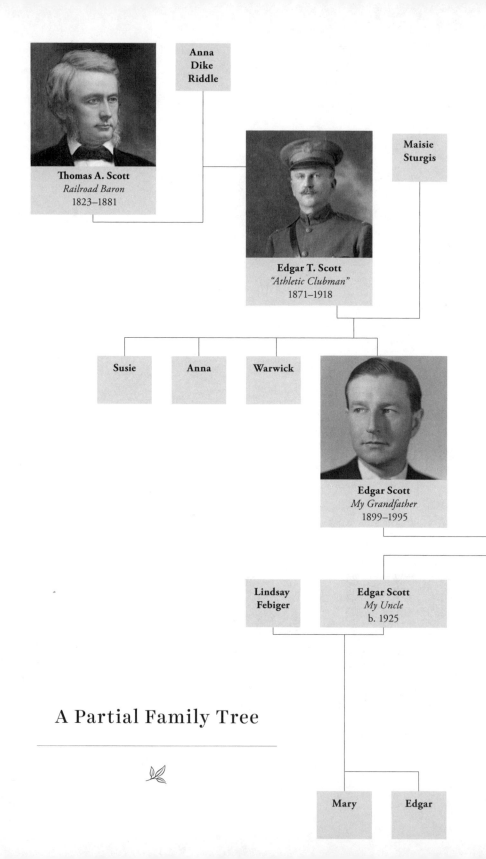

Anna Dike Riddle

Thomas A. Scott
Railroad Baron
1823–1881

Maisie Sturgis

Edgar T. Scott
"Athletic Clubman"
1871–1918

Susie

Anna

Warwick

Edgar Scott
My Grandfather
1899–1995

Lindsay Febiger

Edgar Scott
My Uncle
b. 1925

A Partial Family Tree

Mary

Edgar

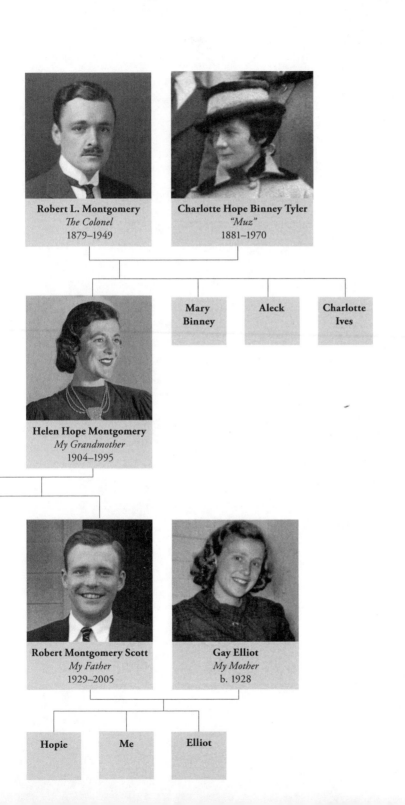

Robert L. Montgomery
The Colonel
1879–1949

Charlotte Hope Binney Tyler
"Muz"
1881–1970

Mary Binney

Aleck

Charlotte Ives

Helen Hope Montgomery
My Grandmother
1904–1995

Robert Montgomery Scott
My Father
1929–2005

Gay Elliot
My Mother
b. 1928

Hopie

Me

Elliot

"There are two parts of me"—yes, he had been moved to go on. "One is made up of the history, the doings, the marriages, the crimes, the follies, the boundless *bêtises* of other people—especially of their infamous waste of money that might have come to me. Those things are written—literally in rows of volumes, in libraries; are as public as they're abominable. Everybody can get at them, and you've, both of you, wonderfully looked them in the face. But there's another part, very much smaller doubtless, which, such as it is, represents my single self, the unknown, unimportant—unimportant save to *you*—personal quantity. About this you've found out nothing."

"Luckily, my dear," the girl had bravely said; "for what then would become, please, of the promised occupation of my future?"

—Henry James, *The Golden Bowl*

Chapter One

On a rainy October afternoon in the early years of the twenty-first century, in the prosperous suburbs that roll west from Philadelphia along what was once the Pennsylvania Railroad's main line, a crowd gathered at a church, founded three hundred years earlier as an outpost of the Church of England, to mark the untimely passing of the Duke of Villanova. After the service, in which men mumbling incantations dispensed wafers and wine to congregants lined up before the altar, the crowd spilled from the church, dispersed into cars, and bolted for what many must have anticipated would be the Duke's final bash. Vehicles lurched out of the parking lot, accelerating past the mossy churchyard where his ashes lay freshly deposited beneath a blanket of mud. A conga line of SUVs, hybrids, and limousines soon stretched the entire two-mile route to the reception, which, as everyone in that crowd could have guessed, was to take place in the fifty-room hilltop pile that had served as headquarters for the deceased's family for ninety-one years. The house had acquired a certain mystique in those parts, not merely for the hundreds of acres of rolling fields and woods over which it still presided at a time when single acres in the area were going for a quarter of a million dollars, but for the predilection of its owners, through three long-lived generations, for carrying on in a vivid, anach-ronistic style, and for throwing some unforgettable parties.

The route from the church that afternoon wound past the traces of a vanishing past, when fortunes made from sugar refining, liquor distilling, and the condensing of soup had made possible the creation, a century earlier, of dozens of country estates modeled unapologetically on those of the British. Most had flourished for a generation, maybe two, before taxation, the Depression, and dynastic vicissitudes did them in. Manor houses, baronial in scale, were hastily demolished or unloaded onto colleges and schools. Some survived as the stately centerpieces of retirement communities, adrift in an archipelago of villas. Where lawns had once spread, present-day palazzi sprouted. Pharm Belt millionaires, flush with profits from the sale of antidepressants and statins, poured in. As the old road from the church dipped and wove, the procession rumbled past home-security-system signs, duck ponds, and the occasional vestigial stone gatepost bearing the name of one more family in the latter stages of being forgotten.

At the top of a hill a mile from the church, cars climbed to a T intersection and slowed to a stop, their drivers idling for a moment to peer down the other side of the hill for oncoming traffic. Beyond the road, a panorama spread before them like the backdrop of some enormous outdoor stage at opening curtain. To the left of the road, a hayfield plunged and majestically rose, its contours undulating like ocean swells. Beyond it, a pasture spilled toward the horizon; another, beyond that. To the right of the road, a cornfield sloped downhill toward the dark margin of a wood. A farm road arced through the rows of khaki stubble. No driver that afternoon, pausing, could have missed the sight—the northeast corner of the largest piece of open land left in the township, vast enough in its golden era to have spanned four unincorporated communities. Each car idled for a moment, then pressed on, accelerating across the opposite lane onto a long, straight road that ran alongside a stone wall stretching as far as one could see. Near the wall's midpoint, a high, wrought-iron gate interrupted the ribbon of gray stone. Cars slowed, turned, and glided through the entrance to the place.

There was no dukedom, of course. The title was a private joke, deployed by his wife and children in moments of exasperation with flights of grandiosity now long forgotten. My sister and brother and I used it mockingly but not without affection; we'd never have let it slip in his presence. He'd been cast in a role in life, which he seemed to have embraced out of duty, filial devotion, family pride. That he'd played the part to acclaim was evident in the funeral turnout, which included people from the dozen and a half cultural and civic institutions in and around Philadelphia that he'd served—all listed on the back page of the program. There were museum curators, philanthropists, smaller donors, musicians, newspaper reporters, men and women who'd spent their lives working in the houses and barns of his grandparents and parents. There were a few rubberneckers, too. He wouldn't have minded; he'd have been flattered. In his later years, he'd taken to sending us copies of articles about himself clipped from city magazines and local newspapers, which never tired of him as a subject. For all their well-intentioned fawning, it seemed to me, journalists rarely got him right. He'd mail out copies anyway, with a note on a Post-it affixed, simultaneously self-mocking and pleased. He knew as well as we did, maybe better, what the scribblers missed. He'd been catching sight of himself for years, as though brought up short by his reflection in a store window. To the extent that his performance was sometimes over the top, he'd never quite managed to look the other way.

A few months before his death, he'd been the guest of honor at a dinner at a private club in the center of Philadelphia, one of those once all-male establishments with a brownstone-and-brick clubhouse and a venerable history dating back to the Civil War. Tuxedoed, with a cabernet-colored waistcoat and a black bow tie, he'd been maneuvered, in a wheelchair, onto the dais to be presented with a slab of glass recognizing his manifest contributions to the arts. He'd been drinking since morning. His face, perpetually boyish, had become, in his last years, blotchy and swollen. His blue eyes, habitually merry, looked watery with pain. Organs were failing. Arthritis had corroded the joints in his knees.

Several hundred friends, former colleagues, civic leaders, and family members watched with curiosity, sympathy, and some trepidation the wheelchair's progress up a wooden ramp onto the stage. The pilot, who was employed by my father and had become something of a surrogate son in those years, pivoted the chair to face the room, locked the brakes, and withdrew. Then, like a man on a high wire, the seventy-six-year-old honoree launched into his acceptance speech. He was winging it, it seemed, lofting sentences out over the heads of the audience—clauses looping, hovering, teetering—and reeling in his catch, hooked by his weather-bitten charm and occasionally self-lacerating humor.

"When I was told that I was being given the Crystal Award," he growled, eyes twinkling, "I thought, 'Perfect. You can see right through it.'"

The line of cars on the driveway dipped through a wood, rumbled over a stone bridge, and came to a place where two approaches to the house intersected. To the left, plane trees made a canopy over a curving drive. To the right, a lane descended through a cow pasture toward a cluster of barns. Straight ahead, atop a small hill, one could make out through the trees the slate roof, stone-trimmed gables, and Palladian dormers of a large English Renaissance Revival–style house. Parking attendants were commandeering cars, racing them back up the driveway, parking in an adjacent field. Guests arriving through a second gate were bailing out of their cars and setting off toward the house in the drizzle. A trolley, leased for the occasion, was shuttling people to the foot of the final hill. From there, they trudged uphill toward a paved circle blanketed in butter-colored pebbles, and entered the house through a massive, double front door.

Inside, the atmosphere was not exactly sepulchral. A large crowd, roaring and chattering, filled a long, walnut-paneled, transverse hall that ran the full width of the main body of the house. To the left of the entrance, a capacious alcove had been converted into an open bar. Ten bartenders stood by, provisioned with what looked like enough booze

to fuel a political convention. Through a set of doors at one end of the hall, waiters beetled from a bustling pantry, maneuvering trays of hors d'oeuvres past the stuffed head of a moose and into the stream of guests. In the dining room, a table, designed to seat thirty, groaned under a payload of hams, seafood, platters heaped with slabs of rare steak. When I try to summon the specifics of that event all these years later, all that comes to mind is a blurry impression of excess. Someone had chosen to believe that seven hundred mourners might turn up, all in the mood for a hearty, multicourse meal at four in the afternoon. Out of the corner of one eye, I could swear I caught sight of a bubbling fountain of melted chocolate. I know for sure that I glimpsed a slab of something, chessboard-size but thicker, the color of cream, embossed with a heraldic shield bearing the first letter of the name of the family or the house. Butter, really?

In the fogbound days between the death and the funeral, the call had gone out to the usual catering company—one that, I now know, had enjoyed a lock on the family's entertainment budget going back to Prohibition. (The founder had been a bootlegger back then; the family, an energetically convivial client with abundant social and political connections.) Arrangements for the reception had been made in grief and haste, a contract signed, perhaps a deposit made. But when the bill landed like a stink bomb sometime later, no one could quite remember having signed off on a banquet of blowout proportions. Economizing had not been my father's style in his declining years. To be fair, the caterers may have known exactly what he'd have wanted. Then again, they may have sensed in his death the end of an era—justification, albeit self-interested, for going for broke one last time. That evening, after the reception was over and the house had gone quiet, my mother, living alone nearby, received an unexpected visit from members of the catering crew. Because her marriage to my father had lasted forty-two years before the two of them had called it quits, the caterers were not strangers. Could she use a few leftovers? they wondered. (A ham, maybe? Six dozen rolls?) She couldn't. A few weeks later, my brother, sister, and I, as executors of our father's will, balked at the caterer's bill and tried drop-kicking it back. The total, after all, exceeded the median household income in the country that year. Not including the $8,200 tip.

Counterintuitively, that house was in better shape on the day of the funeral than it had been during most of my father's lifetime. He'd spent what had proved to be his final years in a protracted, low-grade fever of restoration, lavishing his attention and inherited money on a white elephant whose days, an outside observer might have declared with certainty, were surely numbered. When my parents' marriage had ended, my father had moved out of the fieldstone house where they'd lived together for forty years and into the nursery on the third floor of the even bigger house where his mother had grown up. For a sum that he said exceeded what his grandparents had spent to build the entire house, he'd restored the eighty-year-old slate roof. Next, he'd converted the nursery into a flat for his newly singled self: two living rooms, a dining room, library, kitchen, master bedroom, two guest rooms, two bathrooms. Then he'd set his sights on the ground floor, which had been uninhabited for a decade and a half, used only for occasional weddings, parties, and charitable events. He'd ended up restoring every one of the public rooms on the ground floor with no less attention to detail than would befit a curator of period rooms at the Philadelphia Museum of Art, where he'd been the president and chief executive officer for fourteen years. Ceilings were repaired, light fixtures rewired, draperies reproduced, paintings cleaned and lit. A carpet, bigger than a tennis court, was custom woven for the living room; a round-trip ticket was purchased to send the ballroom rug across the Atlantic for rehabilitation. Furniture was dismantled, rebuilt, refinished, and reupholstered. Needlepoint sofa covers were removed, cleaned, and reapplied. Smoke stains were scrubbed from limestone walls. Plaster walls were not simply restored but "underrestored" to allow the house to look like "the beautiful old lady that she is," as my father put it. The work was scrupulous, no expense spared.

The scale of the undertaking was bewildering—not least because the house didn't belong to my father. It was held by a trust set up by his grandfather, the beneficiaries of which were the members of succeeding generations who numbered in the dozens. Because the trust lacked the cash to keep up with the decay, the manse and everything in it had been deteriorating for years. No one had occupied it in its entirety for a quarter of a century. A cousin of mine was living with her partner and their daughter on the second floor, raising bull terriers in a kennel on the lawn and running a dog-training school out of the basement. My father, from his lair in the nursery, bankrolled most of the restoration out of his own pocket. Privately, more than one of his cousins wondered how he could afford it. He spoke of the house, in those years, with a tone of fond indulgence, as though it were an aging family member with a colorful history deserving deference. "This house loves a party: It was built with entertaining in mind," he'd say, squiring astonished visitors from room to room. "Something like this is too wonderful to let disappear. It represents the last of its kind." Which, incidentally, was not unlike the way he allowed himself to be presented—as the last of a breed on the cusp of extinction. As the years rolled by, the big house, as it was known in the family, looked better and better. Its benefactor, truth be told, looked worse and worse.

By his final Thanksgiving, the contrast between the two was alarming. Some years earlier, my father had begun hosting a Thanksgiving feast on a grand scale in the dining room on the ground floor. To maximize attendance by avoiding any scheduling conflicts with other family members' Thanksgiving festivities, he staged his banquet on the Friday evening after. With each passing year, the guest list grew longer. The acceptance rate was high, in light of the host and the venue: Soon he was feeding nearly one hundred relatives and friends. There were descendants of his maternal grandfather's generation, in which there had been eleven siblings. Cousins on his father's side traveled from Washington and Maine. To summon the troops to the table, he hired a bagpiper in kilt, sporran, kilt hose, and clan accessories. He choreographed the seating on sheets of yellow legal-pad paper. Children cantered along the transverse hall and darted up and down the broad staircase, running their pink palms along its pierced balustrade to where it terminated in finials carved into baskets of fruit. With the dining-room table extended to its capacity, smaller tables filled the rest of the room and spilled into a limestone-walled conservatory next door. The host, red-faced and congenial, seated himself in the middle of one side of the big table, his back to the fireplace beneath a portrait of an august ancestor who'd served for a time in Congress. On his right, he'd seat an aged aunt or other especially honored guest. Across the table, he'd station younger women whom he wanted in his line of sight. On his final Thanksgiving, as his guests circulated through the ground-floor rooms, admiring the polished marquetry chests and a pair of gilded and newly restored Rococo mirrors, he made his entrance late, in a wheelchair, his skin ravaged. Before dessert was over, he asked to be wheeled upstairs on the rattling, sixty-five-year-old Otis elevator; pushed down the long, carpeted hall of the nursery; steered into his bedroom with its oriel window framing the blue-black sky; and helped out of his party clothes and into bed.

In the origin stories, my father's grandfather was the great progenitor. It was said that he'd fallen from a horse on a hilltop in a section of Radnor Township then called Villa Nova while foxhunting sometime around the turn of the twentieth century. He was knocked unconscious, the story went, but promptly recovered. Coming to, he found himself captivated by the spot, with its three-hundred-sixty-degree views of farmland dotted with houses and barns. He resolved to buy the land and build a house to match the scale of his ambition. He was a young investment banker, present at the birth of a new era in the country's industrialization; he'd made a propitious marriage to the daughter of a wealthy, well-connected Philadelphia banker. So he hired the go-to architect to plutocrats of the day. He named the estate Ardrossan, after a town and a castle in southwestern Scotland left behind by his ancestors. He installed nine Ayrshire cows, imported from Scotland, in his dairy barn, and seven mares and a prizewinning stallion from Ireland in his broodmare stables. He hired young immigrants newly arrived from Sweden, Ireland, Switzerland, and France to milk his cows, mow his meadows, drive his cars, clean his house, cook and serve meals for his growing family. Annexing surrounding farms, he soon presided over some eight hundred acres. With the help of French governesses, he and his wife brought up four children in the house. Three of the children married, moved into houses on the property, and reared children of their own, who, in turn, followed suit. By the early 1950s, there were four generations of my father's family living on an estate roughly the size of Central Park, located a half hour's drive from the center of the fourth largest city in the country. It was a nineteenth-century British estate, plucked from the pages of Jane Austen or Henry James, floated across the Atlantic, and wedged in among swimming pools of John Updike and John Cheever. The place—which is what family members called it, applying the blandest of generics to something increasingly sui generis—comprised dozens of houses, a half dozen barns, stables, carriage houses, garages, silos, an ice house, a root cellar, several swimming pools, tennis courts, a kennel, and a couple of one-room schoolhouses, in one of which my grandfather, an aspiring playwright for a time, had labored over the only play of his that, I'm told, he ever got produced. The run is said to have lasted three nights.

As a child growing up there, I couldn't have told you which direction was north. I'd never seen the place on a map or seen an aerial photograph of the patchwork of farms, fields, and woods that stretched away from our house into the distance as far as I could see. I'd never wondered who'd built the stone houses where my grandparents and aunts and uncles lived, or the stone barns where hay bales were stacked to the rafters. I'm sure I never thought to ask who'd come before us in that place—people with names, like Abraham and Sayen, which lived on, attached to a lane or a barn or a quarry, the way words live on in the language long after their original meaning has been forgotten. In the big house, where my widowed great-grandmother still received visitors over tea or cocktails in late afternoon, portraits hung in every room on the ground floor, but I could never make out in those faces any suggestion of ours.

A portrait of the founding father, my great-grandfather, hung over a fireplace in an oak-paneled living room roughly the size of a modest automobile showroom. Chandeliers hung from a thirteen-foot-high, sculpted-plaster ceiling. A set of French doors opened onto a terrace that led to a broad lawn, fields, a wooded hillside beyond. For his portrait, the patriarch had chosen to wear formal riding habit: scarlet hunting jacket, white vest, stock, cream-colored breeches, knee-high leather boots. In his lap lay a silk top hat, gloves, and a coiled whip. The red jacket leaped from the canvas. His short, dark hair showed signs of graying; his eyebrows were thick and perfectly shaped; a small mustache seemed to hover unusually high above his upper lip. His dark gaze and set jaw suggested a forceful confidence, or perhaps insistence, about his place in the world. The surprise, which slightly softened the impression left by the picture, was a liquid shimmer in his large, dark eyes. Though everyone referred to him, a half century after his death, as the Colonel, I never heard anyone explain why.

If the scale of the house and its setting had been intended to make a statement about the Colonel's ambitions, the ubiquitous portraits were surely meant to make a point about the family's history. A seventeenth-century Scottish baronet in a suit of armor, with a voluminous russet mane enveloping his head and shoulders like a fur hood, was the subject of a portrait in the living room. The nineteenth-century member of Congress—a double-duty forebear, claimed by both the Colonel and his wife, who were second cousins—had top billing in the dining room over the mantel. A woman in a lacy headpiece peered from the wall under the light of the silvered lanterns hanging from the ceiling in the long hall. Two well-fed, eighteenth-century brothers with ponytails and muttonchop sideburns faced each other from either side of the living room's French doors. Some of the portraits had been inherited; many had been purchased or commissioned. As the rest of the country tumbled and slouched into the Great Depression, the Colonel sought out the biggest names in European portraiture and shipped off each child, in his or her late teens or twenties, to be painted, three of them across the Atlantic.

Of particular interest to me here is the Colonel's spirited, willful eldest—the captivating character who, more than anyone else, left her imprint, I now see, in the impressionable clay of the child I'd later know as my father. In another time and place, Helen Hope Montgomery might have been one of those outsize women politicians from a place like, say, Texas. She was charming, flirtatious, disciplined, competitive, driven. The only thing she feared, my father once said, was failure. Her formal education, at a girls' boarding school in Virginia that admitted horses along with their owners, had been fleeting; she'd been raised for other things, as she readily acknowledged, like succeeding at parties and marrying well. If there'd been SATs in those subjects, my father's mother would have been a National Merit Scholar. In one evening, at one party, at the age of eighteen, she's said to have fielded (and tossed back) four marriage proposals. A year later, she married the urbane, literary-minded, theater-besotted grandson of a nineteenth-century railroad baron who'd given a young protégé named Andrew Carnegie his start. She went on to become an accomplished horsewoman, able to checkmate even the most highly strung of chargers. She rebuilt her father's declining dairy herd into the highest-producing Ayrshire herd of its size in the country. A connoisseur of filthy jokes and racy stories, she once bought a horse from a friend for a pound of caviar and a dirty story every week for a year. Society columnists and feature writers, whose care and feeding she'd mastered, stopped by regularly to burnish her image. They'd stagger back to their keyboards enchanted, professing amazement at how approachable, how down-to-earth, how earthy she was. By the 1950s, my grandmother—whom I knew, improbably, as Granny—shared her father's estate with her widowed mother, her brother, her sons, and various nieces and nephews. But in the local imagination, the place belonged to her.

Her celebrity, and that's what it was, arose in part from her connection to the 1939 Broadway play that had revived the languishing career of Katharine Hepburn and turned into one of the most celebrated Hollywood movies of the century. In a playwriting class at Harvard, whose alumni included Eugene O'Neill and S. N. Behrman, my grandfather had met Philip Barry, the Yale-educated son of a marble and tile contractor from Rochester, who would become one of the most successful playwrights of his generation. Barry was, as Brendan Gill, the longtime writer for *The New Yorker*, once put it, "drawn to the rich and well born. To their astonishment, he found them interesting and therefore to be cultivated." When Barry married in the summer of 1922, my rich, well-born grandfather, Edgar Scott, was an usher. Barry and his wife, Ellen, became regular visitors to Ardrossan. And when Barry's sixteenth Broadway play opened in New York in 1939, with Hepburn starring as a spoiled Main Line heiress, Tracy Lord, the dedication page of the book, *The Philadelphia Story*, read, "To Hope and Edgar Scott." The movie, released the following year, won six Academy Award nominations, two Academy Awards, and a place on the American Film Institute's list of the top hundred American movies ever made. By the 1980s, my father's mother was rarely mentioned in print without it being said that she was the model or the inspiration for Tracy Lord. When she died in 1995, her obituary was stripped across the top of the front page of the *Philadelphia Inquirer*. "Main Line Socialite Hope Montgomery Scott Dies at 90," read the headline, in very large type. The death of Pope John Paul II some years later got only marginally better play.

A framed photograph of Helen Hope in her midforties resided on a table in the ballroom of the big house. In the photograph, taken by the fashion photographer Horst P. Horst for *Vogue*, she stands in the same ballroom, to the right of her portrait. She's wearing a Dior evening dress with a strapless bodice, a tulip skirt, and a stylishly uneven hem positioned to allow an unobstructed view of her left calf. A greyhound, on a leather leash held in her left hand, presses against her. A choker made of four strands of small pearls rings her neck; a matching bracelet rings one wrist. Her bare shoulders and arms are those of a woman two decades younger. Her dark hair, worn with bangs in the tomboy style she favored, frames a heart-shaped face, turned slightly away from the camera, eyebrows raised, lips parted in a smile. She appears to be listening in rapt attention to someone just outside the frame. It's an expression I remember—an alertness to the possibility of fun. To anyone on the receiving end, it was flattering: She could count on you, of all people, to give her a laugh. It was also intimidating: What if you bombed? Once, after I'd regaled her with the details of an unplanned escapade of my own involving a college-visiting trip, a detour to a boys' school, and a scandalized housemaster at 2:00 A.M., she rewarded me with the roaring-laughter equivalent of a standing ovation. She'd been caught, two generations earlier, in a rumble seat, she said, with the grandfather of my accomplice.

My father was the second of Hope and Edgar's two sons. They named him Robert Montgomery Scott, after the Colonel, who was Robert Leaming Montgomery. He grew up in his parents' farmhouse on his grandparents' place, surrounded by pastures studded with apple trees, and approached by a honeysuckle-lined driveway. He attended the school that his maternal great-grandfather had attended. He followed his father and brother and paternal grandfather to a boarding school in Massachusetts and to Harvard. He graduated from the law school that had trained his great-grandfather and took his place in the law firm that his great-uncle had cofounded. He entrusted his money to the stockbrokerage that his grandfather and father had started. And, after marrying within days of graduating from college, he moved with his Boston-bred wife to his family's compound. They settled into a tiny springhouse beside a brook and in a grove of willows, one field away from the house where he'd grown up—just as his mother had settled, twenty-five years earlier, into her farmhouse a mile from the big house and her parents. When my parents outgrew their little house, they moved into a bigger house one field away. My father rode the commuter train into Philadelphia every weekday morning and out in the evenings, often dropping by for a drink with his parents or his widowed grandmother before returning home. When his grandmother died at eighty-nine, leaving the big house empty, he floated the idea of moving in. My mother—already in a three-story house with ten bedrooms, two wine cellars, a cedar closet, three terraces, gardens, a four-car garage with an apartment above it, et cetera—told him that if that was his plan, he'd be moving there alone.

My parents' house stood on the edge of the property like a handsome doorstop on a curling corner of an antique carpet. It had been built from stone that you could imagine being taken many years earlier from the meadows around it. A barely legible date stone suggested that some house, if not exactly the one we lived in, had stood on that spot since the 1700s. Ours dated from the 1820s, with a kitchen wing added by the Colonel's architect a hundred years later. The house had shutters painted a dark green verging on black, a gabled roof, and a symmetrical, ivy-covered facade. We weren't alone in finding it the most beautiful house on the place. In keeping with family tradition, my parents made no down payment, took out no mortgage, paid neither a security deposit nor rent. Just as my great-grandparents had paid my grandparents' rent—collected to help cover the operating costs of the estate—my grandparents covered my parents'. The rent the month they moved in, in 1955, was fifty-five dollars. For the humblest of houses in that area, which was one of the more desirable suburban zones on the East Coast, that price would have been a steal. It was inconceivable for a "nine-bathroom house," which was the shorthand we used years later, after my mother had become its sole inhabitant, to signal that we weren't oblivious to the absurdity of things.

From a southwest-facing dormer window on the third floor, a child could survey the landscape spilling uninterrupted into the distance. Flagstone terraces on two sides of the house led to a lawn framed by a post-and-rail fence and an L-shaped field. Every summer, corn shot up in the field, walling in the lawn and the house with an impenetrable, green palisade. On windless nights, dance music from a country club a few miles away drifted in, along with the distant roar of the occasional car accelerating down a certain long, straight road. Beyond the cornfield stood a stone barn and the springhouse where my parents had lived in the first years of their marriage. Beyond that were pastures and my grandparents' house; beyond that, more fields, woods, streams, stone houses, stone walls, stone bridges, the big house, dairy barns, the ruins of an ice-skating rink, and an abandoned quarry where we sometimes backed up a borrowed pickup truck and sent some obsolete household appliance somersaulting to the bottom. Up until the last years of the twentieth century, it was possible to ramble the mile-and-a-half distance from one end of Ardrossan to the other—through open fields, up and down hills, across streams, through woods—and cross just one public road. On the byways that traced the meandering periphery of the property, the occasional tractor, driven by one of the farmers, slowed rush-hour and carpool-minivan traffic to a crawl.

"What was he like, as a father?" a writer whom I'd admired asked me once, when we first met, having stunned me with the news that he'd known my father in college. My father had been dead a few years at that time. I was out of the habit of bumping into people eager to report that they'd known him, curious to see where that led. There was something unsettling and touching about its happening now, a feeling I associated with awaking out of the rare dream in which he'd made a cameo appearance. I can't recall the words the writer used to describe what he'd observed back then, but I was left with an image of my father roistering in the diffused light of a streetlamp in the small hours, outside one of those private clubs that men who arrive at Harvard from prep schools seem to feel compelled to join for reasons I'll never understand. The writer appeared to have been more acquaintance than friend, but he'd absorbed an impression that hadn't faded in fifty-five years. Because he showed no surprise at my account of the circumstances of my father's death, I wondered whether he'd glimpsed something premonitory back then. Perhaps not. My father caught people's attention. He had qualities they tended not to forget.

I'd once imagined there was something distinctly American about his looks. I now suspect that was a distortion of the sort that led medieval cartographers to inflate their own continents on early maps. He was good-looking enough. I think of him at six feet tall, though the Pennsylvania driver's license in the pocket-polished leather wallet I salvaged from his possessions states unambiguously that he was two inches shorter. To people from other parts of the country, his accent would have sounded British; to some of his antagonists at city hall in Philadelphia, it stunk of privilege. There was something of the perpetual undergraduate in his face. The angles were soft. He was blue-eyed, pink-skinned, buffed. There was nothing exotic or intimidating about his appearance. Strangers occasionally believed he was someone they already knew—a phenomenon he'd attribute to "my lowest-common-denominator face." We had a pet, a plus-size beagle, with an unusual inherited trait: Caught in the act of pretty much anything forbidden, her upper lip recoiled in a disarming, canine version of a shit-eating grin. Even the tone of a mild reprimand, in the absence of any misdemeanor, would set it off. My father did a good imitation of that smile, possibly because the dog's and his had attributes in common. His grin—a flash of big, well-cared-for incisors—was punctuation, ingratiation, a beat for comic effect. He professed to be shy, which I always found curious; if it was true, he certainly seemed to have perfected a convincing imitation of gregariousness and affability. Also odd was his prediction, more than once when I was young, that he'd be dead by fifty. His parents, well past fifty, were showing no signs of slowing. I should mention, too, that he, like his mum, was flirtatious. He flirted with other people's wives, younger women, babysitters, our childhood friends. The sanctity of marriage was not for him. The unspoken message that we absorbed early was that marital fidelity was an option, not an absolute. It was an option he seemed not to have chosen.

But as a father? the writer had asked. An answer wriggled to the surface of a heap of emotional odds and ends: Not like others, that would be safe to say. No watching sports, no tinkering in the basement. In his twenties and thirties, he kept four polished copper hunting horns marshaled in formation on our front-hall table. He had a pack of beagles—as many as three or four dozen—housed in a whitewashed cinder-block kennel near the main dairy. On Sunday afternoons when leaves were turning and the stubble fields teemed with migrating Canada geese, he put on white shorts and dark green wool socks to his knees, a white shirt and a knit tie, a dark green hunting jacket with brass buttons engraved with the image of a hare, and a black velvet cap. At the kennel, he and a handful of like-minded souls loaded a couple dozen dogs into a two-wheeled trailer, hitched it to a Jeep, and towed it to the open countryside to the west. There was an association of people willing to pay modest annual dues for the opportunity to be out in the countryside, get some exercise, and watch hounds hunt. Dozens showed up. In the tussocky fields around places like Chadds Ford, my father was the huntsman, assisted by a team of whip-cracking subalterns to keep the hounds working as a pack. The rest of us followed in a less disciplined pack of our own. The protocol formalized the natural order of things in our family: my father, master of hounds, jogging into the distance, hunting horn in hand, high socks burred, knees bleeding from thorns; the rest of us trudging, milling, chattering, trotting to keep up, left to interpret the horn calls for clues as to what he'd be up to next. A rapid series of pulsating doubled notes—urgent, exhilarating—announced that some unsuspecting rabbit had bolted from its covert into the open, sending the hounds barreling and yelping in pursuit. A long, tremulous, single note marked the moment the creature finally outwitted the hounds by going to ground. The call played at the end of the day, as the sky was turning indigo and the cold was descending, was a mournful wail of longing and regret.

At home, I practiced those calls on the horns arrayed on the front-hall table. I vibrated my lips against the mouthpiece until they felt bruised and tasted of metal. I mastered one hundred sit-ups, memorized the Gettysburg Address, balanced my father's college dictionary on my head. He'd learned to wiggle his ears to catch the eye of the headmaster's daughter who sat behind him in chapel at school; my sister and brother and I learned to wiggle ours, too. I sifted the detritus that accumulated in the saucerlike base of the brass lamp on his chest of drawers: collar stays, ChapStick, Pep O Mint Life Savers, toothpicks, buttons, Chiclets. In the cabinets that lined the pantry, my parents housed hundreds of glasses. Highball glasses, old-fashioned glasses, martini glasses, shot glasses, brandy snifters, champagne flutes, glasses for white wine, for red, for water. I loved the syncopated swing and thwack of the heavy leaden head of the Tap-Icer, with its flexible red metal handle, as it crushed a cube of ice in my hand. With the sleek martini shaker made of brushed stainless steel, I could produce a martini by age twelve. My father had a silver "tasting cup" on a red and gold ribbon for hanging around one's neck. It was the badge of membership of one of the two wine-tasting societies to which he belonged. I pictured portly, red-faced men sitting around, spitting wine onto a stained floor. He had a wine cellar in the basement of our house. I vied for the assignment to take the steep wooden staircase into the basement, pass the small room on the right full of firewood, pass the furnace, run my hand along a high shelf for the hidden key, unlock the door to the wine cellar, and slip in. The place was a hive, dark bottles stacked horizontally in diamond-shaped cubbies made from plywood, or arrayed in racks with cradles for their necks. I learned how to pour wine, twisting the bottle at the last moment to shut off the flow without dripping on the polished mahogany surface of the dining-room table. I became a collector of labels and corks. I lined the stained corks on the pantry windowsill to dry. I ran empty wine bottles under hot water in the sink until the labels slid off like shed skin, then dried them on dish towels. I saved them in a shoe box as though they were paper currency from countries I'd never visited or postage stamps from faraway places like the Republic of Upper Volta.

The year I turned fourteen, we left Ardrossan. A Philadelphia publishing tycoon, appointed ambassador to the United Kingdom by President Richard Nixon, made my father his special assistant at the embassy in London. We moved into a cream-colored town house in Belgravia with a balcony overlooking a garden square. My father took to wearing bespoke suits and striped shirts from the erstwhile shirtmaker to Winston Churchill. He acquired a small-wheeled bicycle that could be collapsed, like a stroller, for stowing on British Rail. He'd ride it from home to Charing Cross Station, take a train to Kent, pedal to Sissinghurst Castle, tour the gardens, return to London for dinner. It was as if he'd been in training since birth for a sojourn in

England. My mother, a pianist, took up the serious study of music. She found a piano teacher, enrolled in music school, and retreated to rehearsal rooms attached to a Renaissance-style recital hall where Arthur Rubinstein had performed. When a burglar found the trick drawer in a highboy in her bedroom and plundered her jewelry, she spent the insurance money on a second piano, on which Boris Goldovsky, the Russian conductor, later played Chopin's Black Key Étude with a grapefruit, rolling it up and down the black keys with his right palm.

By the time my parents returned from England, my sister and brother and I were out of the house. One after another, we went out into the working world. Newspaper jobs took me from Massachusetts to New Jersey, to California, to New York. The anomalousness of my father's family's place, which we'd never reckoned with as children, began, with distance, to come into focus. The place was a curiosity, a marvel, an awkwardness, too. How to explain? Occasionally, asked where I'd grown up, I'd just say on a farm in Pennsylvania, disingenuously leaving it at that. Once, in college, I accepted an offer of a ride home at winter break, from a friend, without thinking it through. He was a brainy, serious-minded, first-generation American. There was a third person in the car, a football player I didn't know at all. We were approaching my parents' house, passing a wall of evergreens through which one could catch sight of the fenced fields beyond. "Where are the slave quarters?" my friend asked, teasing, sort of. "Do you have your own police force?"

I knew the place intimately. I understood it not at all.

As the twentieth century accelerated toward the millennium, Philadelphia tumbled into the throes of fitful metamorphosis. The old manufacturing industries that had built the city and its suburbs were going or gone. The last traces of the Pennsylvania Railroad had vanished in the biggest bankruptcy ever. Power—economic, political, cultural—was shifting. Across the street from my parents, a trucking tycoon with his own football team had moved in and was landing his private helicopter in one of the fields, with my grandmother's permission, until my father begged him to stop. On the commuter rail line, Ethiopian immigrants were reverse commuting from the city to housekeeping jobs in medical offices in Radnor. At the farmers' market in Strafford, where Mennonite women in prayer caps sold lima beans and lamb chops and scrapple, the onetime preponderance of Main Line matrons in pastels and Pappagallo flats was giving way to a somewhat less monochromatic crowd.

The Colonel's place, however, seemed barely to change. The cows, all direct descendants of the original Scottish transplants, still arrived like clockwork at the barn at milking time, sauntering in from the pastures, udders swaying, in languid procession. Helen Hope would be there, too, on most days, giving every cow the once-over. Around the holidays, she distributed turkeys to the farm families, just as her father had done. My father still commuted to work in Philadelphia, sometimes by bike, the lower legs of his suit pants bicycle-clipped to his ankles. On summer nights when I visited, we'd eat outside on the terrace, fireflies flickering in the fading light.

I know now, but didn't then, that the dairy operation was hemorrhaging money. Helen Hope, it seems, had been covering the losses with income from trusts her parents had set up decades before. Sometime around the early 1990s, she asked her eldest son, my father's brother, to examine the books, ostensibly to diagnose the dairy's condition and suggest a cure. Ed was the stockbroker in his generation. Decades earlier, he'd bailed out of Ardrossan and moved an hour away—not long after his mother had delivered to Ed's young wife four pages of instructions on the proper handling of servants. Ed had risen to the top of the brokerage firm in Philadelphia that his father and grandfather had started in the months leading up to the stock market crash in 1929. Now, summoned by his mother, he spent hours going methodically through spreadsheets and bills. When he finished, he'd remember later, he turned to his mother and delivered the bad news.

"Well, Mum," he said. "It looks to me as though it's costing you three dollars to sell a dollar's worth of milk."

His mother looked uncharacteristically grave.

"If I get it down to two fifty," she asked, "can I keep going?"

It wasn't a question. It was her final offer.

A lifetime on horseback had left Helen Hope with steel and plastic replacement joints. A champagne cork, achieving escape velocity, had done serious damage to one of her eyes. A surgeon had managed to repair that, too, as had been done with the other parts. My grandmother didn't worry about dying, she once told me; what she dreaded was outliving. Blessed from birth with every conceivable advantage, she imagined her long-lived self incarcerated at the end in a cradle—snapping, like a disagreeable baby, at passersby. A month after her ninetieth birthday, she was in a horse-show ring on the back of a long-horn steer, a barrel of muscle on four legs, with a pair of horns like the wingspan of a condor. In a photo taken of her that day, she's wearing form-fitting slacks and a black knit shirt, her physique shown to advantage. Around that time, a nephew of hers, living in a house next to one of the dairy barns on Ardrossan, encountered her touring the barn with the operations manager for the farm. Helen Hope had a bandage on her forehead and a black eye. Because she didn't mention it, her nephew didn't either. But after she'd rumbled off in her Jeep Wagoneer, he asked the farm manager what had happened. Oh, that, the manager said. She'd stopped by one of the barns on her way to a cocktail party in a tight skirt and had taken a header while vaulting a sewage pit.

It was surprising, then, that Helen Hope was one of the first of her generation to go. My grandfather, five years older, appeared to be in worse shape. He passed his days in a yellow-slipcovered armchair near a bay window in the house—memories, in improbable combinations, clattering in his head like old newsreel footage in an ancient projector. Sometimes he was in a grand hotel in Paris where the service, regrettably, was slipping; no one at the front desk was picking up.

Sometimes he was certain some French cousins were arriving in Philadelphia any moment; he needed to meet their boat—the *Mauretania*. My grandmother, by contrast, showed few signs of flagging. The day before she died, in January 1995, her young property manager had arrived early and led her horses and donkeys from her stable to her fields. He'd carried the Sunday newspapers from the driveway into the house, where he'd found Helen Hope in the kitchen, standing beside the stainless-steel-topped table, gazing out the bay window as the temperature rose above freezing. He'd offered to return in the afternoon to bring the animals back into the barn.

"No," he'd remember her telling him. "It's a beautiful day. I'd like to bring them in."

One day later, Helen Hope was dead. Her sister followed her by three months, and Edgar one month after that.

What happened next is the thing I've found hardest to fathom. My father had been the beneficiary of extraordinary good fortune. It wasn't only the privileged life into which he and the rest of us had been born; he'd found work that he loved and for which he was treasured. He'd had the company of his parents for sixty-five years. One might have imagined he'd carry on cheerfully for another thirty, then fade out in midflashback, like his father, at ninety-six, or pop off briskly, like his mother, at ninety, after perhaps a fall from his bicycle and a timely blow to the head. But that wasn't how it went. In the ten years that followed their deaths, my father's marriage dissolved, his job ended, and his health imploded. He spent so much money restoring the big house, which he didn't own, that, when he died at seventy-six, the former trusts and estates lawyer left his estate in something of a shambles. He passed his final days in an intensive care unit, too sick to be transported fifteen minutes home, where he'd hoped to die. His life ended up twenty years shorter than his father's, fourteen shorter than his mother's. Even his grandmother—born the year of the shootout at the O.K. Corral, and middle-aged before the invention of vaccines—had lasted longer than her grandson. I admit I had a selfish interest—a child's interest—in his survival. But I couldn't help feeling he'd made a choice to lop twenty years off his life, and that he'd done it for reasons I'd never understand.

Once, many years earlier, he'd astounded me by promising a rare open window into himself. He told me he intended to leave me his journals when he died. It was no secret that he kept them; he'd once said that my mother's discovery of one of them had precipitated an early marital crisis. When he traveled, he carried with him a notebook and a tin of loose tea; he'd catch up on his diary over cups of China Yunnan. My brother and I, in our twenties, occasionally accompanied him on bicycle trips. The offer of the journals came at the end of one of those. "Why me?" I asked him. "Because you're the writer," he answered tersely. His explanation felt like a verbal shrug. In the decades that followed, neither he nor I raised the subject of the diaries again. Maybe he'd forgotten the earlier conversation. I never did. I couldn't figure out how to make clear my interest without seeming to be counting the days. So the offer hung before me, like a bribe: I was conscious that he could take it back, though I doubt he'd intended it that way. Years after his death, I asked his girlfriend for the journals. After some weeks, she produced a half dozen slim volumes; they were, she said, all she could find. Since they dated from a seemingly random assortment of periods, I couldn't imagine why he'd have kept only those—or why she'd have withheld all the others. Maybe he'd remembered his offer and ditched the rest out of spite. God knows I'd infuriated him sufficiently, in the years leading up to his death, for him to have changed his mind.

He'd been dead about nine months when a manila envelope arrived in my mailbox in New York. I sliced it open with my front-door key before the elevator arrived at my floor. Inside was a nineteen-page list of a thousand items—an inventory, between vinyl covers, of family flotsam and jetsam that, it seemed, had come to rest in an ironing room in the back of the big house. My father's secretary and his girl-friend had inventoried the items. The list enumerated photo albums, scrapbooks, journals, birth certificates, wills, poems written for family occasions, bills from the Ritz-Carlton in 1915, and letters from Andrew Carnegie and Tallulah Bankhead, among others. There was also, it appeared, an extensive record of the original conception of the estate, including bills and correspondence dating from the construction of the house. There was a record of the restoration a century later. I slid the inventory into a desk drawer. When I rediscovered it five years later, the ironing room seemed like as good a place as any to start.

Maybe all fathers are unknowable. Maybe all families are mysterious. If we're lucky, we get interested in ours before it's too late. Memories silt over, lives are cut short. By the time we've come up with the questions, there's no one left to answer.

The world exemplified by my father's grandparents had slid beyond the memory of almost anyone living. Yet a new version of that moment was being born. Technological change had unleashed a new industrial revolution—just as it had a century and a half before. Regulations that had been intended to rein in the excesses of earlier generations were being lifted. In hedge funds, investment banking, and private equity, new fortunes were being amassed. A bumper crop of billionaires was bringing about a new age of disparity and excess. Now they were erecting monster houses and nailing down the class position of their children, like another generation had done a century before. Did they ever wonder how the wealth and position they'd manage to amass would play out in the lives of the generations that would follow?

My great-grandparents' place had survived against the odds from one gilded age into the next. It had persisted, long after others had been dismantled, as a result of wily tax planning, ego, and a romantic attachment to the Colonel's vision. In the wake of its lavish restoration, it had now, in my father's absence, resumed its decline. The heirs to the founders had begun selling off land and houses. The fate of the big house and its trappings remained anyone's guess—its worth in the twenty-first century having been variously estimated at anywhere from priceless to "negative value." Wasn't there some Russian oligarch who might want it? one or two family members wondered in the countdown toward the termination of the trusts. Had anyone considered a business in artisanal cheese? In the aftermath of the making of a moderately sized American fortune lay a parable for others embarking upon that cycle again. For better or worse, the Colonel's fancy had shaped four generations in my father's family. If I could unearth that story, maybe I'd understand what had happened to him.

In my father's final week, his doctors had run out of tricks. He'd been in the intensive care unit for days. His advance directive was unambiguous: no heroic measures. Decisions now fell to his girlfriend and my sister and brother and me. We'd met in a conference room with a social worker and a doctor. We'd agreed he should be disconnected from life support. His bed had been wheeled into an unoccupied room in a sleepy wing of the hospital. My sister and I sat in that room, on plastic chairs, uncertain what to do. Touching had not been part of the language he'd ever used with us. So that simple source of solace felt awkward if not exactly off-limits. His breathing became like groaning, as though he were in pain. A cousin, who was a physician, stopped by and seemed mildly alarmed. She spoke with the nurses, who made adjustments. After that, his breathing slowed. A nurse checked in. All was well, she assured us. Minutes later, his breathing stopped.

I was padding down the hospital corridor to phone my mother with the news when my cell phone rang. It was a reporter for the *Philadelphia Inquirer*. He'd heard that my father had died. Curious, I asked how he'd gotten word so fast; the not-so-old man had been dead for four minutes. Someone at the paper, he said, had received a tip earlier in the day from an affiliated hospital on the same computer system. The tipster, misreading the electronic record, must have jumped the gun. The reporter didn't need much from me; he'd written most of the obituary in advance. But I'd anticipated his question. It was going to necessitate a choice between bluntness and discretion. Faced with those options, I'd figured I should go with the technical answer. That way, I'd be factually correct without saying too much. The more complicated answer remained, at that moment, beyond me.

Could I tell him, the reporter wanted to know, the cause of death?

Chapter Two

As a child, I assumed the place had always been as I'd found it. I probably assumed, too, that it would be that way long after we were gone. Cut off from the march of subdivisions, car dealerships, and drive-through banking, it floated in an eddy, outside the whooshing of time. There were fields where my father had tobogganed as a boy, where he took us to discover the rapture of hurtling downhill on the brink of abandon. There was a hollow tree, which would still be standing when I had children of my own. There were ancient initials carved in the bark of beech trees, the letters swollen by the passage of years. Dug into the side of a small hill, there was a root cellar dating from some prehistoric era, *ante* synthetic refrigerants. Cows had claimed it, paving the dirt floor with dung. A sign nailed to the fence around that pasture warned to beware of a bull. As we passed by on the long driveway, the black mouth of the cellar beckoned. On rare occasions when we dared to slip between the fence rails and venture near, it exhaled dank, cold breath.

Back then, I experienced the place through the senses. I knew the burning of bare soles on baking macadam, and the clammy coolness of the paving-stone path to the pool in the woods. There was the sour sweetness of Concord grapes on the vines along the rusting iron fence that bounded our backyard, and the soughing of window fans buffeting the humidity around bedrooms at night. Mica glittered in the stone walls; mint grew wild beside the stream banks. Stinging nettles lurked beyond the barn. Later, in another country, I could lie in bed and summon the sensation of coasting down the driveway in my parents' station wagon in the sweltering stillness of August. For a time, I had a treehouse in an elm in the field beside our house, where you could try to imagine how the place might appear from another angle. But Dutch elm disease took the tree, and the treehouse with it. The site, bouldered and brambled, became a boneyard for hamsters, dogs, and the ashes of my mother's childless, irascible, out-of-town aunt.

A map of the area hung on the wall in my parents' house for years before I examined it closely. It was in a downstairs bathroom—a powder room, if you used that term, which we didn't. You entered the room from a paneled library, past a stuffed and mounted head of a hare, its incisors visible, stained like a smoker's. The bathroom had a sink and a toilet but no tub. The wallpaper was dark red in a pattern that suggested overlapping slices of an exotic fruit. There was a tall, narrow closet in the bathroom, used as a liquor cabinet, with shelves that burrowed so deep into the wall, I imagined tunneling into the house's hidden interstices. The bathroom light fixture was a wooden hand, flesh colored, jutting out from the wall near the pedestal sink, gripping a red, Statue of Liberty–style torch. Idling on the toilet seat, you could reflect on that curious assortment of bathroom accessories or gaze out the window toward a sea of alfalfa. Under the circumstances, I see why I overlooked the map. But it would have been a gate into the story, an opening to ask questions before the narratives ossified into myth.

The map came from an atlas, one in a series published around the turn of the twentieth century, tracking the buying and selling of land along the Pennsylvania Railroad's Main Line. The railroad company had acquired, from the state, a line known as the "Main Line of Public Works," and had turned in the 1870s to developing land on either side of the tracks. The company built a two-hundred-fifty-room resort hotel in Bryn Mawr for prosperous denizens of Philadelphia, one of the great industrial powerhouses of that age, which was busily spitting out new fortunes made in iron, steel, locomotives, banking, department stores, and shipping, the way Silicon Valley churns out tech fortunes today. Philadelphians took to summering at the hotel, and tycoons began buying farmland for country estates. They built fortresses with crenelated walls, stone-mullioned windows, porte cocheres, banquet halls, gargoyles, buttresses, peaked roofs. By the late nineteenth century, the railroad was running dozens of trains a day between seventeen stations along the Main Line, many of them named after Welsh towns, Welsh counties, Welsh saints. In Lower Merion, an iron and steel magnate erected an Elizabethan manor with seventy-five rooms, on five hundred forty acres landscaped by the Olmsted brothers. Sixteenth-century tapestries, imported from England, hung on the walls. Every five to ten years, a new edition of the *Atlas of Properties on Main Line Pennsylvania Railroad from Overbrook to Paoli* took stock of the rollout of what was becoming the country's archetypal ribbon of railroad suburbs. In doing so, the atlases also traced Robert Leaming Montgomery's conquest of Villanova.

A week before Christmas 1910, I now know, newspapers reported the sale of two hundred ten acres in Radnor, in what was said to be one of the largest real estate deals ever in that part of the Main Line. The land had a pedigree of a sort the buyer would have approved. It had been part of a grant made by William Penn, the founder of Philadelphia and the Province of Pennsylvania, to a family of Welsh Quakers. The mother of a Revolutionary War general, Anthony Wayne, had been born on the property. An outpost of the Continental Army had camped there during the winter of 1777 to 1778, when George Washington was at Valley Forge. The newspapers, for whom high-priced land deals on the Main Line must have been becoming more dog-bites-man than the reverse, saw no need to spell out what the buyer, Robert L. Montgomery, had in mind. They reported simply that he intended to "erect a handsome country residence for his occupancy"—a turn of phrase that I began to see, as I foraged in his correspondence, could have come from the aspiring laird himself.

Six years after my father's death, I began piecing together the story of Robert L. Montgomery—known as the Colonel from World War I on, for reasons that I now suspect had been discreetly forgotten. In my apartment in New York, I'd become interested for the first time in the inventory that had turned up after my father's death. I took to leaving the apartment as the sun was rising against the city skyline, and walking north on Broadway to the garage, passing a man in rags whose permanent home I knew to be the doorstep of Victoria's Secret as I made my way toward the fifty-room ancestral manse. I'd leave the city, drive south on the New Jersey Turnpike, and cross into Pennsylvania, scudding past shopping malls and storage units. Sometimes, approaching my father's family's place, I'd try to see it the way a stranger might if he were catching sight of it for the first time—the way, after years in Southern California, I could still conjure how a certain bend in the Hollywood Freeway had first struck me. In Pennsylvania, I couldn't do it. I'd lived away from the place for forty-four years. But my sense of it was too deeply ingrained to allow even a momentary override.

I'd park in a small gravel parking area behind the big house and enter the silent kitchen with its smell of polished linoleum and dark-stained wood. I'd cross what had once been the servants' dining room and climb the back staircase that my father had used until his legs had failed him, after which he'd ridden the clanking elevator, incarcerating himself behind its gate. On the landing between the second and third floors, I'd turn right into a narrow corridor leading into what had once been the servants' wing. Inside the ironing room, cardboard file boxes lined the shelves. Albums and scrapbooks filled the drawers. Dust swirled in the light from a single dormer window. The only furniture was a stepladder and a child's desk. I'd haul a box off a shelf onto the desk, remove a stack of papers, sit on the stepladder, and read.

The truth is, I suffer from an almost promiscuous inquisitiveness. It's an occupational hazard, I suppose. Though I can't say whether the occupation or the inclination came first: Maybe newspapers were chicken *and* egg. In this instance, I had no idea, when I got started, where my digging might lead me. I knew only that there was a vein of paper to be mined. Arranging a heap before me, I'd angle myself over the pint-size worktable; by the time I'd look up, hours would have passed. By the following spring, I'd begun to sense a story taking shape—a narrative unwinding over multiple generations and one hundred years; spilling from the paneled chambers of the big house to the rice plantations of South Carolina and the palatial "cottages" of Mount Desert Island, Maine; tossing up its characters, from time to time, near the gurge of the historical moment; and leading me toward an answer to the question I couldn't shake.

A story, of course, begins where the teller chooses to begin it. I'm starting this one with the making of a middling American fortune—a fortune that would pale by comparison to many, like those of Rockefellers or Carnegies or Kochs, but one sufficient, if shrewdly managed, to subsidize a generation or two or more to come. This story ends in the final years of my father's life nearly one hundred years later—in his meticulous restoration of a mansion he didn't own, and in his simultaneous self-destruction. The world that the Colonel constructed, and set to spinning on its axis, had shaped the lives of all who'd followed. His aspirations had marked his children, their children, their children's children. If I could piece together the story of the inception of Ardrossan, and some of what followed, maybe I'd begin to see how my father's charmed life had arrived at such a perplexing end.

A word of caution. In my father's family, Ardrossan wasn't the only thing that was passed down. Names rolled from great-grandparent to grandparent to parent to child: four Edgars, three Roberts, three Hopes, multiple Marys, Charlottes, Alexanders, and Warwicks—all of those in just four generations. For that reason, it might help a reader to know that there will be three central figures in this saga—the Colonel; his daughter Helen Hope; and her son Robert, my father. My paternal grandfather and great-grandfather will be important, too. While others will come and go, no reader need keep them all straight, hauling them around, as if in some overstuffed mental roll-aboard, from one chapter to the next.

My father's forebears were not "the sort of people who leave few traces," to borrow the words of Patrick Modiano, the Nobel Prize–winning French novelist who puzzles over questions of identity, gathering remnants of a buried past. The Colonel alone had left behind boxloads of correspondence, invoices, and other detritus that for some reason, or no reason, neither he nor anyone had seen fit to toss. There were communiqués to architects, landscapers, business associates, friends. There were letters drumming up support for a favorite cause, the repeal of Prohibition. Downstairs, in a corner of the library, his wife's drop-front desk sat largely untouched since her death forty years earlier. In it were letters dating from early in her marriage, written by her young banker husband as he crossed the country negotiating financing deals—letters tinged with homesickness and dislocation as he peered into an unfamiliar American future. "I am greatly interested in the Pacific Coast in the way of its development, but the people you see are certainly queer," he wrote from the Palace Hotel in San Francisco four years after the 1906 earthquake wiped out most of the city. "This is a very large hotel, one of the very largest in the country, yet you see the women come in quite dressed up and not a man in a dress suit."

To me, the Colonel was a figure out of ancient history when I was young. He'd died just six years before I was born. But if you'd asked me, as a child, when my father's grandfather had lived, I might have guessed around the time of Lincoln. He was the personage in the portrait, a figure in a fairy tale, a name invoked in toasts on Christmas Eve. When my grandmother occasionally mentioned her Dad, it threw me: I couldn't reconcile the everydayness of the name with that legendary creature, monumental and remote. My aunt once described for me her first audience with him, which had occurred not long before she married my father's brother. The Colonel, ailing, was scheduled to arrive at the Bryn Mawr train station, returning in a private railroad car from his plantation in South Carolina. An ambulance idled near the platform. The train rumbled into view, braked, shrieked to a halt. Then the great man, outsize and prostrate, his chest heaving, emerged on a stretcher, threaded through a train-car window, a camel through the eye of a needle.

Robert L. Montgomery was a proud, ambitious man. In his choice of spouse and business partners, he was strategic or fortunate or both. In his taste in architecture, art, costume, hobbies, sports, he leaned eastward toward Britain. He spent extravagantly but scrutinized every bill. He was capable of generosity, employing some of his less successful half siblings, but philanthropy appears not to have played a large part in

Robert L. Montgomery

his life. As the Depression dragged on, he railed increasingly against government spending. He complained that the township was making life difficult for the owners of big estates. As I pored over his papers, it seemed he'd carried on at times like a cartoon fat cat—not all that different from the present-day private-equity titans whose excesses I'd been contemplating with distaste.

The Colonel, before he was the Colonel, set out early to make a fortune. A great-grandfather of his had invested in property in New Orleans in the late eighteenth century, the value of which had skyrocketed after the Louisiana Purchase. The resulting windfall had benefited several generations but was drying up by the time of Robert Montgomery's birth in 1879. His mother died when the boy was not yet two years old. His father, suddenly a widowed father of three, imported from the young state of Nebraska the daughter of an Episcopalian chaplain in Fort Omaha to serve as governess, then married her and fathered eight more. The blending wasn't flawless. For the only photograph known to have been taken of the whole clan, dating from 1907, Robert's father and stepmother gathered all eleven offspring on their summer farm and lined them up in descending order against the trunk of a fallen tree. The photograph that resulted, known as "The Family Tree," is said to have marked the last time the entire family was together.

Growing up in his father's increasingly populous household in Radnor, where his maternal grandmother would come and go in a carriage with a liveried coachman, the young Montgomery is said to have been conscious of the strain on his father's resources. At sixteen, he left school and went to work as a stock clerk at a merchant bank, a branch of the House of Morgan. By twenty-seven, he'd started his own firm along with two well-chosen partners—a wealthy banker's son, married to a granddaughter of a multimillionaire transit mogul and financier, and a son of one of the founders of the Philadelphia department store Strawbridge & Clothier. Together, the three partners had what it would take to flourish in the clubby world of early-twentieth-century investment banking—social standing and connections. The new firm opened seven months before the Panic of 1907. Soon, it was "buying and selling businesses with good prospects but little success—often very quickly and with enormous profit," a half brother of the Colonel wrote later in a memoir. Robert Montgomery became a millionaire "almost overnight."

"It was almost as though he belonged to another family—a cousin rather than a brother," the half brother, Horace, wrote. "To my proud, wealthy and aristocratic half-sister and half-brothers, it was *who* you are and not *what* you are that counted most. One's family was the all-important criterion. You could be undistinguished, dull, silly, even poor provided you came from or were related to a family that 'belonged'."

The Colonel's talents in finance weren't the sole source of his wealth. At twenty-two, he'd married Charlotte Hope Binney Tyler, the daughter of a Philadelphia businessman and bank cofounder. The latest in a long line of nearly a dozen firstborn Hopes, she was beguiling, stylish, and artistic. Her father served on the boards of corporations his ambitious son-in-law might hope to cultivate as clients; and, Hope's mother having died, her father had married the daughter of a man whose serial successes in produce, oil refining, and transit had made him far richer even than Tyler père. On their first wedding anniversary, the young Montgomerys dined at the White House; Hope's cousin Edith was President Theodore Roosevelt's second wife. Soon, Robert Montgomery and his brother-in-law were in business together. Not long after that, Theodore Roosevelt Jr. joined them. All in all, it was an auspicious union. Asked years later how the Colonel made the money to pull together Ardrossan, a lawyer for the family is said to have answered, "He married Miss Tyler."

The Colonel was thirty-one when he bought his first two hundred ten acres in Radnor. By the time the 1913 *Atlas of Properties* came out, he'd annexed

Charlotte Hope B. T. Montgomery

ninety-nine more. By 1920, he owned five hundred forty-two; in 1926, he had seven hundred forty-two. His name arced like a necklace across a full third of Plate 22 in the atlas published that year; his holdings included manor houses, farm buildings, orchards, and three tributaries of Darby Creek. On the next plate, his latest acquisitions extended across Newtown Road and three-quarters of a mile north. By the time his shopping spree ended, his fiefdom encompassed some eight hundred acres, with frontage on four and a half miles of public roads. He was the biggest individual taxpayer in Delaware County. When a real estate broker wrote to him in 1930, offering to sell him a one-hundred-ninety-acre farm and a stone house near West Chester, all suitable for what the broker referred to as a "Gentlemen's Country Estate," the gentleman answered haughtily, "I am already owner of a vast estate in Villa Nova."

To build a house suitable to his station, he hired a Philadelphia architect with a fashionable practice catering to what Michael C. Kathrens, an architectural historian and author of a book on the architect, has described as the desire of the extremely rich of that era "to flaunt their wealth with more grandiose and more expensively appointed old-world-style houses." The architect, Horace Trumbauer, had made a name for himself in the Philadelphia area at the end of the nineteenth century by designing a forty-room castle for a sugar baron. From that modest beginning, he'd gone on to build a hundred-ten-room palace for a trolley-car titan; a Renaissance-style mansion with frescoed ceilings for the titan's business partner; and an Elizabethan-style house for the business partner's son. With a Trumbauer house, a man might hope to cement his business connections and build what Kathrens describes as dynastic alliances through the marriages of his children. When the Colonel hired Trumbauer, the architect had yet to undertake some of his best-known commissions, including Widener Library at Harvard, and Miramar, a summerhouse in Newport, which he equipped with a twenty-foot stone basin big enough to accommodate two hundred magnums of champagne on ice.

The house Trumbauer designed for the Montgomerys had no champagne basin. But modest it was not. The design was inspired by a house in Surrey that had been featured in *Country Life*, a British weekly read closely by country gentlemen, arrived or aspiring. The Montgomery house would have fifteen bedrooms, fifteen fireplaces, and accommodations for twelve servants. Trumbauer stretched the scale of certain features of the Surrey house to achieve what Kathrens calls a more monumental appearance. For interior decoration, the Montgomerys hired the London firm that had overhauled Buckingham Palace after the death of Queen Victoria. The Colonel's wife hired that firm "with the understanding that everything was to be as plain as possible, but of a quality unsurpassed." Her tastes, it seems, were simpler than those of her husband, whose birthday checks she sometimes parked in a bank account and forgot about for years. Occasionally, she called the palace he'd ordered up "my Taj Mahal."

The Colonel didn't stop at the house. He arranged for a fifty-foot-long swimming pool, fed by springwater that arrived through a spout at one end and spilled out the other end into a chute leading to a passing stream. He built a seventeen-hundred-foot-long stone wall along what was then the northern frontier of the estate. He called for a balustrade of Indiana limestone, decorated with sculptures, matching the trim on the house. He had the driveway circle expanded to accommodate the turning radius of a large touring car. He built a stone water tower—concrete-lined, shingle-roofed—and had water pumped from springs on the property into underground tanks. To design homes for farm employees, he sent his architects a book on British cottage architecture. The semidetached houses were to be surrounded by gardens, fruit trees, hedges, honeysuckle, roses. The architects wrote back, reassuring the client, "The whole group will be quite English in effect."

Because he'd long dreamed of a stable with a clock tower, he sent his architect a pencil sketch of what he had in mind. When the stable was completed, it had a stone tower with a self-winding Seth Thomas tower clock, an indoor exercise track, box stalls, a saddle room, a trainer's room, a trophy room. Grain arrived, and manure departed, via carriers attached to a hanging track. Years later, my grandmother would say the stable was the part of her parents' place she'd loved most when she was a child.

Poking through the Colonel's papers, it occurred to me for the first time that the place I'd known from my earliest years was an invention. It had seemed to date from time immemorial; in truth, it was a creation of a fairly recent vintage—a product of one man's imagination and will. The invention wasn't simply the house with its towering gateposts decked out with lanterns with antique glass panels. The Colonel had ordered up farm roads, stone bridges, walls. He'd had boulders hauled out of the fields and woods, to be crushed into gravel for surfacing the roads in his preferred shade of gray. He'd selected the grasses—timothy, bluegrass, redtop, white clover—which were still growing in the pastures when I was young. He'd insisted upon Norway spruce along the boundary to the north—until he changed his mind and replaced them with white pine. In the heaps of correspondence, bills, and receipts, I could track his restless desire behind the thousands of man-hours spent clearing, blasting, hauling, digging, filling, grading, planting, transplanting, plowing, harrowing, seeding, paving, pumping, fencing. Even the landscape was, to some extent, the Colonel's vision.

A year or two after moving into the house, he ordered up a forest. He enlisted the services of a nursery in New York that had developed a sideline in transplanting mature trees onto estates. The nursery sent a landscape architect to Pennsylvania to design a bespoke forest, then dispatched the superintendent of its tree-moving department to oversee the operation. For three weeks in February 1915, men uprooted trees, swaddled roots in burlap, and hauled transplants from one end of the Montgomery property to another. As George S. Kaufman said of the hundreds of trees transplanted onto Moss Hart's estate, "Just what God would have done if He had the money."

But, several weeks in, the Colonel aborted the maneuvers. The cost was turning out to be much higher than he'd expected. It had taken thirteen days to move just six trees. What's more, the trees, once transplanted, weren't tall enough to fulfill their intended purpose, which, it seems, may have been to erase the sight of another very large house rising on an estate a mile away.

The following spring, the planting extravaganza resumed. Ten thousand rhododendron bushes were ordered for the woods on the Montgomery holdings. Seven hundred linear feet of privet went in along the boundary to the south. On the high banks of the long, straight road that served as the property line to the north, one thousand, two hundred fifty climbing roses took root. Seven hundred fifty honeysuckle plants arrived from a local nursery. In April and May, landscapers installed two dozen purple beech trees, two dozen junipers, three dozen white dogwoods, four dozen hemlocks, and dozens of snowballs, lilacs, forsythias, mock oranges, hydrangeas, and box trees. For the landscaping around the new swimming pool, nine hundred ferns were trucked in. The lawns spilling away from the big house were planted with nearly five hundred trees. Six hundred cowslip, rock cress, white stonecrop, and other small, flowering perennials arrived from a nursery in Vermont, along with instructions from a famous landscape architect in Manhattan to plant them in the cracks of rocks.

The Colonel furnished himself, too, with the ultimate gentleman's accessory, a herd of cows.

When I was young, mine was the only Main Line grandmother I knew of with three hundred cows. But in her father's day, I've since learned, a dairy herd was prized accoutrement for the gentleman farmer on several Main Line estates. Percival Roberts, the iron and steel man

with the Olmsted land-
scapes, had Ayrshires at
his place in Penn Val-
ley and Gladwyne. An-
other estate, with a
house modeled on a
Tudor castle in War-
wickshire, had its own
dairy, too. The Colonel,
who'd already dabbled
in sheep and poultry,
bought approximately
a dozen Ayrshires—
hardy, economical, long-
lived producers of su-
perior milk—from a
friend who'd imported
them from Scotland.

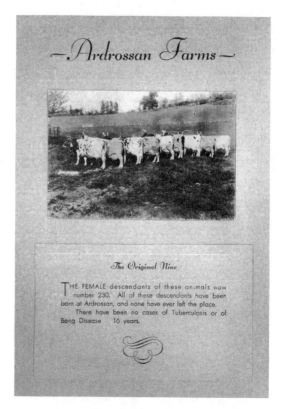

Ardrossan Farms

The Original Nine

THE FEMALE descendants of these animals now
number 230. All of these descendants have been
born at Ardrossan, and none have ever left the place.
There have been no cases of Tuberculosis or of
Bang Disease 16 years.

In a photograph from the early years, the original cows stand in a row,
facing away from the camera, their posteriors on display. The unpro-
nounceable names they brought with them—Auchenbainzie Katie,
Lessnessock Violet II, Muiryhill Sally III, and so on—read as though
lifted from a Scottish gazetteer.

By 1920, the herd had multiplied sixfold with the cooperation of
the Colonel's prizewinning bull. The Colonel wanted his dairy to be
state-of-the-art, so he sent an emissary to gather intelligence at an in-
novative farm in the Hudson Valley. He experimented with crop rota-
tions; he tried a portable barn for milking, to save money on
bedding—then ditched it, having realized his cows were wasting energy growing winter coats. By the time a reporter from *Field Illustrated
Advertiser* showed up in 1920, the farm was said to be turning a small
profit. But the Colonel insisted that making money mattered less to

him than superior milk. To his sister, he wrote, "My personal pride prompts me to sell a better product, if I can, than anyone else, as I never like to have to do with anything unless it is the best."

Brandy from Berry Bros. in London, picnic baskets from Asprey, jodhpurs from Huntsman & Sons of Savile Row: The laird of Ardrossan prided himself on his standards and taste. Once, he instructed his grown son to return forty-one cases of Gordon's gin: Only Bellows would do. He fished for salmon on a river in Canada where Micmac fishing guides escorted the world's richest men. His black cloth overcoat was lined with mink. And when rodents turned up in the big house, no garden-variety pest-control specialist would suffice: Horace Trumbauer wrote to his exacting client, "With reference to exterminating the rats at your residence I have made inquiry as to who did this work at the Ritz-Carlton Hotel."

The big house required a battalion to run it. Thirteen servants—young immigrants from Ireland, Sweden, Switzerland, and France—lived in the house at the time of the 1920 census. When the household was in full operation, my father said, sixteen men and women sat down to the midday meal in the servants' dining room. There were cooks, maids, butlers, valets, chauffeurs, handymen, gardeners, watchmen. The pantry housed enough silver to keep busy a polisher chasing tarnish full-time—candlesticks and candelabras, hot dishes with covers, footed bowls, fish platters, compotes, bouillon spoons, ice tongs, chop plates, toast racks, chafing dishes, gravy boats, candlesnuffers, and old-fashioned glasses etched with the word "Achievement." The staff didn't simply clean, cook, wait on tables, wash dishes, wash laundry, drive, cultivate the gardens. They were essential to the raising of children. My great-uncle Aleck had not one baby nurse but two. When his mother's breast milk couldn't keep up with demand, the family summoned the fashionable wife of the fashionable French chef of a fashionable French restaurant in Philadelphia to fill in as a wet nurse.

Extravagance in genuflecting to the past was not, it turns out, exclusive to our Colonel Montgomery. A distant kinsman of his occupies a rarefied niche in British history for having mounted an ill-fated medieval jousting tournament on the grounds of his imitation Gothic castle in Ayrshire, Scotland, in 1839. At a time of Romantic infatuation with chivalry and other things medieval, Archibald Montgomerie, the thirteenth earl of Eglinton, trained forty earls, viscounts, marquesses, and so on to play the role of medieval knight, and dressed them in medieval costume and armor. He had pavilions and grandstands constructed. A glittering roster of guests, including the future Napoleon III, turned out for the event. Four thousand people were expected; as many as one hundred thousand are said to have shown up. Then, as knights and their entourages pranced forth in the opening-day parade, lightning crackled and a sudden downpour swamped the festivities. Guests ended up having to flee on foot. At the time, the earl's effort was admired for its pageantry and ambition. But ridicule followed. The Eglinton Tournament has been remembered more recently as "one of the most glorious and infamous follies of the nineteenth century." It took a large bite, too, out of the thirteenth earl's cash.

It had never occurred to me to wonder what our Colonel had been thinking. There was the story of his fall from the rented horse and his resolution to build a house on the spot—a story that every journalist who ever encountered my grandmother swallowed whole and served up in print. But that tale didn't really explain the serial annexations or the magnitude of the Main Line Taj. The Colonel hadn't merely bought a hilltop with a view that had caught his eye. He'd made a statement about himself, his family, his place. As decades passed and generations piled up, Ardrossan appeared to embody assumptions about family—for example, the responsibilities of each generation to those that preceded and came after. Had my father's grandparents, both motherless at a young age, shared a dream of an indissoluble, multigenerational clan? "On Ardrossan, unity is strength," the Colonel's wife, whose children and grandchildren called her Muz, wrote upon hearing that her eldest grandson was decamping. When they locked up their land and houses in trusts that couldn't be tampered with for a hundred years, were they envisioning a family compound that would endure intact far into the future?

I ran that hypothesis by my uncle. My father's only sibling (and the third of the four Edgars), he'd known his grandparents longer than any member of his generation. He'd grown up on Ardrossan and returned to it after the Marines, Harvard, and marriage—until it had become clear that his wife's happiness wouldn't survive being cooped up on the same eight hundred acres as his mother. He'd spent his career in the stockbrokerage that his father and the Colonel had founded. He was as likely as anyone to know his grandparents' motivations. When I went to see him, he was in his late eighties, living with his wife and their dogs, cats, and horses at the end of a gravel road in the rolling countryside near the Brandywine River valley in a landscape that three generations of Wyeths had painted. Fifteen years earlier, while foxhunting at age seventy-five, he'd found himself parallel to the ground, halfway out of the saddle, on a galloping horse after it stumbled on a fence. Seeing no alternative, he'd let go and fallen, breaking a piece of bone that projects upward from the second vertebra in one's neck. Thinking nothing was seriously wrong, he'd accepted a ride, from a photographer with a jeep, to a trauma center, where a nurse, wheeling him out of the room where a technician had just X-rayed his back, assured him he was lucky because nothing appeared to have been broken. "Well, I'm certainly glad to hear that," he'd remember saying, "but, I must say, I've never had such a sore neck." The broken bits, he discovered after the nurse executed a volte-face with the gurney, had not displaced. So he'd avoided paralysis and/or death. The day I went to visit, big yellow dogs bounded to the door of his house, tails wagging with enough vigor to upend a small child. We sat in a room with a picture window, beyond which hills plunged and climbed into the distance. When I asked him if he thought his grandparents had conceived Ardrossan and set up the trusts out of a commitment to some idea of the enduring family, he seemed to doubt it. The Colonel was dynastic, he said. But my uncle said what my father, the former trusts and estates lawyer, had occasionally said: Their grandparents' intention was to avoid taxes.

The first trust was set up in 1912—the year before the ratification of the Sixteenth Amendment gave Congress the authority to tax income. The second was dated 1917—one year after the Revenue Act of 1916 created a tax on the transfer of wealth from an estate to its beneficiaries. A third was dated 1933—the year Congress created the gift tax to stop the rich from dodging the estate tax by handing down wealth during their lifetimes. The Ardrossan trusts had other benefits, too. They'd protect the Colonel and his well-situated wife in the event of losses in his business: Any creditor who came after them would have no claim on anything held in trust. In the meantime, the estate might be made self-sustaining. The rents paid on the houses could be used to cover expenses without having to be declared as income. Though many of the houses went to family members for rents that seemed minimal, my uncle told me those rents "damn near did maintain the property for years."

The Colonel had become an investment banker at an opportune moment. He'd gone into finance just as the market for industrial securities was being born. Until 1890, Americans with capital to invest had mostly put it in real estate. If they'd wanted to buy securities, railroad securities had been almost the only option; industrial firms had tended to be small, closely held, and not publicly traded. In the early 1890s, that began to change. With railroads covering much of the country, the demand for investment capital for the rail system had become less urgent, and a market for industrial securities emerged. Dozens of industrial companies issued investment-quality, dividend-paying preferred stocks in the early years of that decade, through mergers, incorporations, and recapitalizations. A business grew up in the distribution of industrial stocks. After those stocks performed better on average than railroad securities during the depression of 1893 to 1897, investors embraced them, enabling manufacturing and other industrial firms to grow. A wave of large-scale mergers took place. By the early twentieth century, investment banking firms were underwriting new issues of industrial securities, selling the stock to investors, and making money on the sales. When Montgomery, Clothier & Tyler was formed in 1907, that was the firm's business.

How successful the Colonel's firm really was proved almost impossible for me to determine. Newspaper articles and advertisements from the period make it clear that the firm was busy with stock offerings, bond issues, syndicates, mergers. But, as a private partnership, it wasn't required to keep records or file reports; how much money the partners made on individual deals was not recorded. Until the advent of the income tax, the partners kept what they made. But because the firm was an unlimited liability partnership, their own money was at stake. If they paid more to underwrite an issue than they made distributing the stock to investors, they swallowed the loss. My uncle, the third Edgar, told me he'd heard that the firm lost money for the first seven years, then more than made up for it in each of the following seven. A cousin of my father's remembered his grandmother, Muz, telling him, "You know, your grandfather went bankrupt twice, and I bailed him out both times."

At thirty-two years old, the Colonel landed at the center of one of the biggest deals of the time—the reincorporation, restructuring, and recapitalization of what had been the leading firm in the locomotive industry. The Baldwin Locomotive Works had for a long time produced more than a third of all the locomotives built; in its best year, 1906, it had turned out two thousand, six hundred sixty-six engines, running its Philadelphia plant around the clock and employing seventeen thousand men. In 1909, Baldwin had incorporated as a privately held company with a capitalization of twenty million dollars. Two years later, the directors took the company public. According to the *Philadelphia Inquirer*, the Colonel prepared the financial plan for the new corporation, whose capitalization doubled overnight to forty million dollars. Though Baldwin's officers eventually enlisted two larger and better-known firms to work with Montgomery, Clothier & Tyler, the Colonel himself was reported to have made a killing. "According to reports current in financial circles at the time, and which were not denied, Mr. Montgomery made one million dollars by his work on the project," the *Inquirer* later reported. A banker who'd advised Montgomery, Clothier & Tyler on the deal resigned as president of his bank amid criticism of his sharing in the profits of the financing. The underwriters were said to have been paid in common stock, and the adviser's share was rumored to be valued at five hundred thousand dollars. Baldwin's net profits averaged 9.8 percent of sales between 1910 and 1915, rising with the advent of World War I.

With war orders surging, the Colonel engineered the merger in 1915 of two major manufacturers of guns, shells, caissons, and other ordnance—advance word of which sent the price of the stock of one of the firms to its highest levels ever. His firm took the lead, with a New York firm, on the reorganization and recapitalization of the world's largest manufacturer of trucks. In 1916, a syndicate led by the Montgomery firm and one other acquired nearly all the stock in one of the oldest and best-known independent oil-refining and petroleum products companies in the East and reorganized it under new ownership. In 1917, it led the restructuring and recapitalization of one of the world's largest consumers of copper, which the company used to produce cable for telephone and telegraph, and electrical, companies. And during the war years, when American machinery firms became targets for Wall Street stockjobbing operations—the buying and selling of securities in pursuit of quick profits—the Montgomery firm was a principal in the purchase, reorganization, and recapitalization of one of the only two United States producers of armored steel, used to make battleships.

On the evening of March 1, 1917, ten years after the partnership had been announced in the *Wall Street Journal*, the firm celebrated itself with a banquet in the ballroom of the thousand-room, French Renaissance–style Bellevue-Stratford Hotel in downtown Philadelphia. Three years earlier, the partners had opened a New York office with Theodore Roosevelt Jr. in charge; a year after that, they'd opened branch offices in Pittsburgh and Hartford. One hundred twenty-five firm members and guests turned out for the tenth-anniversary blowout at the Bellevue-Stratford, described at its opening a decade earlier as the most luxurious hotel in the country. In the two-tiered ballroom, with light fixtures by Thomas Edison and chandeliers by Lalique, the Colonel, in white tie and tails, sat on the stage beneath the proscenium arch, at the midpoint of a feasting table draped in white linen and decorated with floral centerpieces, silver place settings, and candelabras. His cofounders sat on either side. Their fathers, the city's banking and department-store bigwigs, flanked them. Below the high table, men in tuxedos and women in evening dresses sat at round tables filling the room. The menu for the occasion listed nineteen dishes, including fillet of sole, breast of guinea, sweet potatoes, and a dessert called bombe pompadour. A photographer captured the event—the sea of pale faces turned upward toward the camera, frozen momentarily above crystal glasses, linen napkins, oysters on the half shell, dinner rolls yet to be touched. Some seven hundred fifty oysters were consumed that evening in celebration of the Colonel and his firm's dazzling success. I wonder if anyone there that evening imagined even for a moment that the partnership would begin to crumble within six months.

Helen Hope, the Colonel's eldest child and my father's mother, used to say she was raised to go to parties. That's how she put it. "I'm just a party girl," she'd say, chasing the confession with a percussive laugh.

Her parents wanted her to know a lot of people, she'd say; they wanted her career to be marriage. On one level, the declaration was matter-of-fact—a data point along the lines of "Dad flew autogiros." The laugh that followed was an invitation to see the humor in the situation: If you found it funny, good. So did she. By the time I knew her, she was fully aware that changing times had stolen some of the luster from her assigned vocation. But she can hardly have regretted how it had worked out. She'd aced the party-girl exams, no question. As for her career in marriage, she was CEO of a blue-chip domestic union. She'd made herself into a dairy farmer of some renown, disregarding her father's stated position that cows weren't for women. She'd appeared on best-dressed lists alongside Babe Paley. She'd judged horses at Madison Square Garden.

Helen Hope Montgomery, with two of her siblings

She'd honored her parents by doing more than anyone else to keep Ardrossan going, the farm operating, and four generations of family members on much better than speaking terms.

Helen Hope Montgomery had been named for her mother but she took after her father. She had his big, dark eyes, pronounced eyebrows, dark wavy hair. Headstrong and competitive, she had a pony at four, rode in horse shows at eight, competed in jumping classes at thirteen. "I was terribly ambitious," she said. "I wanted to be the top of everything."

She had a fine affinity with animals. In a scrapbook, I find a photograph of her at about eight months, in a white linen dress with puffy sleeves, propped against a long-haired dog named Cauliflower, twice her size. She sits in the curve of the dog's long torso, eyes wide, one tiny fist lost somewhere in the dog's flowing beard. Child and dog meet the gaze of the camera, appearing mildly affronted, as though the photographer has interrupted a moment of intimate consultation between cousins. In a published account of the activities of a local foxhunting club—an enthusiast's diary of miles covered, fences cleared, noses bloodied, port consumed—I find the trail of the Colonel and his then adolescent eldest, Helen Hope. They would set off together before dawn on fall mornings, riding for miles across frosted fields to join the hunt that her great-uncle had founded.

On a cold day in the winter of 1910, the girl who would grow up to sing a naughty song to the Duke of Windsor and win a Charleston contest judged by Josephine Baker gazed for the first time at the rolling expanse that was to become her family's place. Helen Hope was six years old that day. Her family had been living in Haverford, a half dozen station stops out from Philadelphia on the Main Line. Governesses, cooks, maids, chauffeurs—nine in all—attended to the needs of two parents, one auntie, and two daughters. (Two more children were yet to be born.) On that day, which Helen Hope would recall vividly eighty-some years later, the family set off in a French touring car, with an open top and a French chauffeur, to survey Dad's latest acquisition. ("Americans were not supposed to be capable of driving a car in those days," my grandmother would note.) To its six-year-old passenger, the car seemed to tower above the ground. Sunlight flashed on its brass fittings. The party sallied forth in the gravy boat with its uniformed driver. He headed northwest, intending to approach the property from the south, and maneuvered the vehicle onto Godfrey Road. Soon the road, unpaved then, turned into a ribbon of mud. The wheels began to spin, sending clods of dirt shooting into the air, burrowing deeper into the muck. The young gentleman financier with his fancy car, enviable wife, beautifully turned-out little girls, and grand dreams ended up having to summon four horses he'd just bought. Pressed into service as draft horses that day, the hunters hauled automobile, chauffeur, children, wife, and paterfamilias from the ooze.

School in any formal sense was not a priority. Some Main Line parents sent their offspring to boarding school at six or seven, aping the child-rearing customs of the British upper classes; the husband of one of my father's cousins was sent away at five. The Montgomery children were spared that fate. "My mother, a strong believer in both practicality and charm, regarded education for women as a rather unnecessary waste of time," my grandmother once explained. Instead, a French governess taught her to read and write in French. Tutors taught her and her siblings other subjects at home or in the houses of other families nearby. A dance instructor was imported to hold classes in the then unfurnished ballroom in the big house. Boys in knicker suits and dancing pumps and girls in dresses and ballet slippers arrived from neighboring estates. A liveried butler met them at the door, escorted them past several large dogs, and delivered them to the ballroom to shake hands, in front of the fireplace, with Muz. Helen Hope's brother, Aleck, eventually went to boarding school and from there to Harvard. But the first test their sister Mary Binney would later remember having taken was a Red Cross test, during World War II. She was in her midthirties.

Unconstrained by the obstinacy of school calendars, the Montgomery family was free to travel. In December 1921—by which time there were four children, ages seventeen, fourteen, ten, and nine—the family set sail for Europe on the last of the four-funneled ocean liners, the *Aquitania*. On his passport application, the Colonel wrote that the family would return "within eight months." Their itinerary, as Aleck reported it later on sheets of yellow legal-pad paper, was listed as follows: "British Isles, Egypt, India, Gibraltar, Madeira, Portugal, France,

Italy, Greece, Switzerland, Holland, Belgium, Algiers, Czechoslovakia and other countries en route." A year and a half after returning, the family set off again, minus Helen Hope, on a circumnavigation that took them to England, France, Egypt, Aden, Ceylon, Burma, Singapore, Hong Kong, Macao, the Philippines, China, and Japan. During a month-long emergency layover in Hong Kong, the matriarch recovered from what was said by several American newspapers, which saw these facts as newsworthy, to be "an attack of India fever."

In a book about the Bund, the waterfront quarter of Shanghai, I came upon a mysterious reference in a chapter on the Astor House Hotel, which was said to have been the first Western hotel in China, advertised as "the Waldorf-Astoria of the Orient." The author recounted the hotel's history as a magnet for foreigners and expatriates. "Notable Guests"—from Albert Einstein to the Maharaja of Kapurthala and the last Hawaiian king—were enumerated. Buried in that list was the following item: In 1924, a British woman and her daughter stayed at the hotel "pretending to be Charlotte Hope Binney Tyler Montgomery and her wealthy socialite daughter Helen Hope Montgomery." The pair "made a fortune duping Shanghai's foreign community. The daughter, who was supposedly coming into a huge fortune, courted marital proposals and was swift to lose or run off with engagement rings, whilst her mother borrowed many expensive fur coats on the pretense of having them copied, but which were never seen by their owners again. The couple made a safe escape to Hong Kong before the hotel was besieged by their debtors."

When I knew her, my grandmother had a storytelling style that inclined sharply toward antic capers and skillfully calibrated overstatement. But she professed to have been painfully shy as a child. Her mother had cured her, she said, with two pieces of advice—the first, about the importance of always giving people the best possible time; the second, about the futility of excessive self-awareness. "It is stupid to always be thinking of yourself," my grandmother would remember her mother telling her. "Point yourself at something and then get going." Whether she'd really suffered from shyness, I can't be sure. If she did, it seems conceivable that she cured herself by force of will. She had the discipline to override whatever mild anxieties might have caused what she called shyness. If that worked for her, she probably assumed that the rest of us could benefit from similar advice. The language of emotional nuance was not her mother tongue. Once, she turned to a granddaughter, not quite emerging from adolescence, and offered a bit of blunt, less-than-tender grandparental advice. "You know, it's not enough to look good," she said. "You have to *say* something."

By her own account, Helen Hope put her mother's advice to work: "So the first thing I did was to get some girlfriends with plenty of boyfriends. On Sundays our courtyard was full of the most disreputable cars imaginable." Her parents were horrified, at least in her telling: "I had become very interested in boys and I think my parents were worried that I was going to be old news by the time I was a debutante at eighteen." So they found a boarding school that took not only girls but their steeds. They promised her a horse if she'd go. She took the bribe. Before leaving for school, she asked her mother what she should do about Latin, the existence of which was news. No problem, Muz assured her: "You're fluent in French!" The horse arrived at the school first; rider followed. She lasted less than two years. Her parents, she said, "snatched me out to polish me off in Europe. I was delighted about that since I missed the final exams, having cleverly avoided tests in the past by getting chicken pox and pinkeye."

Of Muz's four children, Helen Hope most closely resembled her father. She adored him and, it seems, he adored her. If he had one criticism of his admired eldest, it was that she might benefit from grappling more seriously with life. When she looked in the mirror each morning, the Colonel would say, Helen Hope would ask herself, "How much fun can I have today?" My grandmother liked to tell that story.

But, from the way she told it, you might have concluded that she took her father's critique as a point of pride.

Mary Binney, three years younger, was the artist. A pianist and a dancer, she traveled, as a teenager, into Philadelphia every Friday afternoon and Saturday evening to hear the Philadelphia Orchestra perform under Leopold Stokowski, then at the height of his nearly thirty-year run as the orchestra's music director. Aleck, four years younger than Mary Binney, suffered from an unhappy relationship with his father. Aleck's son described Aleck's Navy enlistment as running away from home: "My grandfather's somewhat brutish personality was not particularly helpful to my father." The youngest of the children, Charlotte Ives, eighteen months younger than Aleck, was the most daring and the most tragic. Widely loved, she rode horses that no one else would attempt, became a recreational pilot, made a spectacularly bad and brief marriage, ended up in a wheelchair for reasons no one ever seemed quite able or willing to pinpoint, and was outlived by all three of her siblings.

To mark my grandmother's 1922 "launch" into society—that's the society writers' vernacular, conjuring visions of a luxury liner gliding decorously down a ramp, champagne bottles shattering across the prow—her parents organized a day of point-to-point races in her honor. An import from Ireland and England, point-to-point racing was new. Amateurs raced hunting horses on a course that took them across open fields and over fences and ditches. In his scarlet coat, top hat, and breeches, the Colonel greeted his guests at the front door of the big house. They sailed across the carpeted hallway, through the living room, out the French doors onto the terrace. One woman, it was reported later, wore a red-and-white-check gown; a black velvet box coat at hip length; a small hat with a black velvet crown and silver metal brim; a fox fur scarf; and high, laced, tan shoes, their fronts embroidered in red. Men and women gathered on the greensward, which stretched into the distance before ending abruptly at a recessed retaining wall designed to keep cows off the lawn without interrupting the view. In a black-and-white photograph apparently taken that day by a photographer hired for the occasion, riders gallop their horses flat-out across a pasture, coattails flying. The house looms behind them on the hilltop, half-hidden by not yet fully grown trees. In a second photograph, a horse and rider clear a high post-and-rail fence, as two more horses approach from behind. In the distance, spectators watch from a ridge. "Never in the annals of society in this city has a debutante been honored in such an unusual way or been the recipient of so much social attention," the *Philadelphia Inquirer* reported breathlessly the following day.

The infatuation of society reporters with Helen Hope, and her attentiveness to their needs, commenced in earnest that fall. Newspaper readers learned that the daughter of Mr. and Mrs. Montgomery would "never grow wildly enthusiastic over a new recipe, or skip with glee over a brand new way to put up tomatoes." She preferred dancing and golf, though she said she was no good at the latter. She was the one debutante who defended bobbed hair; she favored longer dresses over shorter ones because they made her look dignified and tall. Her "crowning shame, of which she is not ashamed," the newspaper said, was a tendency to fall unexpectedly and deeply asleep. "When it comes to the question of husbands, Miss Montgomery tells her preference with the same engaging smile," the newspaper reported. "The ideal HE must be tall, good-looking, good-natured. He must have a million, and, last but not least, he must . . ."

The final qualification for the job had been torn off of the clipping.

At just over six feet, Edgar Scott was tall enough. He was stylishly tailored and slim, leaving the impression of an extra inch or two. My father once described him as resembling "a latter-day Roman emperor— benign, intelligent." He was good-looking, if not in the chiseled, caveman way. He had blue eyes, a fair complexion, a curved nose, and light brown hair combed back from his forehead. His long face, at rest, settled into a slight smile. To me as a child, he had the look of a creature in a children's book—a debonair fox. He was good-natured: What most people saw most of the time was a gentle charm, though he, too, had a temper. If he didn't "have a million" in the year of Helen Hope Montgomery's debut, there was reason to expect that one day he would. His grandfather Thomas Alexander Scott, the railroad president, had left behind a fortune estimated in 1881 at between five and ten million dollars. At a dinner party in Rosemont, Pennsylvania, in November 1922, my father's parents laid eyes on each other for the first time. She was eighteen; he was twenty-three. Refining her account of that evening over the decades that followed, she polished it into the smoothest of romantic chestnuts. "I looked at him across the table," she would say. "I thought he was divine."

They saw each other twelve times before they decided to marry. Or was it six? Maybe four. As a precautionary measure, her parents mandated a nine-month engagement and removed her temporarily to Shanghai. In the first of the scrapbooks in which she preserved the paper record of their life together, mementos crowd the first page. "Looking forward with pleasure to this evening," reads his handwriting on a cream-colored card—the kind that arrives with flowers—which she's annotated, "First token ever from ES to HS." Three place cards, pocketed after a dinner party and fitted into photographic corners, find Mr. Edgar Scott seated between Miss Yarnall on his left and Miss Montgomery on his right. In a telegram sent from Cambridge, Massachusetts, not long afterward, he signs off, "Miss you painfully. Oceans of love." By Thanksgiving: "I'm spoiled by now—and a dinner at which I don't sit next to you seems like nothing on earth." By Christmas, all is settled. "Life isn't what it was; and the most important trouble is that life isn't what it <u>will be</u>," he writes to her. "I can't help thinking and thinking about that—and realizing that every minute of life without you is a minute of life lost." His cousins, he reports, have fired questions and insinuations at him all evening: "God knows how I had the strength not to scream at them: 'Yes! Yes!—And she loves me!'"

The Colonel was evidently not overjoyed. It seems he'd made a point of pinning down the lineage of the man who'd captivated his eldest. He knew that Edgar's mother was a member of an admired Boston family of bankers, writers, and so on. She'd grown up in Philadelphia's desirable Rittenhouse Square. But Edgar's paternal grandfather, the railroad baron and an assistant secretary of war, had started out as a mere tavern owner's son. "At least the mother is from a good family," the Colonel is said to have sniffed, sideswiping the most accomplished forebear in memory on either side of the family.

That wouldn't be the last dig he'd take at a man one of his daughters hoped to marry. Mary Binney, who played at Carnegie Hall at seventeen and recorded the *Carnival of the Animals* with the Philadelphia Orchestra, fell in love with Stokowski. Divorced and twenty-five years older than her, he'd go on later to marry an heiress, divorce again, and marry another heiress. Visiting the big house, he's said to have been so appalled by the piano in the ballroom that he bought Mary Binney a Steinway. "He may have bought it, but I paid for it," the Colonel is said to have snarled. Stokowski was not the husband the Colonel or Muz had envisioned for their second daughter. A butler at the big house would later tell the story of a visit by Stokowski. Heading out for a walk, Mary Binney offered him one of her father's hats. Later, after Stokowski had returned the hat, her father instructed the butler to have it cleaned—and, once it was cleaned, is said to have commanded, "Now burn it." The Montgomerys forced Mary Binney to break off the affair with Stokowski—an act said to have nearly killed her. "I will not have you marry a fiddle player," the Colonel is said to have told her. In another version of the story, he says, "I will not have you marry that Polack." Maybe he said neither, or both.

Edgar Scott was not from Poland and he didn't play the fiddle. But his grandmother on his father's side was the daughter of a banker and onetime mayor of Pittsburgh named Riddle. The Colonel, it seems, had doubts about the Riddles. Perhaps the prospect of his eldest daughter leaving the nest had gotten him thinking. Maybe he was feeling, at that moment, that he'd accomplished much of what he'd set out to do. He'd reversed the sagging trajectory of the Montgomery family fortunes. He'd married a woman with the temperament and inheritance to indulge him. He'd constructed a world grand enough to match his sense of himself. He'd created a structure, in property and trusts, that could minimize the exposure of his wealth to taxes and hold his family together into the future. Did the prospect of his eldest child's marriage leave him to wonder about forces beyond his control?

"She can't marry him," the Colonel is said to have fumed. "He's a Riddle, and the Riddles are drunks."

Chapter Three

A few months after my grandfather's death in 1995, his sole surviving sister paid me a visit. She was eighty-eight years old, widowed, and living alone in an apartment on the Upper East Side of Manhattan. I was a half century younger, on maternity leave, with a newborn baby, living in an apartment across town. She arrived by taxi as the afternoon sun was turning the faces of the apartment buildings along Broadway a rosy pink; when I answered the doorbell, she was standing on the elevator landing, leaning on a cane. She had the legs of a shore bird, which I'd always admired. Her expression was humorous: Expect the unexpected, it seemed to say. She'd taught drama and literature at schools in Manhattan for years—so memorably that, when her eldest son took his children to tour boarding schools in New England, teenagers loped over to report that his mother had introduced them to Shakespeare and they'd remember the experience as long as they lived. After a successful stint in rehab in her seventies, she'd found a late-in-life calling as a pillar of the recovering-alcoholic subset of the summer population on the island in Maine where she had a house. Now, in my sparsely furnished living room, my father's aunt Anna settled into a high-backed chair and accepted tea. When I asked if she'd mind if I nursed the baby, she chortled. "Mind?" she said. "I'm envious!"

After the tea had been downed, she extracted from her bag a black-and-white photograph. In it, four people were seated on the steps of what appeared to be a large house constructed in part from massive blocks of stone. The group included a man, a woman, and a small boy seated between them. A uniformed nurse sat nearby. The man looked like a character out of an Edwardian drawing-room comedy: Tall and soigné, he was appareled in a boater hat, bow tie, vest, jacket, light-colored trousers, and dress shoes so well polished they gleamed. A walking stick rested in the circle formed by his folded hands. The woman, more handsome than beautiful, sat straight-backed in a high-collared shirt, bow tie, and ankle-length skirt. She smiled toward the camera, but her body was oriented toward the child. Beneath a broad-brimmed hat, fine blond bangs parted across the boy's forehead. Something familiar winked at me from his small, round face. I squinted at the photograph, puzzled. I could identify no one. I was certain I'd never seen the house.

"Chiltern," my great-aunt said. "Nineteen hundred. The first summer."

The early life of the boy in the photo—my grandfather, the eldest brother of Anna—was unknown country to me. Looking back now, it seems as if his history had been packed in a hatbox and stashed in an attic. Like a Punjabi bride, he'd moved in with his in-laws, Helen Hope's parents, upon marrying her in 1923. He'd lived with them for more than a year while the Colonel's architect built a home for him and Helen Hope out of the ruins of an eighteenth-century stone farmhouse. Six years later, he'd gone into business with his father-in-law. He'd spent his entire career in that firm, just as he'd spent all of his adult life on his father-in-law's estate. If people came to think of the Montgomery place as the Scott place, it was only because Helen Hope had taken Edgar Scott's last name. There was no mistaking the fact that she was in charge—of the farm, of the place, of their household, of him. He was the Duke of Edinburgh, absorbed into the Windsor family fold. The arrangement appeared to suit him just fine. But I now know that my grandfather, Edgar Scott, never lost sight of the fact that the house he lived in wasn't his. A few days after Helen Hope's death, their eldest son stopped by to see his newly widowed father. At ninety-six, his father was losing his marbles. Nevertheless, he maneuvered briskly to the point. To my uncle, he said, "Now you can throw me out, if you want to."

At the time of my great-aunt's visit and the presentation of the photograph of my grandfather as a small boy, I knew only a few facts about his earliest years. Born in Paris in 1899, he was said to have spoken French before English. He'd grown up largely in Lansdowne, Pennsylvania—a place I'd never been, though I now see it was only eleven miles away. He'd had a brother who'd died in the Pacific in World War II. His grandfather had been president of the Pennsylvania Railroad; I knew that because my father had said Lincoln had ridden in Thomas Scott's private railroad car. It wasn't until I was in my early twenties, killing time in a bookstore and flipping through the index of a book on robber barons, that it dawned on me that Thomas Scott had been one himself. As for the robber baron's son, my great-grandfather, I barely recall anyone speaking of him, ever. In all my grandfather's letters to my grandmother, I found he mentioned his father just once. The silence was so complete, it had never entered my mind to ask why. As my uncle later told me, "The Scotts were people who could just erase."

It would take me years to figure out what had been expunged from the record.

An almost life-size portrait of Thomas Scott, robber baron/forebear, hung on a wall in the library of my parents' house. In the portrait, he's a pink-faced man with muttonchop side whiskers the color of smoke, in the style favored by steamship and railroad tycoons. Scott also happens to have been partially disabled as a result of injuries suffered when an engine in which he was riding derailed, tossing him out of the train and onto his head. You wouldn't know that from the portrait. He looks every inch "the Pennsylvania Napoleon," as a New York newspaper editor once called him, "ambitious to take possession of the republic under a nine hundred and ninety-nine year lease." After my father's death, my brother, Elliot, entertained himself over the years by hanging the enormous portrait in a series of unpretentious apartments and houses he occupied in river towns along the Hudson. Once, after a store-window designer saw it in Elliot's living room and rented it from him for a couple of months, the Pennsylvania Napoleon could be glimpsed through a thicket of three-piece suits, twill trousers, and dress shirts in the window of a Ralph Lauren store in SoHo—a Gilded Age apparition returned to help sell haberdashery to aspiring nabobs of the new gilded age.

Just about the only detail I seemed to retain about Thomas Scott was a single, unforgettable quotation. It was said to date from around the time of the Great Railroad Strike of 1877, the first major rail strike, described by Albert J. Churella, the author of a history of the Pennsylvania Railroad, as "the beginnings of the age of industrial and class warfare in the United States." Four years into the longest recession in American history, and in response to new wage cuts and work rules, train crews in Maryland and West Virginia walked off the job. Then a strike broke out in Pittsburgh, where railroad workers blockaded the yards. People with other grievances against the railroad joined the protest. So did factory and mill workers and others whom the recession had left homeless and unemployed. After National Guard troops were called in, members of the crowd attacked them. Troops fired back, killing at least ten people and wounding many more. Protesters looted gun shops, seizing weapons. Someone lit a freight car on fire, and the blaze spread; other cars, filled with coke and oil, burst into flames. Roundhouses, an engine house, a machine shop burned. Troops killed more rioters. After three days, one hundred twenty-six locomotives and sixteen hundred freight and passenger cars had been destroyed. The railroad estimated the damage to its property at two million dollars. Ever since that time, Thomas Scott, then in his third year as the railroad's president, has been quoted as having suggested the rioters be given "a rifle diet for a few days, and see how they like that bread."

He was perhaps, some have said, the quintessential railroad man of his generation. Yet neither a biography nor a major collection of his personal papers exists. He's said to have appended to his business correspondence, like a postscript, the words "Destroy this letter." In the ironing-room archive, I exhumed no more than a dozen pieces of correspondence involving Thomas Scott, nearly all dating from the last years of his life. At his death, he even managed to keep secret the valuation of his estate. These days, the Pennsylvania Napoleon is largely forgotten. Among the few who still recognize the name, he's remembered primarily as a mentor to Andrew Carnegie, Scott's telegraph operator, chief assistant, and secretary at age seventeen. Others know only the rifle diet—or variations on that theme. In the 1970s, when labor history was on the rise, a fellow Harvard undergraduate, presenting himself as a man of the people, asked my sister, Hopie, whether she was a descendant of "Thomas 'Machine Gun' Scott." It was the first time she or I or Elliot had heard the story. From then on, on the infrequent occasions when Thomas Scott was mentioned in our presence, we'd snort knowingly, "Give 'em a machine gun diet!" The snort was a performance of worldly-wise cynicism—a hedge against being implicated in a history we'd barely begun to understand.

Thomas Scott, I now know, was the sixth (or possibly seventh) of the nine surviving children of a tavern owner in a hamlet on the turnpike that ran between Philadelphia and Pittsburgh. By birth and circumstance, he was endowed with charm and a capacity for ceaseless work. Orphaned at twelve, he went to work as an assistant to the collector of tolls on the state road in Columbia, Pennsylvania; he was chief clerk by eighteen. Hired at twenty-seven as a station agent for the Pennsylvania Railroad, he became general superintendent at thirty-five. A year later, he held the second-highest administrative position. Over the next fifteen years, he and J. Edgar Thomson, his predecessor as president, turned what had been merely a Philadelphia-to-Pittsburgh carrier into a six-thousand-mile system of railroads stretching from the Atlantic coast to the Mississippi River and the Great Lakes. Speculating in real estate, lumber, and other lucrative enterprises along the railroad's right-of-way, they became key figures in a high-powered investment group with interests in transportation, oil, minerals, and coal. Their influence eventually extended as far as New Orleans, Colorado, Arizona, and Mexico. At the height of their careers, they controlled not only the biggest freight carrier in the world but the most profitable corporation in North America.

Operating out of an office next to the state's legislative chambers, Scott applied the full force of his personality, as well as bribery, to bending the Pennsylvania legislature to his will. As vice president of the railroad, he masterminded a successful campaign to convince the legislature to repeal the tonnage tax levied on the railroad, in part by promising to send branch lines through elected officials' communities in return for their support. The railroad became, as William G. Roy puts it, "a single force so formidable that the government became its subject rather than its master." It developed a reputation, Churella writes, "as a company whose officers—particularly Scott—would stop at nothing in their efforts to manipulate the political process." As assistant secretary of war during the Civil War, Scott was in charge of all military railroads and government telegraphs. Though he resigned after a year amid allegations of conflict of interest, he returned to service the following year as an Army colonel and oversaw the transport of thirteen thousand troops with artillery wagons and horses from Virginia to Chattanooga—"the greatest mass movement of troops by rail up to that time."

Thomas Scott had his share of disasters, too. His failed attempt in the 1870s to build a transcontinental railroad through Texas and the Southwest brought huge losses upon himself, Edgar Thomson, and the Pennsylvania Railroad. During the disputed presidential election of 1876, he's been said to have played a pivotal role in the Compromise of 1877, the deal that settled the election in favor of Rutherford B. Hayes and resulted in the withdrawal of federal troops from the South and the end of Reconstruction. In light of which, it may seem trifling to note that he may never have uttered the words "rifle diet." The infamous quotation first appeared in a Chicago publication affiliated with a short-lived antimonopolist party in the late 1870s. It resurfaced in labor journals and anticapitalist diatribes but, it seems, not in the mainstream press. The most thorough contemporaneous account of the riots—the report of a Pennsylvania General Assembly investigating committee—makes no mention of any such statement. "Tom Scott was one of the most consistently and thoroughly vilified business executives in the nineteenth century," Churella told me when I asked him about the story. "Some of this he brought on himself, but much of this was undeserved—call it 'sour grapes' from people whom he outwitted." When dealing with any quotation attributed to Scott, Churella suggested, "It is useful to remember Yogi Berra's line about 'I really didn't say everything I said.'"

One year after the 1877 railroad strike, Scott suffered the first of a series of strokes that would eventually kill him. In what's been said to have been his one and only vacation, he took his wife and two of his children abroad to try to recover. When recovery eluded him, he resigned from the presidency of the railroad just six years into his tenure. By May 1881, he was dead at fifty-seven. Two thousand people turned out to watch the sixteen-carriage cortege that accompanied Thomas Scott's casket from his country home in Lansdowne to a cemetery carved out of an eighteenth-century estate overlooking the Schuylkill River in West Philadelphia. Railroad men from the Union Pacific, Texas and Pacific, Baltimore and Ohio, and other railroads were present. Railroad presidents and vice presidents carried the coffin. At the graveyard, where winding carriageways meandered beneath English elms, Scott was buried among the tombs of Civil War heroes, surgeons, artists, architects, and inventors. For thirty days, the locomotives, railroad cars, stations, and offices of the Pennsylvania Railroad were draped in black.

My father had some interest in his great-grandfather's story. He hung the portrait of Thomas Scott on the library wall. A fading back issue of *Pennsylvania Magazine of History and Biography*, with an article about Thomas Scott, had a permanent berth on a magazine table in the living room, where lesser periodicals were regularly culled. I regret now my lack of curiosity about old Machine Gun back then; I'd have liked to have asked my father what the family tie meant to him. I have the impression that the famous forebear's ghost occasionally stalked at least a few of his descendants. If Thomas Scott was a source of pride, he was also a reproof. The tavern owner's son, after all, wasn't simply the original self-made Scott: You might also wonder if he was the last.

Thomas Scott's son, my great-grandfather, had his father's charm but none of his drive. Whether the reason was nature or nurture—I'd only be guessing. But it's safe to say that the son's choppy course through his abbreviated life contrasts sharply with the father's pyrotechnic rise. The railroad king was in his late forties, and on his second wife, when the boy was born. They named him after his father's business partner, J. Edgar Thomson—a choice that strikes me, albeit from a great distance, as peculiar. What's it like to lug around the name of your famous father's famous, onetime boss? Would a contemporary equivalent be Tim Cook naming a son of his Steve Jobs Cook? My own first name was plucked from my mother's side of the family. But then the firm started by my father's father and grandfather merged with one called Janney, with an *e*. Ever since the new firm took the name Janney Montgomery Scott, I've been distressed on occasion to discover that there are people who believe my parents named me after a stockbrokerage.

Young Edgar Thomson Scott's opulent childhood bore zero resemblance to his father's humble beginnings. He started off in his parents' fifty-two-room mansion on Rittenhouse Square, a part of Philadelphia then thick with railroad, banking, and manufacturing notables. After his father died when the boy was just nine, his mother joined the exodus of adventurous Americans flocking to Paris, in the last half of the nineteenth century, for intellectual and artistic education. Under the guidance of a second cousin from Pittsburgh, Mary Cassatt, whose family was also in Paris, Anna Dike Riddle Scott began collecting Impressionist paintings. She shipped her little son off to a boarding school in England where, I'm told, lordlings wrote home on stationery engraved with their families' coats of arms, and Edgar, denied a coat of arms by birth, invented his own, featuring a locomotive rampant. "Has apparently never been taught how to work," his Latin and Greek teacher remarked witheringly on an early report. Three years later: "His weak points are that he never will muster the courage to face a difficulty fairly." At fourteen, he returned to the United States and was sent to the Groton School for Boys, founded two years earlier in Massachusetts on the British model with the aim of instilling the virtues of character, leadership, and service in the scions of the Gilded Age. The headmaster, a twenty-nine-year-old minister just back from shepherding Episcopalians in Tombstone, Arizona, after the shootout at the O.K. Corral, detected immediately that the railroad heir lacked his father's steam propulsion.

"Fair scholar but idle," Endicott Peabody, the headmaster, noted.

It seems only fair to acknowledge that the boy's early years had not been painless. He'd been born into a household of great wealth and privilege, but his older brother had died when Edgar Thomson was just seven. He was fatherless at nine. In the archive at Groton, I searched the headmaster's notes on his lackluster student for some foreshadowing of what was to come. The boy was "taken ill" in his senior year, Peabody wrote; he left school for a time and studied with a tutor. He entered Harvard in 1889: "Bad record there." Harvard sent him away after freshman year, telling his mother that he'd failed to open a book—a development that's said to have left Edgar depressed. After more tutoring, he returned to Harvard in 1891. "Left at Easter, ill again," Peabody wrote. He never went back and he never graduated. Perhaps he could see no compelling need to excel. But the headmaster's repeated use of the word "ill" made me wonder: Was Peabody covering for a privileged slacker? Or was the boy somehow suffering?

Here, the story takes a singular turn. In what I've been told was an attempt to cheer up her dispirited son, his mother helped him acquire a steam yacht—one hundred eighty-five feet long and rigged as a three-masted topsail schooner. At age twenty-two, Edgar T. prepared for a two-year circumnavigation of the world—an unusual regimen, in any decade, for a newly fledged college dropout. From a British passenger service, he hired the commander of an ocean liner that operated along the route between Liverpool and New York. He enlisted a crew of twenty-five Norwegians, a chief steward, and a valet. He took along traveling companions including a couple of cousins, his mother, his younger sister, a German governess, a physician, a young minister from Groton, and Warwick Potter, the son of a Civil War general and Edgar T.'s closest school friend. A nephew, Hugh Scott, fresh out of Groton, went along, too.

Hugh kept a diary of the voyage of the *Sagamore*—that was its name—which survives to this day. It's a novella-size journal of the expedition, which took the Scott party from Southampton, England, in the summer of 1893 to Norway, Denmark, France, Portugal, Spain, Gibraltar, Italy, Corfu, Albania, Greece, Egypt, Suez, Aden, Oman,

India, Ceylon, the Andaman Islands, Burma, Malaya, Singapore, Brunei, the Philippines, Hong Kong, China, and Japan—with overland side trips to London, Paris, Madrid, Granada, Seville, Toledo, Olympia, Cairo, Ahmedabad, Jaipur, Delhi, Agra, Cawnpore, Lucknow, Calcutta, Madras, Mandalay, and so on. Abruptly and unexpectedly, the trip ended in Yokohama eleven months in. With the First Sino-Japanese War looming, high-quality coal was in demand. How "the *Sag*" would get back across the Pacific was unclear. Edgar Thomson and company sailed home on a Canadian Pacific Railway steamer, leaving the crew to figure out what to do about the yacht.

Hugh Scott's journal reads like a cross between Jules Verne and Evelyn Waugh, SparkNotes edition. Reindeer shooting in Norway, boar hunting in Avlona, burning corpses in Benares. Mosques, monasteries, ostrich farms, opera houses, temples, tea plantations, pagodas, bullfights, the finest brothel in Paris. "Drunk!—Drunk again—and without hilarity," the diarist recounts grimly. Even the clergyman is occasionally unconscious. In the harbor at Copenhagen, the party encounters the yachts of Czar Alexander III, the King of Denmark, and the Prince of Wales. Prime ministers, sultans, dervishes receive them. "Women with such large nose-pendants that they have to bring a lock of hair from their forehead down and curl it around the pendant to take the strain off their noses," Hugh notes in Karachi. Off the coast of Oman, the night sea glows with phosphorescence: "Surf breaking on shore all aflame. Can pick it up by handfuls." At Christmas, the masts and bowsprit are decked with evergreen trees. For the costume dinner, Edgar's mother makes her entrance as an Oxford don. She and the girls sail off up the Nile. Edgar gallops a donkey through Cairo bazaars. "Mandolinist in stateroom while we smoke and shave," Hugh reports. In a hotel in Delhi, a sign catches his attention: "Please do not strike the servants." Shooting clay pigeons near the mouth of the Rangoon River, "Scott's gun goes off, tears hole in deck." A census of the *Sagamore's* passenger manifest: "Cows, polo ponies, a pack of fox hounds, a monkey, a dozen sheep, lots of geese, hens, parrots, small birds, etc etc." In the Andaman Islands, the travelers encounter a man named Portman, sent by the British Museum, to "take charge" of the pygmies: "He tames them and teaches them. They speak English, French and Italian." In Mandalay, Hugh reports that the Burmese had begged the English not to allow the use of liquor. A futile request, it seems: "The consequence is the Burmalese are falling off a bit in quality while the English grow richer."

Two months into the voyage, tragedy strikes. While heading for Lisbon in rough seas, members of the party fall ill. "Potter very sick from diarrhea and sea-sickness combined. An awful night," Hugh writes. The captain changes course and steams toward the harbor at Brest. A French doctor is summoned. "Potter gets worse and nothing much can be done," Hugh reports. Potter's brother hastens to the ship from Paris. Warwick rallies—but only briefly. "Poor old Warwick died at about ten o'clock in the morning without regaining consciousness," Hugh writes. "Fearfully sad."

"Colors are at half-mast," he added.

American newspapers attributed the death of the general's son to "the effects of seasickness" or "an inflammation of the stomach." From Hugh Scott's journal, it seems the French authorities may have suspected cholera. Edgar and the elder Potter accompanied the body back to New York on a French steamer after a service on the *Sagamore*'s deck. George Santayana, the Spanish-born poet-philosopher, who'd known Potter at Harvard, was moved to write four sonnets, titled "To W. P.," now among Santayana's best-known works. "We shall not loiter long, your friends and I; / Living you made it goodlier to live; / Dead you will make it easier to die."

Nine years later, Edgar Thomson Scott would name his second son Warwick Potter Scott. After Warwick Potter Scott's death, his younger sister would name her second son Warwick. But back in 1893, Edgar T. and the elder Potter rejoined the group on the *Sag*. And carried on.

If Thomas Scott rarely took a vacation, his son almost never held a job. "Principal occupation: None." That's how I found his employment history summed up in alumni records in the Groton archive. "Occupation: None at present." An exception occurred briefly in his late twenties when he worked for two years in the United States embassy in Paris as second secretary under an ambassador whom it seems likely the family knew from railroading circles. There, the second secretary occupied an eight-bedroom apartment in the sixteenth arrondissement, capacious enough to have an *office de maître d'hotel*—a butler's office—and a room called a *froisserie*, apparently devoted to the polishing of shoes. But in June 1899, in a letter to the secretary of state, the second secretary announced he was taking a leave of absence and would be resigning upon its expiration "for urgent family reasons." Before and after that fleeting period of gainful employment, his life was one of vigorous leisure. He raced sailboats, owned horses and carriages, bought speedboats and the latest automobiles. He was a champion racquets and tennis player. He belonged, at one time or another, to eighteen private clubs. He drank a lot. He enjoyed women. ("Poor Ma," his daughter Anna would sigh to her children.) I had to admire the resourcefulness of the headline writer who, called upon to sum up the railroad heir's life's work for the one-column head on his obituary in the *Philadelphia Bulletin*, settled on "Athletic Clubman."

The ghost of the athletic clubman, like that of his father, may also have stalked his descendants. Otherwise, how to explain the silence? It was not until my late twenties that I heard anything about my father's paternal grandfather—and, even then, it wasn't much. My father and I were in Ireland that summer, bicycling south to north. One evening, in a place called Kesh, I badgered him over dinner to tell me stories about his relatives. Eventually, the conversation turned from Montgomerys, some of whom I'd known, to his Scott grandfather, who'd never crossed my mind. He'd died eleven years before my father's birth. But my father said his own father had never spoken to his sons of their grandfather. When I pressed my uncle, years later, to explain how that could be, he told me, "The subject just didn't come up."

Edgar T. Scott, you'll have detected, was not a devotee of the simple life. Like Colonel Montgomery, he craved a grand country seat. And, like the Colonel, he turned to Horace Trumbauer, the architect of the moment, to build him a humongous house. The house was to be built on the Lansdowne property where the railroad baron had kept a relatively modest rustic abode, but it was to be "of a size suitable for an American plutocrat of the era," as Michael C. Kathrens puts it. The house, called Woodburne, was in the style of a late-eighteenth- or early-nineteenth-century American house—differing, Kathrens says, only in "its enormous size." Visitors entered through a high-ceilinged vestibule leading into a "gallery" the length of a basketball court. Off the gallery were a living room, drawing room, dining room, and library. French doors opened onto a four-columned portico and an oceanic lawn. The floor plan, come to think of it, resembled that of Ardrossan. Upstairs, there were eight large bedrooms, with adjoining bathrooms, for family members and guests; there was a nursery and playroom on the third floor. The "service wing" rivaled the main part of the house in size: In addition to a kitchen, butler's pantry, china pantry, walk-in safe, elevator, dumbwaiter, and so on, there were sixteen bedrooms for servants. Edgar T.'s sensible wife, Maisie, found the house oversized and pretentious. But he soon sold the Rittenhouse Square house, where the family had been living. In 1913, a syndicate bought and razed it, clearing the way for a fifteen-story apartment house, the first skyscraper on the square.

The house in the photograph given to me by my father's aunt Anna on her visit to my apartment wasn't Woodburne. It was yet another huge house, the athletic clubman's summer palace. If Ardrossan was the Montgomerys' Taj Mahal, this one was the Scotts'—except that, instead of a mausoleum for a dead wife, this *mahal* began as an inducement to marriage. Edgar T. Scott had spent summers in Bar Harbor on Mount Desert Island in Maine, a place that had once appealed to "rusticators" with an appetite for simple living. But, by the 1880s, Bar Harbor was transforming itself into an alternative to Newport, Rhode Island. Wealthy families from Boston, New York, Philadelphia, and Chicago began building palatial "cottages," accessorizing them with hanging gardens, heated swimming pools, a motorized dining-room table. There, the railroad president's son took an interest in the youngest daughter of a high-minded widow from Philadelphia, a Unitarian of Boston Brahmin stock. It was an unlikely pairing—the dashing socialite with lavish appetites and intemperate habits, and the disciplined bluestocking, whom Warwick Potter had considered the Platonic ideal of woman. Edgar pursued Maisie Sturgis unsuccessfully for years. Finally, in the mid-1890s, he bought fourteen acres of wildwood and swampland on the water—Vanderbilts to the north, Pulitzers to the south. There, he told Maisie, he'd build a house where, if she refused to marry him, he'd retreat from the world and think only of her. He'd call it Chiltern—an allusion to an esoteric procedure, called "taking the Chiltern Hundreds," for resigning from the British House of Commons. Maisie surrendered. Nine days after their marriage in 1898, the newlyweds sailed for France. Over the next two years, while they lived in their eight-bedroom apartment in the sixteenth arrondissement, their summer "cottage" took shape above the rocky crescent of beach at Cromwell Cove.

Chiltern, where my grandfather and father would spend childhood summers, was built to last. The ground-floor stonework resembled, as one newspaper put it, that of a modern fort. The cellars and foundation were blasted out of solid rock beneath a clearing that sloped to the water. Granite hauled from a nearby quarry was cut into squared blocks and fitted into place by thirty masons. The windows were mullioned, panes leaded; the upper stories were shingled. Inside, there were two living rooms; a dining room; a study; an octagonal, glassed-in porch; thirteen big bedrooms, and twenty-two smaller ones for servants, servants' servants, and the servants of guests. At a time when most American homes were lit with gas or candles, Chiltern had four hundred fifty electric lights—not to mention an interior telephone network, a state-of-the-art security system, and a room devoted to flower arranging. "Chiltern was a landmark in Bar Harbor, with the highest budget, if not the most creativity, of Longfellow's designs in Maine," Margaret Henderson Floyd observed coolly in a book on its architect, A. W. Longfellow, the poet's nephew. The house was intended to look, as one newspaper put it, "as old as the Mount Desert hills."

Even the landscape designer had a pedigree. To create a garden, Edgar Thomson Scott enlisted a niece of Edith Wharton, Beatrix Jones—who, under her married name, Beatrix Farrand, would become known as the first American woman to break into landscape architecture. The latest in a line of five generations of gardeners, Jones was hired, at twenty-four, to conceive and plant a ten-acre garden for the Scotts. Out of the spruce and birch forest, she and a hundred-man crew cleared an oval canvas on which to paint. They created a circular lawn with grass paths approaching from three directions, separating drifts of summer flowers in washes of color—scarlets, yellows, and blues on one side; purples, crimsons, pinks, and white on another. The planting plan looked like a quilt with nearly one hundred seventy patches of flowers: columbines, black-eyed Susans, heleniums, and on and on. "I set myself to work out a scheme of color, absolutely by instinct," she wrote later. She designed a semicircular bench and a table, for afternoon tea overlooking a small pond. Evergreens enclosed the garden. Only the chimneys, gables, and roofline of the house were visible above the tops of the trees. "It is, in a way, the most original garden I have tried and it has been a success," Jones wrote. Patrick Chassé, a landscape architect who's written about Farrand's work, calls it an Alice in Wonderland garden, "dwarfing the visitor to childlike proportions."

The family would arrive from Philadelphia by train—parents in one car; children and French governesses in another; horses in a third. There were sailing races, tennis tournaments, moonlight picnics in places like "the ballroom"—a mountain plateau where yet another Scott once hosted a dance, orchestra included. There was an annual children's pageant, too, in the garden. In a photograph, a cluster of tiny cousins costumed as winged creatures—dragonflies or fairies, maybe—cast shadows in the grass, ringed by billowing beds of flowers. A photo of a Sturgis family reunion in 1913 shows twenty-nine members of three generations—men in boaters, boys in sailor suits, girls dressed in white. In the back row—identified as "inlaws" in a handwritten key on the back of the photograph—Edgar Thomson Scott stands, sporting a dark mustache, his face having thickened in the years since the picture taken that first Chiltern summer. In the middle row, among the "original" Sturgises, I find Maisie in a broad-brimmed hat. In the front two rows—identified as the nineteen "descendants"—my grandfather, age fourteen, sits cross-legged, a faraway look in his eye.

They'd named him Edgar, after his father, but he took after his mother. He shared her passion for literature, poetry, and the theater. How, his sporty père is said to have wondered aloud, could any son of his have ended up so athletically inept? On sojourns in Paris, Maisie Scott took my grandfather and his three siblings to La Comédie-Française. The year Anna turned twenty, the books shipped to Bar Harbor for her summer reading included Dante, Molière, Racine, Proust. Years later, Susie, the youngest, would amuse her sons by reciting all seventy stanzas of Thomas Babington Macaulay's "Horatius at the Bridge" from memory. She and my grandfather, in middle age, were overheard fencing over a line from a classical French tragedy. The encounter, her son Rick recalls, went something like this: "Remember that wonderful line of Polyeucte's?" Susie asked, rattling it off. "I remember the line, but it's Pauline's," Edgar answered. "*Polyeucte*," she insisted. "*Pauline*!" he countered. Act two, scene three! Act four, scene two! "Do you remember act two, scene three?" Susie asked. Of course, he answered. "Then let's go through it," she dared him. Which they did.

Young Edgar, my grandfather, was close to his mother. "Tremendously intimate and companionable," his father called them. Confined to bed for a time at age ten, he received from his mother everything he needed to pursue his youthful passion for binding books. She harvested lining paper, from bureau drawers, for him to cut into pages; and she supplied him with hundreds of lines of poetry, aphorisms, and quotations—an adage for each day of the year—with which he filled every page. After her death, my grandfather had the handmade book reprinted and gave away copies. He was impressed, he said, by how much of his mother's spirit—her religious faith, her delight in lyric poetry, her ethics, her feeling for children—lived on in that book. When I came upon a copy, it was hard to miss one recurrent theme— the dangers of excessive leisure. Blessed are the horny hands of toil. No one is so weary as the man who does nothing. Procrastination is the thief of time. And,

Stretched on the rack of a too easy chair,
And heard thy everlasting yawn confess
The pains and perils of idleness.

Maisie, it seems, intended to steer her eldest son toward a life un-like that of his father. She was the Model T of helicopter mothers. My grandfather's name hit the Groton waiting list the day he was born. When he turned twelve, Maisie arranged for him to skip the first year, saying it would be "better for his character" and would keep him from developing "loafing habits." Six months before he was to enroll, she told the school that he was fluent in French, spoke ade-quate German, and was reading Caesar in Latin. Should he know algebra? she inquired, as the family headed off to Europe. What his-tory should he study? She hired a tutor, to travel with the family, with what she considered top-notch credentials—a Bostonian with a Har-vard degree. Later, she'd track the monthly academic averages of both of her sons. "I am distressed about Edgar's Greek," she'd write to the Groton headmaster. "I hoped that he would be a really good classical scholar."

His separation from his mother was rocky. In humorously melo-dramatic letters to "dear Mamma," he pleaded for deliverance. "If you don't come soon, I shall curse some teacher, and get expelled, even if it is a disgrace, I would do it just to see you!" he wrote. He was insolent to the mathematics master, the headmaster reported. He engaged in roughhousing—explicitly forbidden—and used "foul language" with other boys. The headmaster, Endicott Peabody, suspected "an aversion to effort," or "a lack of moral perception," or both. Sentenced to spend an afternoon copying passages, Edgar instead satirized his plight by writing "The Divine Tragedy"—then, when busted, failed to appreci-ate the gravity of his crimes. In time, however, he found his niche. On Edgar's sixteenth birthday, Peabody wrote approvingly of his student's "unusual ability." He'd become an editor of the literary magazine, an actor in school plays. An underclassman would remember him years later as "the Noel Coward of Groton."

My mind wanders to the subject of sons and mothers, fathers and daughters. My grandfather, named for his father, was closer to his mother; my grandmother, named for her mother, was close to her father. Rightly or wrongly, she'd say she'd been his favorite. I, too, was named after my mother's side of our family, but was thought to take after my father. My parents were scrupulous, I was sure, in avoiding the appearance of preferences. But after I finished a draft of this book and gave a copy to my brother, he said, "Don't you think you should say that you were his favorite?"

There was a time in my thirties when I wrestled with an aversion to marriage. I took the matter to a psychotherapist in Santa Monica, whom my future husband took to calling Joan Lightbody, though that wasn't her name. Joan Lightbody steered her conversations with me around to my father: Was something about my relationship with him getting in the way? In giving that hypothesis some thought, I found myself reflecting on my father's relationship with his mother. There was a quality to their oft-stated mutual admiration that I couldn't define. That got me thinking about my grandmother and the Colonel. Were there patterns in relationships between certain parents and certain children that reproduced themselves from one generation to the next?

Had I known anything back then about my grandfather's parents, I might've wondered, too, about the relationship between father and son—the sportive, leisured man with his sailboats and coach horses and racquets, and his literary-minded, soon-to-be-aspiring-playwright son. What role, if any, did a yearning for filial bonding play in the decisions that the son and the father each made to travel together to the battlefields of World War I? Later, my grandfather must have looked back over all the pain that flowed from those decisions. Was he unable to avoid dwelling upon his inadvertent role?

If I hadn't discovered an identification card issued to my grandfather the year he graduated from high school, I might have missed that chapter of his life completely. The card identified Edgar Scott, at seventeen, as a member of an ambulance service in France in the summer of 1916. A passport-size photo showed him on the cusp of adulthood, hair combed back off his forehead, his cheeks not yet visibly acquainted with a razor. The card led me to the Manhattan offices of an international exchange organization that grew out of an ambulance service formed in Paris in the early months of World War I. In the archive of the American Field Service, I found a photograph of fourteen men reclining on an overgrown lawn behind a large house in Paris that long-ago summer. They were dressed in the field service uniform: belted military-style tunic, breeches, leather leggings, boots, visor cap. My grandfather was among them. He'd served at the field service's headquarters that summer, I'd learned from a roster of volunteers.

In the spring of 1916, Endicott Peabody received a letter from a supporter of the American Ambulance Field Service in France. Would Groton raise money, the writer asked, to pay for an ambulance to be used to assist the French? The United States still had a policy of neutrality toward the war. But after the German invasion of Belgium in 1914, three volunteer ambulance corps had formed, including the American Ambulance Field Service, as it was then called, which had grown out of a small hospital maintained by Americans living in France. By late 1915, the field service had become essential to the French army. All three ambulance corps recruited heavily from what George Plimpton, in the foreword to a book on the subject, called the "upper-class gentry." Hundreds of students from boarding schools and Ivy League colleges volunteered, many of them raised to revere French culture. Some felt a sense of national indebtedness because of France's support in the Revolutionary War. Others went for the adventure. By the time the United States entered the war in 1917, more than three thousand, five hundred Americans had served in the ambulance corps, playing a role in almost every major battle. They'd also helped sway American public opinion in favor of declaring war.

The request appealed to Peabody. Soon, the Groton vehicle was in the field. In late June, my grandfather and three other Groton students sailed for France to volunteer. Too young to drive an ambulance, Edgar was assigned to the field service's headquarters on the Right Bank, where the service had been given the use of an eighteenth-century mansion "surrounded by acres of romantic and deserted gardens," as the inspector general of the service described it. Balzac had lived across the street. Rousseau, Voltaire, and Zola had idled in the gardens. My young, literary-minded grandfather worked as a mechanic's apprentice; he also unpacked and transported Ford chassis, arriving from the United States, from Bordeaux to Paris. Less than two hundred miles away from the compound in Paris, the Battle of Verdun raged on the western front, leaving some seven hundred thousand French and German soldiers dead, wounded, or missing. A month after my grandfather left Paris for Harvard, a German shell landed a few feet in front of a field service ambulance near the front, killing another young volunteer from Philadelphia.

Back from Paris and ensconced in Cambridge, young Edgar plotted his return to France. His father and mother were leery. Edgar the elder had attended a voluntary preenlistment training program organized by private citizens in Plattsburgh, New York. But Edgar the younger had to appeal to his old headmaster to make the case to his parents that he should be permitted to go. Peabody said he couldn't "take responsibility" in a matter of such gravity. So young Edgar not only made the case to his parents for himself—he proposed that his father go, too.

"I want to have you let me go, of course—but, as I've told you, it would be wonderful for you, too," my grandfather wrote to his father in January 1917. "It would be awfully hard to say goodbye to the family for so long, and that part of it would be darn unpleasant. But after you got back you'd never be sorry you'd gone away.—Really. And I bet

Ma sees it that way,—although I don't know: I haven't mentioned it seriously."

By late April, it had been decided. The son would take a year's leave of absence from Harvard, and would return to France to enlist with an ambulance corps. The father, twice the age of most volunteers and with no battle experience, would go along, too.

Edgar the elder, the railroad man's indulged scion, prepared to set sail for Paris late that spring buoyed by an unfamiliar sense of purpose. He had a deep affection for France, rooted in his childhood and in the earliest years of his marriage. What was more, it had been his eldest son and namesake who'd urged him to go along. "I quite realize I have never been a father of boys before, and I am reveling in it," he'd written two years earlier, on a father-son trip to the West Coast with his two boys. "Father and Son to Enlist," a headline in the *Philadelphia Bulletin* announced. The article stated that the father had become "enthused" by his son's accounts of his work in Paris the previous summer; by volunteering, the father hoped to free up a younger man for military service. Thomas Scott's pleasure-loving heir, it seems, had come to regret some of his past choices. "Well, *my* sons are going to work," he'd taken to saying—a declaration in which it's difficult not to detect some personal dissatisfaction. In a letter to Peabody several years earlier, he'd written, "Life indeed does seem to be terribly short especially to one who begins to realize how much time has been wasted."

Sixteen summers had passed since Edgar Thomson Scott and Maisie had been photographed on the steps at Chiltern. Now, in the spring of 1917, a photographer arrived at the house in Lansdowne. Maisie, forty-five and graying, settled on one end of a heavy sofa, a tapestry on the wall behind as a backdrop. Her second son, Warwick, sixteen, pressed close to her on her left. My grandfather, two years older, sat with Anna, age ten, in his lap. Susie, age eight, balanced on the knee of her father, who was seated in a chair to Maisie's right, slightly apart. His left elbow rested on the couch behind Maisie. Their marriage had not been easy.

"Your grandfather was the most attractive man I've ever known—when he was sober," one of his grandsons remembers hearing from an older cousin. The duties of Edgar T. Scott's valet included bundling him discreetly into his "dressing room" after nights of carousing. "They were trying to hold things together," a granddaughter, Maisie Adamson, told me. "They were hoping it was going to be all right." There's evidence of tenderness in the portrait taken that day—a feeling you might miss if you didn't linger over it, half-conscious of the trauma to follow. It's in their expressions and the language of their bodies—an arm curled across a shoulder, a hand in another's lap, the angle at which one leans toward the next. To his wife, the father is said to have vowed in a letter from France months later, "When I come back, it's all going to be different."

On the back of the photograph, in my grandfather's writing: "Just before the 2 E's sailed to war."

They arrived in Paris in early June. In an unorthodox route to the battlefield, they alighted first at the Hotel Meurice, opposite the Jardin des Tuileries with easy access to the Louvre. Paris was changed, though not entirely. There were alarms and zeppelin scares; restaurants closed at 9:30 P.M. Hotel rooms had a single light, and hot water once a week. A room and bath at the Plaza Athénée went for fifteen francs. Yet, theaters were open. "Saw Edgar several times and went to the theater with him and several others," his nephew and former classmate, Hugh Scott, the *Sagamore* diarist, wrote of the elder Edgar in a letter home. "On Sunday I stopped to see him and he had been 'tite' the night before at a goodbye dinner." There were chance encounters with friends. In a letter to Peabody, the younger Edgar reported having run into another Groton graduate: "Among his present friends is a young lion cub which he keeps at the Ritz."

My young grandfather went to work, as planned, as an ambulance driver attached to the French army at the front, working twenty-four hours on, forty-eight off. "To date, I have narrowly missed being killed once, been under fire twice, visited the front lines once," he wrote cheerfully from an orchard where his ambulance section had camped. ". . . If I can only take part in the evacuation behind some real attack, I promise you a less 'dry' letter." To his disappointment, however, his section was replaced in mid-October, after the United States forces militarized the ambulance corps. "We all stood in front of our camp in the evening watching the big shells land," he wrote. ". . . That was the night before we left—you can imagine our disgust that they didn't let us stay till after the attack!" From there, he went to work as driver, mechanic, and secretary for his cousin Hugh, the field director for the American Red Cross at Chaumont. And before returning to Harvard the following summer, he spent several months at the front as a canteen officer in the French army zone, having been given the rank of second lieutenant.

His father, meanwhile, appeared initially to flounder. He worked in the office of one of the ambulance corps, then went off on an assignment for the Red Cross liaison with the French army. "Edgar senior is a wonder at wiggling out of one thing into another," Hugh wrote home to his wife. For months, Edgar was, as Hugh put it, "more or less on the bum"—waiting for a job as an interpreter and "losing confidence in himself and everything." Hugh offered help, but the elder Edgar declined it. He was too fussy, Hugh concluded. Finally, the job he'd been waiting for came through: In January 1918, he was hired as an interpreter and aide to the inspector general for the American Expeditionary Forces. Commissioned as a first lieutenant, he was quickly promoted to major. Even Hugh was impressed. My grandfather's pride in his father is touching. "He's been working terribly hard," he wrote to his brother, before leaving France that summer. "And, by

George, I wish you could see him, and be with him, and hear his talk. He's the peach of peaches now; wide awake, and in the game heart and soul, for the best motives."

Edgar Thomson Scott, it seems, had glimpsed the possibility of salvation. In an envelope labeled in his wife's handwriting, "To be destroyed <u>unopened</u>" (which, by the time I came upon it, had been opened), I would find, nearly a century later, a single sheet of French hotel stationery, dated February 3, 1918. On it

The two Edgars in France

was a pledge, in black ink, made by the elder Edgar to himself: "My object in life at present is—," he began. First, "to serve my country in this war to the best of my ability, to be absolutely faithful to General B., to <u>develop</u> myself in every way in order to be <u>energetic</u> and in the job and useful to him when he wants me. To learn all I possibly can about the administration of the Army, to keep my mind and body lithe and active for the purposes of the service, and to gain the General's confidence and trust, and to be worthy of them. To do my best for the war." Secondly, "to develop a sense of responsibility, and a desire to assume it. To concentrate and absolutely master the thing before me."

The third object concerned his family:

"To make myself worthy to take my place at the head of my family if I return to America," the wayward husband and father had written.

"To keep in loving touch with all of them, and to be worthy to be loved by them."

I find myself lingering over the multiple repetitions of the word "worthy." The word reads to me like one uttered in prayer. Consumed by the conviction that he's unworthy, the man vows to prove the opposite to his commanding officer, his family, himself. How could the pampered heir to a railroad fortune ever have felt worthy in the absence of work? Were racquet sports expected to help? Was he to have derived a sense of his own value and purpose from commissioning palaces for himself, using money made by the father he'd barely known? I'm speculating here, but it seems likely that Edgar Thomson Scott wasn't unacquainted with the feeling of shame. He'd failed in school and in college, twice. His friend had died pointlessly on their grand tour. He'd held just one job in his entire adult life—for just two years. It's telling that the leisured scion had pledged that his own sons would work. It's telling, too, that he'd confessed to his old headmaster, looking back, that he'd come "to realize how much time has been wasted."

Now, it seems, the prodigal son may have believed he had a shot at redemption. Did he fear, at forty-six, that it might be his last? He wasn't blind to his shortcomings: The virtues he aspires to, in the letter, are the flip side of the vices he knows too well. He'll be *absolutely faithful, energetic, responsible, useful,* he promises. He'll *concentrate, master, serve.* He'll *develop a sense of responsibility, and a desire to assume it.* It's not clear that he believes he can pull it all off. Why would such a letter—the resolutions of a despairing man who'd found himself suddenly with the possibility of hope—end up preserved in an envelope marked "to be destroyed <u>unopened</u>"?

Eight months later, the letter writer was dead.

"Following a brief illness," the *Philadelphia Bulletin* reported, citing friends of the family. Edgar Thomson Scott had died of pneumonia, the story went, having worked himself into a state of exhaustion. "Unceasing work, with insufficient sleep during nights passed in damp, unhealthy billets combined to cause a severe strain, under which his health finally broke down, and which ultimately caused his death," read a florid report published by Harvard after the war. ". . . Edgar Scott gave his life for his country, and we who are his classmates and who knew him are glad that he found such a happy fulfilment of his life; and we shall ever be proud of the example that he left behind him of patriotic service and unswerving devotion to duty."

In the clubhouses to which upper-crusters still flock to this day, the name of Edgar T. Scott took its place in gold on plaques memorializing the clubmen killed in the Great War. As the years passed, his children rarely spoke of his death. His grandchildren grew up taking it for granted that their grandfather had been a hero. When I asked the youngest what he'd been told of the circumstances of his grandfather's death, he said, "Just that it was unclear, that it was in the trenches and it was pretty awful and nobody was quite sure exactly what he died of." My grandfather, who in his determination to return to France in 1917 had swept his father along with him, never spoke to his own sons about the circumstances of their grandfather's death. It fell to Helen Hope, never one to mothball a good story, to unceremoniously spill the beans.

My uncle, the third Edgar, was old enough to have a driver's license at the time—a fact that places this memory of his during World War II. He was at the wheel of a car, driving his mother home from Philadelphia, when the conversation turned to his paternal grandfather.

"He died in the war. He was a hero," Ed would remember remarking matter-of-factly to his mother.

"Nonsense," she scoffed, of the father-in-law she'd never met.

Then she let fly the long-obscured truth.

"He shot himself," she said.

Chapter Four

The swimming pool lay in a clearing a quarter mile from the big house. You reached it through a padlocked gate in a high, chain-link fence at the bottom of a steep hill. The mossy paving-stone path wound through a wood to a small bridge over a creek, then climbed toward the light. The pool was long and deep and the bleached blue of a beach towel after many summers' use. Tall trees hemmed in the glade, littering the surface of the water with leaves. A buffer of ferns grew between the shallow end and the encroaching forest; a terrace extended along one side. If you lay on your back on the heavy wooden bench on the terrace, the patch of sky above, framed by treetops, mirrored the pool's mattress shape. But because sunlight only briefly struck the pool head-on, the water temperature rarely broke sixty-three degrees. We called it the cold pool—not a pejorative, a term of respect. The cold pool wasn't one of those oversized bathtubs where other people poached until their fingertips wrinkled. This pool flash-froze your nether parts.

My father, in navy swimming trunks, would balance on the slippery lip of the deep end where water lapped out of the pool into a spillway and ran downhill to the creek. He'd sway in the August heat, sweat trickling down his hairless chest. From a pocket in his bathing suit, he'd remove rubber earplugs and fit them into his ears; he'd swum in frigid Maine water as a boy, and had paid for it, he said, with some fraction of his hearing. Arms outstretched, he'd dive noiselessly, cleaving the water. He'd emerge one-third of the way down the pool, and press on in a methodical front crawl. Hopie, Elliot, and I preferred to fling ourselves out over the deep, limbs rigid, slamming into the surface. In the churn, we'd bob up, gasp histrionically, bolt for the side. Once, when I was small, I flipped upside down in the cold pool in an inflatable ring, like a capsized sailboat—mast underwater, centerboard in the air. My grandfather, standing nearby, fished me out by the ankles. I like to imagine that I remember that moment, though maybe all I remember is the story. A swim at the cold pool wasn't just a substitute for air-conditioning. It was a test of mettle—preparation, I now think, for the future, including a leap, decades later, into the sea off Greenland, in a bathing suit, just to say I had.

My grandparents were regulars at the cold pool. Sometimes, after my parents had wrangled us into the wayback and driven up the long driveway toward the big house, after we'd turned onto the farm road that descended steeply between pasture and wood, and after we'd left the paved road to rumble across grass toward the gate to the pool, we'd catch sight of one of my grandparents' cars, parked under an elm beside the post-and-rail fence. They drove Humbers—the car favored by Viscount Montgomery of Alamein in the African campaign. Their cars smelled like leather; their red seats were crazed, like the glaze on old ceramics, by wear and tear. If there was a Humber parked under the tree, my father would slam our car doors, clear his throat, bark orders, rattle the gate in the chain-link fence. Our grandparents, we came to understand, liked to swim naked. Years later, I learned, too, that they'd found a use for the big wooden bench other than keeping towels off the ground.

Helen Hope and Edgar, it was often observed, had a rare sort of marriage. They were one of those couples off whom stories fly like sparks from a fast-moving train. Which of those stories were entirely true, I'm still not sure. They were true enough. In one, my grandmother happens upon her darling in bed with another woman. Instead of taking some more pedestrian course of action, she wedges herself between them, inquiring, "You don't mind if I sleep here, do you?" I've heard it reported that she turned up at a costume party wearing a rooster on her head. She's said to have entertained dinner guests by wriggling into an antique metal chastity belt—a gift from a congenial friend, repurposed by my grandmother as a cachepot. They made an eye-catching pair, my grandparents did, down to Helen Hope's black-and-white calfskin coat by Pauline Trigère. ("It's pure Holstein. I'm afraid I've been unfaithful to Ayrshires.") In a picture taken before a trans-Atlantic crossing in 1938, they stand side by side, camera-ready, at the gangway to the *Île de France*. He's in a dark overcoat and a fedora. She's in a fur-trimmed coat, openwork heels, and a broad-brimmed hat that could well be a Stetson. They look like some Hollywood couple—maybe William Powell and Myrna Loy. If they ever got seriously bored with each other, my guess is few people

knew. "To quote Winston Churchill," my grandfather liked to say, "'My most brilliant achievement was my ability to persuade my wife to marry me.'"

Their union was legendary. After seven decades together, they still talked about how crazy they were about each other. But it wasn't easy, as a grandchild, to see the inner workings. Once, scanning a bookshelf in their bedroom, I stumbled upon a lead. I took down a small, slim volume with a cartoon in the style of *The New Yorker* of the 1950s on its tattered cover. A perky-looking housewife, high heels cast aside, feet on a footstool, was sitting at a desk, poring over a ribbon of tape. At first glance, it seemed she was sewing. But, upon closer examination, the tape turned out to be spilling from a ticker tape machine: The lady, phone at her elbow, was studying stock prices. The book was *How to Lay a Nest Egg: Financial Facts of Life for the Average Girl*, a humorous introduction to investing, by Edgar Scott, published in 1950. The back cover carried testimonials from improbable authorities whose names I vaguely recognized as belonging to my grandparents' friends—Helen Hayes, Katharine Cornell, Anita Loos. Inside, my grandfather had inscribed the copy to my grandmother, "a friend of the author." An engraved calling card dropped out. "Darlingest Bee," he'd written. "One inscription is not enough for You, who are my inspiration in this as in everything else."

If I want to fathom my father, surely I need a better handle on them.

Their house on Ardrossan was unlike the mammoth houses in which they'd each grown up. It nestled in the folds of the surrounding landscape, instead of eyeing it from above. The rooms were modestly sized and intimate, though the living-room fireplace was wide enough to accommodate dozens of Christmas cards on a string pulled taut between the two ends. A painted wooden carousel horse stood in a bay window, a potted plant on its saddle. Along with the paintings by Degas, Manet, Renoir, Boudin, Cassatt, Corot, and Toulouse-Lautrec, most of which my grandfather had inherited, there was an Al Hirschfeld caricature of Hepburn in *The Philadelphia Story*; pewter tankards from a visit to Damascus; a spinning wheel said to hail from some ancestor's 1772 trousseau; framed cartoons by Charles Addams; and dozens of editions of books by John O'Hara, the novelist and short-story writer, remembered these days for having limned the finest of social distinctions once discernible only to members of a now vanished upper class.

My grandfather had met O'Hara at Philip Barry's house in Easthampton in the 1930s and had become a collector of his books—an avocation in which O'Hara assisted by annotating my grandfather's copies, and insinuating into manuscripts occasional inside jokes like "a three-gaited bay mare owned by some people called Scott."

In *The Big Laugh*, a book Fran Lebowitz once called the greatest Hollywood novel ever written, O'Hara slipped the lesser-known Scotts into a roll call of (real-life) luminaries invited to a (fictional) actress's imaginary closing-night party—"which was attended by her friends the Lunts, Woollcott, Katharine Cornell and Guthrie McClintic, Noel Coward, Beatrice Lillie, Alice Duer Miller, Philip Barry, Ina Claire, Jack Gilbert, Marc Connelly, Deems Taylor, the Damrosches, Jascha

Heifetz, Condé Nast, Carmel Snow, William Lyon Phelps, Charles Hanson Towne, Walter Prichard Eaton, Sidney Howard, Elisabeth Marbury, Gerald and Sara Murphy, Neysa McMein and John Baragwanath, and the Edgar Scotts from Philadelphia."

O'Hara, not above making a joke of his famously thin skin, told my grandfather, "Now, Edgar, you have to tell me all about that party because, of course, they would never ask me."

In an era before Rolodexes and Google Contacts, my grandparents had a staggering abundance and variety of friends. There was Henry McIlhenny, the Philadelphia curator and collector whom Andy Warhol is said to have called "the only person in Philadelphia with glamour." There was Anita Loos and Tallulah Bankhead and Claudette Colbert. There was the British First Sea Lord, Sir Caspar John. There were horse people, cow people, burghers of the Main Line, and successive generations of men who ran Angelo D'Amicantonio & Son, the shoe repair place on Lancaster Pike. Walter Annenberg, the press baron and philanthropist, was the source of the chastity-belt cachepot. Once, when I was backpacking around Europe, my grandparents invited my boyfriend and me to lunch in Venice, where we found them hanging out with Jack Profumo, the disgraced British cabinet minister who'd been forced to resign a decade earlier over an affair with an aspiring model with ties to a Soviet naval attaché. In a pile of condolence letters sent to the family after my grandmother's death, I came upon one from the Ayrshire Society of Stavropol, Russia. The undersigned remembered fondly how the mistress of the Ardrossan herd had once kissed him and told him he was a very unusual man.

The stories my grandparents told teemed with names I should have known and sometimes didn't—names like Josephine Baker, the Stork Club, the Duke of Windsor. (My grandmother had persuaded him to stand on his head, it was said, so she could find out what he wore under his kilt.) "I was stuck with Winston Churchill one Christmas on Aristotle Onassis's yacht," was the sort of thing she sometimes said (and once did). "I didn't know what to say. I asked him about the weather and he just grunted. As they handed him a double martini, I said, 'Sir, I heard it was a very windy crossing at Gibraltar. Were you seasick?'" She had a rollicking narrative style not unlike the voice in *Eloise at the Plaza*: People in her stories were always throwing a fit, falling right down with apoplexy, going mad. A flight attendant was "a buxom stewardess with a hangover, who looks like a sow"; a man with designs on her was "so tight he could barely dance." In the service of a laugh, she had few qualms about making herself look preposterous: "He asked me did I know Goya," she once said, recalling her first encounter with the portrait painter Augustus John. "I was so shy. I said, 'Yes, I often see him at parties.' I thought Goya was a gigolo!"

At its inception, my grandparents' union looked to some like an unlikely coupling. At Harvard my grandfather Edgar had been a student of the nineteenth-century French comedy of manners and had translated a period play into English verse for its first American production. His circle of acquaintance included young writers and playwrights like the Algonquin Round Table regular Robert E. Sherwood. One of his former girlfriends was Helen Hayes (who my grandmother liked occasionally to suggest was the real love of his life). My grandmother Helen Hope was the product of a less cosmopolitan, somewhat more provincial upbringing. After an initial encounter, my mother's Boston Brahmin father pronounced her "ravishingly beautiful and spoiled rotten." Her future husband once wrote to her, "I realize what an overwhelming responsibility you're going to be—if, every minute you're alone, men dash up and converse with you! (It's nice, though—and, in a funny way, makes me proud.)" In an unsigned list of their respective personality traits, preserved in a scrapbook, I find my grandfather characterized, in his midtwenties, as sensitive, adaptable, altruistic, even-tempered if moody. His young wife is gay and hospitable but also hot-tempered, competitive, intuitive, tenacious, with an appetite for power. When Maisie Sturgis Scott learned that

Helen Hope Montgomery had taken Maisie's eldest son out for a ride, she deduced that he had to be in love. If he weren't, she told his sisters, he'd never have been caught dead on a horse.

"According to Mom," one of their nephews told me, "everybody gave that marriage six months."

But my grandparents were magnetized by a ferocious mutual attraction. As a child, I couldn't have appreciated the high-voltage current that leaped between them; but, long after their deaths, I witnessed its traces, still sparking on the page. My grandmother saved the vast majority of the written communication that passed between them—hundreds of love letters, sonnets, postcards, humorous poems, erotic poems, erotic cartoons, cablegrams, scribblings on menus. "My keen, glorious, desirable, and desirous, and perfect woman," he writes. "My arms—and everything else—just ache for you!" Their ostensibly chaste nine-month engagement practically killed them. Over seven decades of marriage, their correspondence was amorous, adoring, reproachful, ravenous, jealous, penitent, aching. They tantalized and tortured each other with the specter of other lovers—bewitching theater companions, lascivious train conductors, old flames imagined and real. "The wolves seem to sniff your absence," she writes to him, away on business. "Wright has been frantically trying to get here all last evening." My grandfather to her: "You're much too attractive to be a thoroughly safe proposition in spite of your A1 loyal-type heart." They imagined the worst, hungered for reassurance, begged forgiveness. "A confession, darling," he writes. "I did kiss her—on the cheek—very brotherly." They engaged in outlandish flattery. "Your telegrams almost made me jump out of my skin with excitement," she writes, "but I got so lonely that I almost chewed the sheets and blankets—and really seriously thought of calling the conductor." Beware stallions! he warns. Behavior excellent but dangerously lonely! she reports. "The train is a flop," she writes. "No one has accosted me. Could I be slipping?"

The summer before their wedding, I find her spending several weeks as a houseguest of her future mother-in-law in Bar Harbor. Her sixteen-year-old sister, Mary Binney, has been sent along as chaperone, a mission impossible. When Helen Hope boards a sleeper train at Ellsworth, Maine, for the trip home in late July 1923, she and her betrothed are facing a month-long separation. As the train barrels south, she fires off letters and telegrams from every station—Bangor, Waterville, Portland, and beyond. Upon arrival at home, she dispatches a special-delivery letter in an envelope plastered with stamps: "It seems like a year and it's only yesterday at quarter of four that I left you." He sleeps with her letters in his pajama pocket; she keeps his under her pillow. If a day passes letterless, they panic, fear the worst, telegram for relief. "I imagined someone had kissed you all of a sudden," he writes, "and you didn't know how to tell me." Her letters are full of wild hyperbole: Life is disgusting without you! You are engaged to a perfect lunatic! Please miss me like the devil and have a rotten time! His are ardent, steamy: "O, I just want you, want you, want you with every inch of me!"

A thousand wedding announcements and invitations sailed off that summer to addresses as remote as Argentina. Orders went out for initialed cuff links for the ushers, monogrammed luggage, calling cards for the soon-to-be Mrs. Scott. The scene in the big house in those weeks bore an unmistakable resemblance to the opening scenes of *The Philadelphia Story*. Tables sagged under the weight of wedding presents delivered daily—silver platters, engraved pitchers, volumes of Ibsen, a complete set of Shakespeare. Helen Hope dedicated herself to writing thank-you notes—when not rushing to the train station to intercept incoming mail from Maine. Newspaper reporters, idling through August, telephoned for wedding news. Old boyfriends, said to be bent on blowing up the engagement, dropped in; some stayed for a ride, a game of bridge, a swim in the pool. Mary Binney warned her older sister that regaling her fiancé with tales of her socializing in his absence would soon leave her "minus a husband." But Helen Hope had no patience for a premarital cloister: "Otherwise, it's so, so lonely and I think I would go mad." My grandfather, in Maine with Mamma, had little choice but to agree. "But please, my Angel, love me <u>best</u>."

He has a nightmare about the upcoming wedding: He finds he's to be married in a crumbling ruin that bears some resemblance to the chapel at Groton. His old headmaster has rented a basket of dress suits, every one of them much too big, from which the groom is to choose. Collars dangle like life buoys around his neck. An aging French retainer scurries off to find a more suitable costume for the groom. In a sweat of distress and shame, Edgar awakes, reaches for the engraved stationery, confides all to Helen Hope. Oh, the misery!

"Imagine being married in a dress suit!" he writes.

He was married in a cutaway that September in a Gothic Revival church with gargoyles carved into the masonry. Helen Hope wore a sleeveless white chiffon gown, trailed by a satin train, and carried a bouquet of orchids and lilies of the valley. Bridesmaids, flower girls, and ten ushers abounded. The church was packed; fall blossoms adorned the pews. When the ceremony was over, the crowd headed to the big house for the reception.

It's hard not to wonder what it must have been like to be the offspring of such a match.

My grandfather longed for a literary life. At Harvard, he'd gravitated to the circle of students around George Pierce Baker, whose playwriting workshop for graduate students, the 47 Workshop, had trained the likes of S. N. Behrman, Sidney Howard, and Eugene O'Neill. By the summer before the wedding, he was shopping a drawing-room comedy, set in a Manhattan apartment and a country house on the Main Line, to Milton Shubert and Helen Hayes. In his letters, I find him marooned in Bar Harbor, vowing to devote himself to rewriting the opening act. He'll rise early and work diligently every morning, he swears to Helen Hope. Instead, he stays up until 2:00 A.M., "drinking sloe gin fizzes and chatting." He sleeps until noon. More resolutions follow. "Tomorrow morning I start," he writes, as though putting his intentions in writing will solve all. "I'll sit at my study desk and write or pace in solitary thought about the study floor piecing together scenes and dialogue." But dinner dances intervene. So do whiskey, and bridge at 1:15 A.M., and twenty-one guests arriving imminently for tea. The aspiring dramatist scales back his plans. It's more important, he assures Helen Hope, for him to get in shape for the wedding.

She counsels discipline.

"I want you to be a very great playwright, and the only way you can achieve that is by really working," she writes. In a second letter the same day, she tries another tack: "I want a famous husband."

He had a brief run as a newspaper reporter in Philadelphia. Then he was an editor and critic for a short-lived theater magazine. Then his financier father-in-law appears to have grown impatient. By 1926, the struggling scribbler unexpectedly turns up on the boards of directors of a gas company in New Jersey and of an oil and coal company in West Virginia. Next, he's on the floor of the New York Stock Exchange, as an independent broker. In January 1928, he buys a seat on the exchange, using three hundred thousand dollars of his inherited money plus a loan from the Colonel. A year later, a new stockbrokerage, Montgomery, Scott & Company, opens in Philadelphia. The founding partners: my grandfather and his father-in-law, the Colonel. The offices are in a building on Broad Street owned by the bank where the Colonel's father-in-law is a director. No coincidence, I suppose, that the bank rents space to the new partners on highly favorable terms—and gives them its brokerage business. Nine months before the stock market crash, the firm opens its doors.

The partnership, it turns out, had been an enticement. A bribe, you might say. In October 1927, my father's parents had made plans to embark upon their own circumnavigation. They were imagining a month in Paris, several weeks in Italy, a sailing trip around the

Mediterranean, a month in Egypt, a stop in Ceylon, a voyage across India before sailing to Singapore via Rangoon, then onward to Java and Siam, with a detour to Angkor, a motor trip to Saigon, and a boat to Japan via Hong Kong. "From Japan our plans are vague," my grandfather wrote to his brother, Warwick, that August. "Our mammoth ambition is to get to Peking, and back via Moscow on the Trans-Siberian. If this fails, we shall probably take a boat around Africa which makes many stops." But Colonel Montgomery seems to have had some uneasiness about his son-in-law's life prospects. The Colonel, not one to stint on due diligence, must have known of the voyage of the *Sagamore* and the exploits of his son-in-law's father at a similar age. So he made my grandfather an offer: If Helen Hope and Edgar would cut the trip in half, he'd make Edgar his partner in a new firm. The couple got only as far as Damascus before returning to New York, where her parents were on hand to meet them. Helen Hope and Edgar were so annoyed, she once told me, they made sure they were the last passengers off the ship. They disembarked drunk, fled to the Ritz Tower, and sent her parents home to the big house.

A feature of my grandparents' farmhouse, by the time I knew them, was their collection of work by Augustus John, the Welsh-born bohemian who was as fashionable a portrait painter in his time in the 1920s as John Singer Sargent had been in his. A four-foot-high John portrait of Helen Hope hung in the living room above a library table stacked with books. In the dining room, there was another he'd painted eight years later. There was a drawing of my grandfather, done in London in 1950, and a landscape of Connemara, inscribed in one corner, "Hope from Augustus." Images by John of women were all over—women alone, women with children, nude women, a woman in peasant clothing, a woman in a wide-brimmed hat, a girl in red harem pants. There was a painting of John's muse, Dorelia, the mistress he'd insinuated into his married life. There was a self-portrait, too, titled *Portrait of a Bearded Man.* Red mustache, graying Vandyke, a slight scowl: The artist seemed to glare from the painting. From time to time, my grand-mother alluded fleetingly to various adventures that had taken place the summer when they'd first met—stories that seemed to involve il-legal whiskey and the artist's fondness for his models, not least of all her.

It was her father, the Colonel, who'd chosen John for his eldest. He prided himself on the portraits in the big house. "Not only have I some really beautiful family portraits of different generations dating back for many years," he boasted, "but I have also kept up this generation more completely than anyone of my acquaintance." In the mid-1920s, he'd invited a British society portraitist to move in and paint him, his wife, her unmarried aunt, and her father. An earlier subject of that painter had been Queen Victoria. Twice, the Colonel traveled to Spain to prevail upon an elusive Basque painter to paint Mary Binney (re-covering in Paris, at the time, from a breakdown precipitated by her parents' blackballing of Stokowski). To paint Aleck, his only son, the Colonel enlisted the most prolific of the official artists sent to the western front during World War I. For Charlotte Ives, he hired a Hungarian-born painter of aristocrats and royals, who painted her seated on a horse. At seventeen, the Montgomerys' spirited youngest couldn't sit still. The painter is said to have enlisted a model as a body double.

A figure of mythic magnetism, Augustus John was as famous for his insatiable womanizing as for his draftsmanship and the originality of his early work. When he appeared at the Café Royal in Piccadilly, it's said, young models had to be carted away, fainting; by the end of his life, he was rumored to have fathered as many as one hundred chil-dren. "He seems to regard the world as a magnificent house party, rich in gypsies, intellectuals, artists, celebrities and, above all, aristocrats," a *Time* magazine journalist once wrote. Influenced by Whistler and Rubens, he'd spent much of the 1920s painting writers, public figures, and celebrities from James Joyce to Tallulah Bankhead. His portraits were admired for their psychological insight. "I don't know if that's what I look like, but that's what I feel like," Thomas Hardy is supposed to have said of John's painting of him. Not every sitter, however, was enchanted with the final product. The founder of Lever Brothers sliced the face out of his. Gerald du Maurier, the actor and a friend of the artist, put his portrait up for sale. "The best description of the thing was made by a woman friend of mine who said it showed all the misery of my wretched soul," du Maurier was quoted as saying. To hang it in his house, he said, "would drive me either to suicide or to strong drink."

In the summer of 1930, Helen Hope and Edgar, at twenty-six and thirty-one, set off for the west coast of Galway where the moody, beguiling artist was holed up in a rural hotel with an entourage of artists, admirers, and comely young sitters. His American subject and her husband barreled across Ireland in a black limousine—metamorphosed, in my grandmother's telling, into a hearse. She was anxious: If John disliked her, she professed to believe, he might refuse to paint her. "When we drove up in the late afternoon, there were his two eyes shining out of the ground-floor window where he had his studio," she'd say later. "The car door was flung open, and I fell out on my head."

Lively, bored, indulged, and self-dramatizing for humorous effect—she complained bitterly in letters home to her mother. "You ought to see this dump we're in, it is the most god-forsaken hole in the world!!" she wrote. Ten days into the visit, she declared she was "sick to death of the picture and more than sick of old John, and his temperament, and he is even sicker of me." But there was tango music on a purloined hotel Victrola, whiskey, and outings with the artist and Oliver St. John Gogarty, the poet, playwright, and surgeon whom James Joyce had reinvented as stately, plump Buck Mulligan. Painter and subject warmed to each other, and then some. "We were shy on meeting for the first time, but this soon wore off," John wrote in a memoir years later, "for Mrs. Scott proved to be as sympathetic as she was beautiful." He painted her twice that summer, and a third time in London eight years later. When the first portrait was exhibited in a gallery in New York in 1931, a critic wrote, "Choicest of all its elements is the sweetness of expression. John seldom permits himself, as here, to celebrate the sweetness of life."

Asked long afterward about talk that John had painted her naked, Helen Hope smiled opaquely—an expression her inquisitor told me he took to mean, "I'm not confirming or denying. But I don't want you to think it wasn't a possibility."

In the heavy bottom drawer of a cupboard in the big house, I come upon the scrapbook in which Helen Hope preserved a record of the attachments that formed on the windswept fringe of Connemara that summer. I pore over the scattered puzzle pieces of that never-forgotten visit—letters from John, cablegrams, postcards, photographs, magazine articles, exhibition catalog pages, newspaper clippings. In grainy snapshots taken that summer, John is in his early fifties, leonine and brooding. Out there on the edge of the Atlantic, he's costumed in a homburg, a three-piece suit, and a caped coat like something worn by Sherlock Holmes. In one series, he stands apart, watching members of the house party, half his age, cavort on a lawn. Helen Hope is barefoot, in midair when the shutter snaps. In other photos, the two of them sit together in the bow of a wooden boat. "I was 26 and had been married seven years," she writes to John's biographer four decades later. In the years that followed, she stuffed the scrapbook full of mementos, including newspaper articles written at the time of John's death in 1961. "His personal legend, also his flair for elegant bohemianism and wit, remained undiminished throughout his life and remains undiminished now that he is dead," reads one clipping. "His portraits gave this same immortality to the people who were fortunate enough to be painted by him—the immortality not of remembrance through record, but of perpetual vigor."

I come upon a sonnet in John's handwriting, ending with the lines,

But armed only with my staff
I'll leap my darling's trenches,
And in my fury tear in half
The last of her defences.
Till I achieve the utmost Prize
And force the Doors of Paradise!

Back home in Pennsylvania, Helen Hope trained, hunted, and showed horses, hers and others'. She ran her own stable, sometimes two. Newspaper reporters chronicled her exploits: I find her wrapping up a sixteen-jump course in one show, in record time, to wild applause—only to return on a second horse, turn in another flawless round, and walk away with first and second place. Her smashups added to her local renown. Thundering toward the finish line in a point-to-point race in the 1930s, she's thrown from her horse in a head-on collision, rolled on by the horse, knocked unconscious, and carried off on a stretcher. By the mid-1930s, she's developing a paying sideline as a horse-show judge. She shuttles between capitals of the horse world—Middleburg, Virginia; Aiken, South Carolina; Saratoga Springs, New York.

Anyone who rode with Helen Hope was expected to meet her exacting standards. Never hurry, never take shortcuts, never overwork a young horse. If you're exercising one while leading two more, all three horses must trot evenly, never breaking stride. If the horse you're mounting fails to stand absolutely still, God help you. During foxhunting season, she was up at dawn; she lunched in her kitchen on Campbell's soup and a few leaves of lettuce. If she was at the theater in New York in the evening, she'd take the last train home in order to be up to hunt the next day. Pushing herself to the point of exhaustion, she had a tendency to be harder on other people's mistakes than on her own. When a younger protégé, maneuvering a horse trailer backward into the garage from behind the wheel of a Jeep, scraped the trailer against the side of the garage, "You might have thought I'd burned the place down," the woman told me, laughing. ". . . There's nobody that your grandmother didn't bring to tears."

My grandfather, meanwhile, mastered the legalities of the brokerage business. He had the kind of memory that might have enabled him to recite much of the stock exchange constitution by heart. He was good at managing the relationships that stockbrokering entailed, and he became a governor of two exchanges. He was not, however, perfectly cut out for investing itself. Instead of buying, for example, General Motors, he'd be swept off his feet by the likes of Dymaxion Dwelling Machines, mass-producible houses, invented by Buckminster Fuller, which tanked when postwar home buyers turned out to have no appetite for sci-fi yurts. From his letters, I find him in Washington in February 1934, a supernumerary in the New York Stock Exchange's campaign against President Franklin Roosevelt's stock-exchange reform bill, introduced after the 1929 crash. Intended to protect the individual investor and help stabilize the economy, the bill had become the target of what Sam Rayburn, the Texas congressman, later called "the biggest and boldest, the richest and most ruthless lobby Congress had ever known"—the New York exchange. Edgar dined with bankers, met with senators, socialized with assistant secretaries of the treasury during those weeks in Washington. He was awed by the industriousness of Tommy Corcoran, the young New Deal strategist who'd helped draft the bill. "A capacity for work I never saw among my contemporaries," he marveled tellingly in a letter home. Even higher praise went to the vice president, "Cactus Jack" Garner, said to have once called the vice president's job "not worth a bucket of warm piss."

"The VP is <u>divine</u>," Edgar wrote to Helen Hope. "You would love him."

No doubt.

Their marriage was not uncomplicated when my father was young.

During an especially bitter fight during the thirties, his father heaved a kettle across the kitchen. If Helen Hope was the target, Edgar missed. But, shocked by his own behavior, he swore off alcohol for a decade. Ten years into their marriage, I find angry references, in Helen Hope's letters to Edgar, to "your affair with R." There's a tense stand-off over his intention to take out a woman while Helen Hope is away. "If you need a screw for goodness sakes get it, if you think it will straighten you out and make you happy," she writes. A fight erupts over his refusal to reconsider his intention to take another woman to the opera.

"Darling," she begins sweetly, leading into an explosion of upper-case expletives. "I am sorry that I was so upset and made such an issue. . . . If you have it in your heart to take Jean to the theater, go ahead and do it. I do not want to feel that I asked you not to. . . . It seems extremely unlucky to me that I am taken away at this time as it associates this great pleasure that the opera's given you with someone other than me. And I am jealous of someone else's sharing it with you—especially as it seemed to mean so much to you when I sug-gested not taking her. You used to love to go alone, so you said, but now you say she is the only one you like to go with. So if it means that much go ahead. . . . I feel very sorry for myself. Please be extra strict with your system."

She wakes from a dream in which he's told her he no longer loves her. She's out of town, her bed is damp with tears. "I do hope you still love me," she writes sadly. He writes back, "If I have done any foolish-nesses, or badnesses, you've always understood it had no effect on my adoring you. . . . And, to come to cases, I have done nothing at all naughty since you left."

BEHAVIOR PERFECT, she telegrams two days later. HOPE YOURS SAME.

Third day: TELEPHONE ME THIS EVENING ANY TIME MISS YOU TERRIBLY.

Day four: She's aborting her trip and catching the first flight home. RIDICULOUS THINGS OF NO IMPORTANCE SHOULD NOT BE TAKEN SERIOUSLY, reads her final cable in the series. MUST BE COMPLETELY CHANGED OTHERWISE MANY PEOPLE HURT.

My grandfather's literary life was now strictly extracurricular. He read voraciously, in English and French, and met with other men to read Shakespeare aloud. He wrote thank-you notes in rhyming couplets. In his Christmas Eve poems, he'd include a tip of the fedora to every in-law, horse, dog. In one of my grandmother's scrapbooks, I happened upon a learned paean, in my grandfather's hand, to female genitalia—which turned out not to be the work of E. Scott, playwright manqué, but that of a British humorist, A. P. Herbert. My grandfather, I'm told, would occasionally rise from the table during some convivial dinner and, to the ostensible delight of his guests, recite this version of Herbert's poem aloud.

> *The portions of a woman which appeal to man's depravity*
> *Are constituted with considerable care,*
> *And what appears to you to be a simple little cavity*
> *Is really an elaborate affair.*

> *And doctors of distinction who've examined these phenomena*
> *In numbers of experimental dames*
> *Have made a list of all the things in feminine abdomina*
> *And given them delightful Latin names.*

> *There's the vulva, the vagina and the jolly perineum,*
> *The hymen that is found in many brides,*
> *And countless other gadgets you would love if you could see 'em,*
> *The clitoris and God knows what besides.*

What a pity then it is that when we common people chatter
Of the mysteries to which I have referred,
We should use for such a delicate and complicated matter
Such a very short and unattractive word.

I come upon a scrapbook of my grandmother's labeled "Miscel letters and funny letters for old age!!" Inside the front cover, she's pasted a
studio photograph of a man I've never seen. Receding hairline, soft
face, full lips. I find nothing unlikable—or especially likable—about
his looks. He's in military uniform, circa World War II. On the following pages, I find hundreds of letters, postcards, telegrams, and phone
messages—mostly from the same man. "Hopey honey darling," he begins. He signs off, "I adore you my sweet." The recipient, I notice, has
dated phone messages, after the fact, in her looping hand: July 27, 1944;
August 14, 1944; September 12, 1944. "Major Burden called," many
of the messages read. "Please call Major Burden when you come in." I
imagine the housekeeper who must have taken the messages, standing
at the phone in the pantry, in her white uniform and white shoes. What
went through that housekeeper's head? Would Helen Hope have cared?
The correspondent's sense of humor is in sync with hers: He sends postcards of the Empire State Building, Nelson's Column, other marvels of
upright engineering. "Looking forward to seeing you Friday with vast
anticipation," he writes from New York City. Or, "Looking forward to
seeing you again on Friday with constantly renewed anticipation." His
stationery is as fine as his Park Avenue address. But I find nothing
clever about his letters. Because of their frequency, I entertain the fan-
tasy that my grandmother, in her thirties, had a psychoanalyst on the
Upper East Side of Manhattan. Is it possible she had a shrink named
Major Burden?

A more plausible explanation, of course, is that Major Burden was
arranging assignations with the woman we called Granny.

That nickname was never a perfect fit.

By the early 1940s, Major Burden is writing or calling weekly or biweekly. "So please, please manage to come up here next week," he implores. "I need you and want to see you so badly." Another week: "Honey darling . . . Looking forward to seeing you on the 17th all agog." He tells her he's recently encountered "the author of the rumor that I am violently in love with you, which I at once admitted." My grandfather, it becomes clear, is acquainted with his wife's admirer: Respectfully, the man addresses his Christmas cards to Mr. and Mrs. Scott. My grandfather writes home from Midland, Texas, "My best to Jimmy." He tacks on a cautionary send-off: "Goodbye, good luck, good habits." But by the late 1940s, I sense, the major's star is waning. "Darling, Your crushingly disappointing wire received," he writes. Or, "Darling. Your wire received last night but what were you still doing in Philly on Tuesday if you left for West Virginia Monday PM?" It's as if, he complains, "some annoying demon or Nemesis" is interfering— some nemesis whose "initials are not ES, as they normally are." Helen Hope, meanwhile, is reassuring Edgar. JIMMY BEEN AND GONE VIRTUE INTACT LOVE AND KISSES, she reports in a telegram. And, in a letter: "Jimmy remained in perfect control and didn't even get his toe in my door." A year or two later, Burden is writing from Paris. "Brace yourself for a shock," he tells Helen Hope. She's to keep the news secret until the announcement arrives, which it does, a few days later, addressed to both missus and mister. Everyone is pleased with "the new dispensation"—Burden's phrase. Two weeks later, he and his bride, fresh from Paris, arrive in Villanova for a cozy weekend with honey darling and her husband.

For their twentieth wedding anniversary, Helen Hope and Edgar checked into a suite at the Ritz-Carlton in New York. I study the paper trail, including a *Playbill* from the original Broadway production of *Oklahoma!* Their marriage had proved, as people would describe it to me decades later, durable enough to survive conflict and whatever else happened along. Asked, near the end of her life, about the "secret" to their long marriage, my grandmother would give a deceptively simple answer, the complexities of which I've barely plumbed. "Both of us wanted to stay married," she'd say. Their twentieth-anniversary letters to each other survived in a scrapbook. Hers was exuberant, all superlatives. His was a love letter.

"Temperamentally, spiritually, physically you have been the perfect companion—captivating, devoted, passionate," he wrote. "In the small things as in the great you have charmed my senses, possessed my thoughts and inspired my actions. . . . If during the next twenty years one of us dies, let the other remember gratefully and humbly the magic of our time together. The most important thought will be, not that it has ended, but what it was while it lasted."

The play dedicated to them, *The Philadelphia Story*, had opened on Broadway four years earlier. My grandfather and Philip Barry had met at Harvard after Barry's arrival as a graduate student in 1919 to study playwriting under George Pierce Baker. A newly minted Anglophile, Barry had worked for the State Department in London during World War I, after being rejected from the ambulance corps and the military because of poor eyesight. "He was partial to palaces and to the people who dwelt in them," Brendan Gill would write of him later; and he was even "more partial to people who might have lived in palaces and who chose instead to live in pavilions and pleasances, accepting with light hearts the responsibilities that their good luck imposed on them." In the years after Harvard, Barry was a regular visitor to Ardrossan. Of the twenty-one plays of his that were produced on Broadway, the most successful were drawing-room comedies set in what a character in the play *Holiday* called "a general atmosphere of plenty with the top riveted down on the cornucopia." The day before *The Philadelphia Story* opened in an out-of-town tryout in Philadelphia, a theater critic reported in the *Philadelphia Record*, "We understand that 'The Philadelphia Story' is concerned with a Main Line family who 'manage their vast modern estate, hunt, fall in love and laugh much.'"

I'd been foraging in the ironing-room papers for months before it occurred to me to read the play itself. I started scribbling notes and page numbers inside the back cover of the actors' edition. Soon, to my amazement, a list of recognizable details was spilling backward into the dialogue, littering the margins. The setting of the play is a country estate on the eve of the wedding of the eldest daughter of "the Philadelphia Lords." There's a dairy and stables, like the Colonel's, and a gatehouse built "for a summer place when they all lived in Rittenhouse Square," as had the Scotts. The curtain rises on the sitting room, "a large, comfortably furnished room of a somewhat faded elegance containing a number of very good Victorian pieces"—a solid description of the sitting room at the big house. "I suppose that's contrasted to the living room, the ballroom—the drawing room—the morning room—the—," the interloping reporter in the play remarks. Glass doors open onto a porch—again, like the big house; a portrait by a famous painter hangs over the mantel; cardboard boxes are strewn about, "indicating an approaching wedding," as in the summer of 1923. The bride's father is in finance—with a controlling interest in the company that employs his future son-in-law. Ring a bell? His eldest, Tracy, has been writing thank-you notes. Her younger sister—fifteen, not yet in school—spouts off dreamily about, yes, Leopold Stokowski. "She's out schooling a horse somewhere," the reporter remarks. "It's the horses that get the schooling hereabouts." There's even a swimming pool in a grove of trees. Late in the play and late at night, Tracy ends up undressed and in the pool—with the reporter, not the man she's about to marry.

For the last thirty years of my grandmother's life, she was often reported to have been the original Tracy. "The real-life model," said *Vanity Fair*. The *Sunday Telegraph* called her "the inspiration"; a slightly confused local paper alluded to "the role of Mrs. Scott." Yet, Tracy is priggish in a way Helen Hope never was. For much of the play, Tracy is judgmental, scornful, intolerant of weakness. "You'll never be a first class woman or a first class human being, till you have learned to have some regard for human frailty," her ex-husband, C. K. Dexter Haven, whose weakness is drinking, tells her. Her father, who's having an affair with a Broadway actress, is a target of Tracy's scorn. Only after she drinks too much champagne, ends up naked in the pool with a stranger, and has to be carted off to bed on the eve of her wedding does she become capable of appreciating that, as Barry puts it, "the occasional misdeeds are often as good for a person as—as the more persistent virtues." That wouldn't have been news to Helen Hope.

Even she, it turns out, may not have believed she was the original Tracy. Barry had taken the idea for the play to Katharine Hepburn, who was in need of a comeback, having been branded arrogant and "box office poison" after a string of flops. Together, they made the character of Tracy the booster rocket for Hepburn's redemption. "Make her like me but make her go all soft," Hepburn is said to have told Barry. Tracy became a redheaded graduate of Bryn Mawr College, like Hepburn, with an ex-husband idling on the outskirts of her life, like Hepburn. "Indeed, Tracy Lord *is* Kate Hepburn," A. Scott Berg wrote in *Kate Remembered*. Donald R. Anderson, in a book on Barry's plays, said, "There is no question that Tracy Lord was not only designed for Hepburn but also shaped by her." The play became the most enduring of Barry's plays, running for more than four hundred performances in New York, plus two years on the road. It was revived in New York in 1980, in London in 2005. The movie, starring Hepburn and Cary Grant and released in 1940, is an American classic. Tracy Lord and Hepburn had made Helen Hope "almost famous," my grandmother wrote years later. Occasionally, though, she'd say the character might have been based on her youngest sister. She was even quoted, on at least one occasion, saying, "I don't really think Tracy Lord was much like me."

But for feature writers, the story was too good to check. And their subject, it seems, never went out of her way to correct the record.

Why not? I asked my uncle Ed.

He shrugged.

"She started to value the importance of being 'Mrs. Philadelphia Story.'"

Chapter Five

My father was never one to linger over tales of his childhood. I see that now, looking back. If it had ever occurred to me to ask him why, he might've said, with a look of amusement, that he'd never given the question any thought. It was just, he'd have said, who he was. In our house, there were photographs of my mother as a child with her parents. We knew about their family camping trip to the Canadian Rockies, and the progressive elementary school to which her mother had wisely sent her, and her childhood friends, and the family dogs, and the French nurse, Marie. Of my father's early years, we heard fewer details. There was a studio photograph of a towheaded child with a look of impish anticipation, and a picture of him as a boy in the "Alice in Wonderland" garden at Chiltern. We'd heard of the pet dove he won at a church fair, and a horse for whom he'd saved his wartime sugar rations while away at school. We knew that he adored his parents: He said so often when people brought them up. You couldn't spend time with the three of them and not come away with the impression that the son was as taken with the parents as the parents were with him. I must have assumed I knew the story, since the setting of his childhood, and the cast of characters, overlapped with mine. Only late in his life did it begin to dawn on me that the emotional terrain had been more rugged than I'd understood.

Six months before his death, he let slip a story that none of us remembers hearing. He was speaking to an oral historian, a stranger. I learned of the interview only years later, after his death, when I was given a recording. The opening question was routine, but I was surprised by my father's answer. Asked where he'd been born, he gave his date of birth and the name of the hospital—then went on to say that his mother had left him there at one day old. She'd delivered her first child at home and would have preferred to do the same for her second. So she agreed reluctantly to hospitalization, then checked out as soon as she could, leaving her newborn in the nurses' care. Sometime later, an ambulance pulled up at the house in Villanova and dropped off the infant. I'm sure this is a myopically twenty-first-century thing to say, but I can no more imagine voluntarily leaving my healthy, day-old baby behind in a hospital than I can imagine, say, abandoning him or her on the banks of the Tiber to be suckled by a she-wolf.

In keeping with family practice, my father was placed in the care of a French governess. He came to adore her, he said long afterward, while everybody else disliked her "rather cordially." The summer he turned six, during an extended stay in the Bar Harbor "cottage," his Scott grandmother unceremoniously canned the object of my father's devotion, giving neither of them the opportunity to say adieu. (The governess had been venting her aggression, I'm told, by clobbering my father's older brother, Ed.)

From then on, my father passed many days and nights, not unhappily, in the company of his parents' Irish butler, Irish cook, and Irish maid. (A cousin of my father's, who spent his early years on Ardrossan, told me, "If there are any redeeming qualities in me, it can be attributed to the fact that I was raised by Irish cooks and maids.") Years later, my father professed to have spoken English with an Irish accent until the age of nine—"to the consternation of my grandmother Scott who was a Boston Brahmin and did not approve of her second grandchild speaking in the tongue of the people who had taken over Boston from the likes of her family."

His parents were an intermittent presence. During his first decade, they kept an apartment in Manhattan for proximity to the stock market, the theater, clubs, New York friends. They had a cottage, too, for a time, in the open country to the west of Delaware County, to which the foxhunting crowd was increasingly heading. Piecing together the timeline, it dawned on me, for the first time, that my father was fourteen months old when his parents sailed off to Ireland for their first, month-long encounter with Augustus John. When they left again for Europe the following summer, he'd just turned two. By the time they embarked for London for the third John portrait, he and Ed were old enough to accompany them on the train to New York for the privilege of seeing them off. Back in Villanova, aunts, uncles, grandparents, maids, and cooks pinch-hit. The big house was, my uncle told me without any trace of self-pity, "a resource that was used at such times to ship off the kids and go away." My father used the same tone—an irony so finely planed as to almost slip by undetected—when he wrote, in his sixties, that his parents "returned from time to time to look after their Philadelphia life, including their horses, their dogs, their donkeys and their sons."

I study the margin between said and unsaid.

"My mother and father were wonderful parents," he told a journalist after their deaths. "Enormously kind and caring, in their way.

"But quite . . ."

He hesitated.

". . . distant."

He ventured further.

"Unused to children.

"Busy with their own lives, entertaining and so forth.

"But very decent, loving people."

As a young boy, he had what one teacher called in a report card "considerable social charm." He was lively, talkative, funny. "Such a personality," his father marveled. In elementary school, he could be found amusing his classmates instead of attending to the teacher. "Bobby never walks into a room," his Boston-bred grandmother remarked frostily. "He *makes an entrance*." He had an interior quality, however, that his mother diagnosed as a "slight shyness." Perhaps she passed along to him her own mother's miracle cure. For, by the time he'd reached adulthood, my father gave every appearance of having absorbed the imperative to "always give people the best possible time." He seemed to have vanquished whatever surplus of self-consciousness his mother had labeled shyness.

He alone, I now see, knew better.

For all her charm and gifts, Helen Hope had limitations as a parent. She was self-centered, she liked recognition, she was quick to take offense. One of the few episodes from my father's childhood that my brother, sister, and I all recall him recounting concerned her fury after he, as a small boy, compared her midriff to a wrinkled paper bag. Though she worked tirelessly at many things, that energy and focus came at a price: She was not, it seems safe to say, overly involved in the lives of her sons. In the event of some run-of-the-mill screwup, she could be less than scrupulously honest in assigning blame. Once, after skidding into the side of a stone bridge while driving to the big house with Ed when he was a boy, she took to fulminating against her father—presumably for bridge misplacement thirty years before. Her approach to discipline was tough. "Toilet training was particularly rigorous," my father wrote in a rare confession many years later, "my mother treating the process like housebreaking dogs."

He was careful, I now see, in what he said about her.

"I adored my mother, but she was not easy," he'd say, leaving it at that.

Or, "It was a pleasant existence, if we were careful not to cross my mother."

Or, "When the light was shining on us, we were very much there. When it wasn't, we made do."

In my grandfather's letters, his pleasure in his sons is evident. "The boys were perfect," he writes to their mother, after taking them to a baseball game. "I'm always so happy with them, and so proud of them." Having decided not to wake his youngest to say good-bye as he leaves on a business trip, he's afflicted with remorse. He sends a telegram to Helen Hope, then a letter. "I'm still worried I may have hurt Bob's feelings," he writes. "He's so nice, I'd hate to." But my grandfather's life was busy, too, in those years. Alighting in Pennsylvania for a meeting of the sewer commission on which he's serving, he recaps the day's events in a telegram to Helen Hope, who's also out of town: TOO BUSY OFFICE TENNIS SEWER OPERA WITH MAMMA BOBBY THREW UP SCHOOL LUNCH TODAY FINE NOW DOGS HORSES FINE.

My father didn't share his mother's passion for horses. When his brother asked to resume riding at age eleven, having quit at six, she offered him a donkey, not yet broken, to ride for the summer. Come September, they'd see if he was ready for a horse. Ed rode the donkey, bareback, all summer, trailing his mother, who was on horseback, up and down hills. By fall, he had the donkey clearing small jumps—a feat that I take it is not entirely unlike teaching a dachshund to dance. Impressed, Helen Hope gave her elder son a horse. From then on, they rode together, as she passed on to him everything she knew. Once, when a horse she was breaking kicked her in the stomach, she surprised Ed by handing him the horse to complete the job. In a sphere that was central to her life, she and her eldest connected. In a household dominated by the personality and interests of his mother, my father sometimes found himself on the sidelines. He went through, Ed told me, "a sort of wintry period in his youth."

His maternal grandfather, it seems, left a deep impression on my father. When he dreamed, as a small boy, of living in a palace, the palace in the dream was the Greek Revival temple that the Colonel's architect, Horace Trumbauer, had designed for the Philadelphia Museum of Art. When, many years later, my father would remember his grandparents' house, he'd remember the white-gloved, blue-waistcoated footmen—"like something out of a Revolutionary War–themed painting"—and library shelves lined with Kipling and Trollope. Other grandchildren kept their distance from the irascible, oversized, unnerving Colonel, but my father would look back on the Colonel's fits of temper with fond amusement. He'd remember, with the same indulgence, the Colonel's practice of piloting private planes after a wine-fueled lunch. "I was the first of his grandchildren to be named after him, and I absolutely adored him," he'd tell the oral historian who interviewed him late in life. The words he used to describe his grandfather: successful, opinionated, aristocratic. "Wonderfully enough, I was probably his last great friend," my father said. He'd recall sitting with him after lunch—the older man with his cigar and brandy; the child, age eleven, drinking rum. In his midtwenties, stupefied by the tedium of his newly chosen profession, the law, my father would daydream about writing a novel based on the character of his grandfather.

The two of them understood each other. That's how my uncle Ed put it.

The Colonel was in his early sixties when my father was a boy. A quarter of a century had passed since he'd built his Xanadu beside Darby Creek. What had become of him in the decades following his heyday was a question I hadn't considered until I came upon a letter from a former business partner of his, written after the Colonel's death. "Many times I have tried to figure out what caused the great change in him," the man confided to my grandfather, the Colonel's son-in-law and a business partner himself. The change had come on gradually, the man said, through a series of setbacks. In the years immediately after World War I, the Colonel's partners in the investment banking firm had turned against him. "He was so used to being recognized as the Captain of the ship, which he certainly was, that it was impossible for him to understand how any of us could challenge his leadership," the man wrote. The resulting dissolution of the firm, in 1921, was a mistake, the former colleague wrote. It had left the Colonel, "a man of action," becalmed.

There'd been another blow, too—a public humiliation. A month after the United States entered the war in 1917, President Woodrow Wilson had set up a five-man board charged with stimulating the rapid production of three thousand, five hundred military aircraft. My father's grandfather, appointed to the new Aircraft Production Board because of his experience in finance, was soon in charge of finance for the equipment division of the United States Army Signal Corps, then head of the division, briefly. He was commissioned as a colonel. Congress had appropriated $640 million for the production program; another $840 million had followed. But by the time the war ended in November 1918, the program had failed to generate a single American-built combat plane, pursuit plane, or bomber at the French front. With thousands of trained aviators ready to fly, the United States had had to borrow or buy planes from the Allies. All the aircraft-production program produced was a couple hundred observational planes. Investigations—by Congress, the Department of Justice, and news organizations—traced the debacle to inexperience, errors of judgment, and what the congressional report called "a record of stupidity and stubbornness that involved an inexcusable waste of men and money, and invited military disaster."

In the letter three decades later, Michael Gavin, the Colonel's business partner, wrote to my grandfather, "Some called it a scandal, and some demanded criminal prosecution. You can easily understand how that sort of thing would stagger Bob."

At the height of the uproar, the Colonel summoned his business partner to Washington. Gavin found him "in bed looking tired and worried." The Colonel had been detached from aviation duty and assigned to cooperate with the Department of Justice in its investigation. Aware that Gavin was acquainted with the new chairman of the aviation board, the Colonel asked Gavin to see what he could learn. The new chairman told Gavin to tell the Colonel that "he thought all the talk about scandal and criminal prosecution would die down and be forgotten," Gavin wrote. But the scandal, understandably, hit the Colonel hard. "He seemed, after that, to gradually lose some of that boldness and confidence," Gavin said, "which was a great asset in anything he undertook to do."

The story of the Aircraft Production Board fiasco wasn't one I'd heard in the family. I learned of it from the letter, then newspaper archives, then government records. Did the Colonel's children ever know the details? Did his grandchildren? It was not a descendant but a son-in-law, Edgar, who preserved the lone clue—the business partner's ruminations on "what caused the great change." A century later, I'm unable to determine the Colonel's precise involvement in the crack-up. Was he personally to blame? Or not? Did he belong on that board? Maybe it was perfectly reasonable to appoint a man with experience in industrial finance. All I'm left with is the irony of the Colonel's eternal title and that story: Rank lives on when the facts are forgotten. In the family, Robert L. Montgomery remains "the Colonel" to this day. The title is like one of those stately gateposts, still standing after all other traces have disappeared.

So the Colonel withdrew from what he called "active business" at forty-two after the dissolution of the investment banking partnership.

He turned to managing his investments, serving on boards, and pursuing miscellaneous personal interests. In anticipation of Prohibition, he laid on enough champagne, my father would later say, to last the family for decades. He became active in the campaign for Prohibition amendment repeal, set up the bar manager of his men's club in the bootlegging business, and tried his hand at home distilling. He took up flying, having been warned off of foxhunting and steeplechasing for health reasons. He bought several airplanes and an autogiro. And, in one of the more curious stories I heard, he had mature oak trees shipped across the Atlantic after hearing they were to be felled on some distant Scottish relative's estate. He stored them in a hay barn, where they sustained a colony of termites for a time before finally being hauled away.

The crash of the stock market put a dent in the Montgomerys' wealth. But the extent of the damage is unclear, at least to me. In the 1930 census, the big house was valued at two million dollars. Later in the decade, I find the Colonel asking the township to slash the entire estate's valuation to just four hundred thousand dollars. Turning down a tenant's request for a rent reduction, he says the rental income from his properties is barely covering operations and upkeep. As for his investments, he tells a friend in 1933 that their market value is a fraction of what it once was—"but today they have kept up their income payments and I am no worse off." The same year, he cuts his employees' pay by 20 percent, blaming shrinking dividends and rising taxes. He tells a friend that his income has been "substantially reduced" and that he's worried about an income tax hike. Yet he says the new brokerage, started with his son and son-in-law, has done "very well and, indeed, transacts one of the comparatively large volumes of such business on the New York Stock Exchange." It has "neither made nor lost any great amount of money."

The election of President Franklin D. Roosevelt finds the Colonel increasingly politically active. A local newspaper called him the township's Republican boss. By 1933, he was heading a taxpayers' league, bent on slowing the rise in the cost of county government. Meanwhile, legislation passed in Washington in response to the crash and the Depression put an end to a business practice that had helped make the Colonel rich—a practice my father called "kiting public utility companies." The Public Utility Holding Company Act put a stop, in 1935, to the creation of huge utility holding companies. The Colonel, professing to champion the interests of small stockholders, railed against Roosevelt: "We ask for a square deal, not a New Deal."

By the late thirties, the Colonel's lawyer was telling township officials that the value of the Montgomery property was plummeting. Nearby estates were being unloaded onto the market, he said; even the foxhunters were leaving in search of open land to the west. In 1939, I find, the Colonel flew in from South Carolina in his private plane to testify against a neighbor's plan to donate her estate to be used for a home for twenty "convalescent crippled children"—a move, at least partially philanthropic, that would have removed her thirty-six acres from the tax rolls. "Why, I could give my estate to Delaware County and save all these taxes, enough for me to live on my South Carolina plantation," the county's largest taxpayer thundered, in what sounds quite like a veiled threat. "The schools are piling on new things and additional buildings all the time, and taxes are always advancing. It is very difficult to maintain a large estate nowadays."

Ardrossan wasn't the only white elephant imprinted on the consciousness of my father. There was Chiltern, the four-hundred-fifty-lightbulb fortress on the Maine coast, to which he was dispatched during childhood summers to stay with his widowed Scott grandmother and various cousins, uncles, and aunts. Each of those houses loomed on the horizon of his emotional landscape, each with its family legend attached—the tale of the aspirational future Colonel, horseless on the hilltop, espying his future, and the story of the doomed railroad heir's vow to build himself a gilded cloister if he couldn't snare the woman he loved. Over the decades, my father observed his elders shoring up those monuments. If he ever entertained the possibility that the cause was lost, he must have concluded it was not. Otherwise, why would he embark, as he would do near the end of his life, on the grandest restoration campaign of them all?

By the 1930s, Bar Harbor had changed since the days when Edgar the elder had used his vision of luxurious rustication to entice Maisie Sturgis. With the advent of the income tax and World War I, "cottagers" had begun pulling up stakes. The arrival of automobiles on the island had brought a new class of tourist, and the stock market crash and the Depression made it harder to pay large staffs to operate dinosaurian summer homes. But my father's grandmother Maisie Scott retained a romantic attachment to Chiltern. In 1929, she'd extricated herself from the king-size house that her husband had built in Lansdowne, Pennsylvania, and moved to a more manageable place on the Main Line, freeing herself to pour her money into perpetuating Chiltern. In the style of a benevolent despot, she presided over a rolling open house for four months every summer. In the first thirteen summers of my father's life, his parents regularly packed him off to Chiltern. He and his cousins were often long-term guests. Years later, they'd remember those summers as idyllic.

My father rode the Bar Harbor Express up from Philadelphia, often unaccompanied by parents, and with or without his brother. He shared a bedroom with his cousin Mike Kennedy, in the children's wing on the third floor. From a playroom window, they could gaze across the crescent-shaped cove to a small island, Bald Porcupine. In the early morning, grandchildren would visit their grandmother in the sitting room adjoining her second-floor bedroom. At sit-down lunches in the dining room, marrow bones came individually wrapped in linen napkins, ready to be mined for their marrow with a long-handled spoon. There were steamed clams on Sundays, consumed competitively by the bushel. At dinnertime, the children dined in the playroom. Downstairs, long dresses were de rigueur. During long July and August days, the cousins played in the rocky tidal pools at the water's edge. They climbed mountains, chauffeured to the trailhead with their grandmother and her Irish setters. Charlie Chaplin movies played in the Bar Harbor theaters. The house library was stocked with Dickens and Sir Walter Scott. There was tea on the octagonal porch. There was a vegetable garden where, during the Depression, the less fortunate could help themselves. "It was total security," Mike Kennedy told me. More than thirty years later, as a hostage in Iran for four hundred forty-four days, Mike dreamed of Chiltern.

A feature of those summers was the beguiling presence of the children's uncle, Warwick, my grandfather's younger brother, named for their father's friend who'd died on the *Sagamore* circumnavigation. A born parodist and performer, Warwick had gravitated to theater in school. After studying Shelley at Oxford, he'd become a lawyer—a courtroom showman who relished the formality of the interplay with judges and other lawyers, and made a fetish of being correct. At six foot four, with gray-blue eyes, he was a memorable courthouse figure, attired in a long coat and in gloves that he removed theatrically, for maximum effect. He was a tennis player and a competitive sailor. When the United States entered World War I, he'd begged his parents, at age sixteen, to let him join the Coast Guard. Thwarted on the grounds of youth, he'd arranged instead to do his bit for the war effort by raising sheep on the Chiltern lawn. His nephews and nieces adored him—a childless uncle with a fanciful imagination and a sense of humor rooted in the ridiculous. On racing days, he'd climb to the second-floor balcony, brandishing a red megaphone and uniformed in a blazer and cap, and call across the water to the family's boatman. By the time he and his crew had crossed the lawn, his racing boat, *Artemis*, would be waiting at a neighbor's dock. He'd take along a small nephew as ballast.

In a photo, I find my father, at two, against a backdrop of billowing flower beds in the garden at Chiltern, in the company of his parents' cook and maid. From a letter written the summer he turned nine, I find he's requested his parents' permission to stay an extra month—a request that, it seems, was promptly granted. His parents themselves spent little time at Chiltern: Edgar worked during summers; Helen Hope spent those months developing young horses for the fall. She had no interest in sailboat racing or tennis. In fact, she appears to have detested Chiltern. THRILLED TO BE COMING HOME, she cabled my grandfather from the train, after leaving my father, age two, and his brother, six, in Bar Harbor. COULD NOT STAND IT THERE. She didn't entirely trust her darling at home alone, it's evident from letters. Plus, relations with her mother-in-law were frosty. Maisie Scott disapproved of the fast life Helen Hope favored, and Helen Hope had no intention of knuckling under to her mother-in-law's house rules. Once, I'm told, Maisie excavated a wayward corset buried beneath a sofa cushion; on another occasion, Helen Hope may or may not have been the prime suspect in the case of a newspaper that her mother-in-law found unfolded. The final blowup is said to have come one summer when Maisie tore into her daughter-in-law, newly arrived in Bar Harbor, for her deficiencies as a mother. The rupture was so deep, it's said, that my father's parents walked out. From then on, they returned only for occasional, awkward, duty visits.

As a boy, my father sensed that he was somehow sullied in the crossfire. Years later, he'd describe his grandmother as terrifying—a person who, he said, disapproved of him because he was "too Montgomery." He suspected she preferred his brother, her firstborn grandchild and her late husband's namesake. It seems she felt my father could have benefited from some parental attention. Ensconced in the Oak Room, she once observed an intimate moment between my father's cousin Mike and his father, talking quietly on a window bench, the son nestled in the curve of the father's arm. Turning to her elder daughter, Maisie said ruefully, "If only Bobby had that."

In my father's childhood letters to his parents, I'm struck by how hard he worked to please them. There had *never been* a better Christmas, a more wonderful vacation, more popular parents. "There are lots of people who keep mooning over the fact that 'the most attractive people on the face of God's earth aren't here,'" he wrote from Maine at seventeen. "And since I found out long ago that it always means you, I thought you'd maybe like to hear it." In his letters, he inquired after every aunt, uncle, grandparent, cook, maid, horse, and dog by name. He solicited his parents' views on the Bretton Woods Conference and the presidential election, and gently ventured his own. "Please don't think me fresh, or criticizing your opinions," he wrote. "I don't, but merely vehemently express my humble ones." Toying with the possibility of taking up pipe smoking, he gave them veto power. Instinctively, he knew which stories would pique their interest: "The possibilities and actualities of my love-life are most glowing and very bewildering. I'll tell you about it all someday."

At boarding school, he was his own harshest critic. In report cards, teachers praised his "powers of imagination, and his lightness of touch, combined with his seriousness of purpose." They remarked on his "keen interest in philosophical ideas and problems of man's life." Yet, writing to his parents, his self-criticism was savage—albeit in humorous, hyperbolic terms. His grades would be "putrid," he predicted: "I know they'll stink, or at least radiate a pungent odor." They never did. He called himself "this x&*!#& lazy oaf of a stinking son of yours." He castigated himself: "I have been so damned, damned, damned lazy all term, and am furious with myself. I am terribly sorry and <u>will</u> do <u>better</u> next half term." Maybe he was managing their expectations, or his own. Or perhaps he was more attuned than others to the many ways he imagined he could fall short.

One relative whose affection he cannot have doubted was his mother's artistic sister. As a child in their father's horse-centric household, Mary Binney had taught herself to fall off so she'd be allowed to go back inside to resume doing the things she loved. When the Montgomerys had traveled as a family, she'd packed a portable encyclopedia. She'd studied piano at the Curtis Institute of Music, founded a dance company, worked as a choreographer, and taught dance. Because she was not yet married and longed for children when my father was young, he became, one of her daughters told me, "her first child." She took him to the orchestra and the art museum. He spent afternoons at her dance studio after school. "She is having him again Saturday a.m., at his request, to watch her class," his father reported to Helen Hope. "(Is this good for young lads?)" When Mary Binney, as a single woman, adopted the first of her two daughters in the early 1940s, she made my father, age twelve, a godfather. And when Mary Binney died at eighty-eight, my father confessed to her younger daughter that he, too, felt he'd lost the only person who'd always believed he was perfect.

In the fall of 1943, my father's brother, Ed, left Groton after his junior year to join the Marines. Because he'd go from the Marines to Harvard to marriage, he was out of his parents' house at seventeen. In his absence, Helen Hope turned her attention to my father. "Fate having taken one son away from her influence made her think, 'That's not going to happen again,'" Ed told me. "'We're going to make sure we see a lot of this son.'" She worked hard at becoming close to my father; she also groomed him for the glamorous circles to which she was drawn. "I think she would have been pleased to see him marry a countess," Ed told me dryly. My father, surely, welcomed his mother's renewed interest. ("When the light was shining on us, we were very much there. When it wasn't, we made do.") He was also endowed by nature, it seems, with the social skills she intended to impart. By the time he graduated from boarding school, he'd aced her tutorial. In his high school yearbook, the story chosen by the editors to illuminate his true self concerned a formal party he'd evidently hosted: An interloper, caught crashing the party, is chagrined to receive a personal invitation from the host to stay.

"The act was a revelation of the essential Scott," the editors wrote, "since it involved humor, urbanity, appropriateness, and, above all, society."

When I was a child, my father's widowed Ardrossan grandmother, Muz, would disappear from Villanova every winter. Her destination was a plantation near Georgetown, South Carolina. I was too unworldly to question why this birdlike creature, descended from Puritan stock, made her annual migration to a rice plantation in the Deep South. My parents went rarely; even my grandparents made other plans. Only my grandmother's youngest sister, Charlotte Ives, spent much time in that part of the country; she lived year-round near Georgetown, in a house not far from her mother's. When Charlotte Ives came north to visit, she materialized in a lumbering black limousine, which rolled like a pirate clipper into the circular driveway in front of the big house, scattering yellow pebbles in its wake. From the limo would emerge a piebald Great Dane, the size of a small horse, its unnerving mouth foaming, and this perplexing auntie who, then in her fifties, appeared to be unable to walk. On the rare occasions when we asked why, my father would say she'd fallen off horses once too often while riding without a hat. Or he'd say she'd been bitten by a mosquito in the cypress swamps of South Carolina, and had come down with something he called cerebral malaria.

In my thirties, I found myself in South Carolina for the first time. The strongest and costliest hurricane in the state's history had made landfall a few weeks earlier at a shrimping town south of Georgetown. I was a reporter in California, visiting a friend a few hours' drive from Georgetown. On a whim, we decided to find out what had become of the Montgomerys' plantation, which I knew had been sold, after the death of Muz, to an engineer who'd helped design the interstate highway system. On the outskirts of Georgetown, we found the entrance to the driveway—an unpaved road that ran for two miles through piney woods, strewn with fallen branches, before turning into what had once been a handsome avenue of live oaks. Tumbledown wooden cabins, some dating from before abolition, lined what was called, in that willfully nondescript plantation terminology, "the street." The driveway came to a stop in front of an unprepossessing white plantation house. Its lawns were littered with branches and debris. The impression left was one of unimpeded decay.

An elderly African American couple emerged from one of the slave cabins. They'd worked on the plantation, they told me, in the Colonel's time. They'd stayed on in the cabin after the plantation was sold, receiving a small pension from Helen Hope. Inside their house, aqua-colored walls were partially covered in fading snapshots. Peering at the round face of a pale-skinned, curly-haired woman on horseback in one of the pictures, I recognized Auntie Ives. The big house in Villanova loomed behind her. She was young—the wild child in the portrait in the ballroom, who'd ridden show jumpers for people with names like Guggenheim before whatever terrible thing that had happened to her had set in.

On the field trip that day was the man I'd marry a few years later. He had no reason for sentimentality about this moody, decrepit outpost with its murky connection to my father. He'd spent his life in Southern California, the shimmering land of insistent novelty, the starkest of contrasts to this Southern Gothic rot. Yet the abandoned rice fields, the mangled trees, the devoted couple seized his imagination. An irrational impulse—to rescue, to restore, to reclaim—washed over even him. Encountering my grandmother some months later, he announced gallantly that, if he ever had money, he'd buy back the plantation, rejuvenate it, and return it to her family—in whose possession he imagined, for whatever reason, it belonged.

A look of irritation crossed my grandmother's face.

"That's a terrible idea," she snapped, with a sharpness that took me aback.

Then she added, in a line that lodged itself deep in some recess in my head, "People went down there and drank themselves to death."

Georgetown, I now know, was once the heart of one of the most productive rice-growing regions of the world. Because of the surrounding area's climate and terrain, and because of the exploitation of staggering numbers of enslaved people, South Carolina low-country landowners became, in the first half of the nineteenth century, among the richest people in the United States. After the Civil War, emancipation helped put an end to large-scale rice growing in the region. Abandoned rice fields became vacation homes for hundreds of thousands of overwintering birds. Land prices plunged, opening the door eventually to rich Northerners eager to spend some trivial fraction of their wealth on plantations for use as hunting retreats. In the early twentieth century, there were Vanderbilts, du Ponts, and Huntingtons spending the winter months on plantations in the Georgetown area, along with Bernard Baruch, the financier and an adviser to Woodrow Wilson, and Isaac Emerson, the inventor of Bromo-Seltzer. Visiting a friend near Georgetown in the second year of the Depression, Colonel Montgomery saw a seven-hundred-eighty-acre plantation, called Mansfield. He made a lowball offer. Confident that it would be rejected, he and Muz left for the West Indies—only to discover, upon returning home, that Mansfield was theirs. Muz is said to have had grave misgivings.

The resuscitation of that neglected remnant of the age of slavery gave the Colonel a project—just as the extravagant resuscitation of the Colonel's Edwardian estate to the north would give his grandson, my father, a project sixty years later. The Colonel converted the plantation house's freestanding kitchen and its school building into two-story guesthouses. He built a third guesthouse from scratch. To the main house, he added a basement kitchen with an oyster bar where his

The street

houseguests could congregate before lunch to gorge on oysters and another local delicacy, the tiny crabs that lived in the oysters' gills. He modernized the slave cabins, adding several more, to house his employees. He restored a historic rice-threshing mill. For navigating the rivers, lagoons, and bays, he bought a small fleet of motor cruisers. He installed a boathouse, dredged a canal to the Pee Dee River, and erected a glass pavilion as a picnic destination. Soon there were stables, kennels, an autogiro hangar, and an airstrip—used for, among other things, flying in lettuce from the greenhouse in Villanova. He tried his hand at growing rice—until it proved to be costing him twenty times what he would have paid to buy the same amount. After that, he flooded one of his rice fields, making a large, shallow lake, ideal for unsuspecting ducks. With a rich friend from the North, he's said to have sent the owner of a Georgetown fish house to Russia for a crash course in caviar preparation—an approach the man then used to produce caviar from the Atlantic sturgeon that swam in the Great Pee Dee

River and Winyah Bay. For years, homegrown caviar, packed in mason jars and shipped north by the case, arrived at houses on Ardrossan. My parents stored theirs beside the Popsicles in the freezer. Jars would be taken out and thawed for special occasions, when the caviar would be spread, like grape jelly, on toasted rectangles of Arnold Hearth Stone white, to be circulated on platters to guests.

The operation of Mansfield, like Ardrossan, depended on labor. There was a full-time foreman, a team of laborers, and a roster of local women who could be called up for duty in the kitchen and the houses at a moment's notice. Maids, butlers, and the chauffeur from Villanova would make the trek south. The "inside tipping list," used as a guide for guests, enumerated eleven hardworking souls. In the depths of the Depression, the arrival of a new employer near Georgetown didn't go unnoticed. The purchase of Mansfield was front-page news in the *Georgetown Times*. Men, desperate for employment, wrote to the new owner, begging for work or financial assistance. ("Coming to the point instantly, I need a job," one letter began.) Though the Colonel turned down requests from strangers for money, he did help employees by, for example, fending off a mortgage foreclosure or posting bail. But in the spring of 1933, having cut the wages of his Pennsylvania employees by 20 percent, he did the same at Mansfield. By the midthirties, some of his unskilled laborers were taking home just forty cents a day. In a letter to the president of the power company, the Colonel expressed a suspicion that the families in his cabins were squandering electricity. Each cabin had a four-lightbulb allotment. "If the darkies have been imposing on me, I will cut the power off and use it only in the hangar and laundry," the irritated Northerner wrote. When his loyal foreman asked that the pay cuts be lifted in 1936, he received a dismissive response from the Colonel's secretary. "He would be very sorry to have you go," the secretary wrote, "but it is altogether all right if you want to."

The foreman, I assume, knew nothing of the Colonel's haberdashery budget. It appears from the evidence that, though the stock market crash and the Depression may have dented the Colonel's wealth, they had not yet cramped his personal style. In a cardboard box in the ironing room, I found a heap of receipts dating from a mid-Depression shopping spree in London. Why the records were kept, I cannot know. Did someone anticipate that they'd be of interest? More likely, no one saw a reason to throw them out. As a result, I now know that on July 4, 1936, the Colonel and Muz settled in at Claridge's, the London hotel, which was doing double duty as a refuge for European royalty in Mayfair. At least one purpose of the trip, it seems, was to replenish the squire's wardrobe and inventory of hunting paraphernalia. Over a ten-day period, his purchases included, but weren't limited to, five double-breasted suits, four pairs of jodhpurs, three riding coats, a dozen neckties, nine bow ties, a dinner coat, a "smoking suit," patent leather pumps, seven foulard stocks (whatever those are), a pair of string gloves, three hats (deerstalker, Shetland fishing, Donegal), a silk muffler, suspenders, twelve pairs of silk and lambs' wool socks, and thirty-three shirts. Also acquired in the same ten-day period: a pair of Chippendale mirrors, a Chippendale settee, a pair of mahogany chairs, one hundred twenty-five yards of chintz, two cases of thirty-year-old brandy, one hundred clay birds, four monogrammed pigskin cartridge bags, and a twelve-bore shotgun.

How to square the four-lightbulb allotment with one hundred twenty-five yards of chintz?

The Colonel was not entirely satisfied with his purchases. He complained to his shirtmaker, Edouard & Butler, that he'd been overcharged. The store's managing director, with a mannered solicitousness barely disguising his disdain, called the colonial's bluff. "We are very sorry to learn that such a longstanding and valued customer should be in any way dissatisfied with our prices," he wrote, "but would point out that the materials we supply are the best it is possible to procure, as also are our cut and workmanship. If however you should require cheaper materials we could of course obtain them, but naturally in our class of business it is our policy to supply only the best unless specifically asked to the contrary."

The Colonel, it seems, didn't take up the offer.

Life on the plantation was quiet in the extreme. My father's brother, Ed, who was packed off by his parents to Mansfield for three months while recovering from bronchitis at age nine, remembered it as "very comfortable, very beautiful, really dull." He recalled having seen not one child of his age during his recuperation—though once, after the call went out for roast pork for dinner, he saw a decapitated pig running in circles. In an album, I find a photo of my father, by himself at about the same age, balancing on a joggling board under a canopy of Spanish moss. From Mansfield, his mother had written to his father, several years earlier, "Really this place bores me stiff." The antidote was houseguests. Acquaintances traveling by motor yacht were invited to dinner; friends and relatives arrived from the North by overnight train or made the two-day trip by car. On a set of typed driving directions, I happen upon this admonition: "Do not ask Negroes for directions. Always ask White People, preferably a woman."

There were boat trips, picnics, duck hunting, socializing with neighbors. Charlotte Ives, the youngest Montgomery, whose taste in potential husbands cannot have escaped her father's judgment, finally eloped, at thirty, with an unsuitable South Carolinian about whom all details have been erased, except that he may have been a stable hand.

How long were they married? I asked my uncle.

A week? he ventured.

"I was told it happened," he said. "Everybody was aghast. And then it un-happened."

In the Georgetown County Judicial Center, a clerk directs me to a rack of red leather-bound volumes listing marriage licenses by year. In a volume labeled "White," I find a listing for the marriage of Charlotte Ives Montgomery and Edward Mitchell. No one seems to remember, or be willing to say, why the union soured. Whatever happened, and it cannot have been good, the bride's mother came hastily to her daughter's rescue. In the big house, I find a flurry of letters between lawyers for the family in the immediate aftermath of the elopement, full of cryptic references to "the unexpected marriage" and the need to put certain property in trust. There's later correspondence, too, referring to a car accident and the near impossibility of insuring Charlotte Ives in the event of an accident such as a fall downstairs. There are vague allusions to "her present condition" and the "undesirable risk" she presents for insurers. Her mother reports that Ives "hobbles a bit further" each day but that "it is very painful and aches most of the time." She is happy with her animals and her house, her mother writes, but "if she lost those there would be very little in life for her." Later, in her mother's letters, there are mentions of difficulties with balance, and a reference to her being on the wagon.

Food and drink occupied much of the day at Mansfield. For houseguests, there was the option of an early breakfast before being paddled out onto the lake for duck hunting at dawn. A full breakfast, including eggs and grits, awaited them upon return. Midday: oysters, cocktails, lunch. An afternoon nap, tea, more cocktails, dinner, bed. In the Colonel's papers, I find he's kept his orders for bourbon, cognac, Jamaica rum. "You know my weakness," he writes to a friend in Georgetown. ". . . There is nothing more delightful than Johnnie Walker Black Label."

The lifestyle took a toll on the host's health. The Colonel, who'd given up foxhunting after a heart attack possibly precipitated by his having ridden two point-to-point races in one day, slid into an increasingly sedentary state. He ate, drank, gained weight. In the winter of 1935, a Georgetown doctor, alarmed by the Colonel's blood pressure, ordered him to bed. The patient resisted, insisting the condition was a passing result of excessive entertaining and drinking—a problem he'd be unable to address until he got home. Back in Pennsylvania, he went to bed for a week in his second-floor bedroom, uninterrupted by social obligations. His blood pressure dropped to close to normal. The Georgetown doctor was informed of the good news. With what seems like a surplus of deference, the medical professional wrote back to his wealthy patient, "I can see my mistake in trying to rest you at Mansfield. It is impossible, and I think the few days you tried it made you worse instead of helping you."

At the "cottage" in Maine, a shadow fell over the summer of 1941. War was raging in Europe and Asia. The United States would soon join. My father's uncle Warwick had joined the Naval Reserve and was now a naval intelligence officer in the Pacific, deputy to the director of the port at Manila. Maisie Scott, the Scott family matriarch, was unwell. On the advice of a doctor, she departed from Chiltern in midseason, leaving her eldest daughter in tears. Back in Pennsylvania, a surgeon found, in Maisie's intestines, a cancer so advanced, he simply took note of it, then stitched her back up. "Don't bring me back to any half-life," she'd instructed him in advance. When she died that fall, at sixty-nine, the town of Bar Harbor shut down for the afternoon of the funeral. The selectmen turned out to pay their respects. My grandfather and his sisters carried their mother's ashes to the top of Newport Mountain, then scattered them on the rocky slopes where she'd hiked, her voice slicing the still air as she called to her dogs.

Manila fell to the Japanese that winter. With the rest of the naval forces, Warwick retreated to Corregidor, the largest of the fortified islands protecting Manila Bay. American and Filipino soldiers held out there for four months against Japanese bombing and shelling. "I note one thing," Warwick wrote to his family, two months in. "—that I love you all very much. Don't <u>ever</u> forget that! I note another thing—that this existence being unguessable from day to day and not free from danger, does <u>not</u> inspire me to write you great things about life and death or to memorialize myself in some poetic effort about self giving his all in distant Asiatic sea or shore or wherever it is I am." On May 6, 1942, the commander of Allied forces in the Philippines, Lt. Gen. Jonathan M. Wainwright, surrendered. "There is a limit to human endurance, and that point has long been passed," he radioed to President Roosevelt. Taken prisoner along with seven thousand other Americans, Warwick was listed as missing in action.

Human endurance was to be tested further.

For nearly a year, the family received no word of Warwick. My grandfather, courteous by temperament and training, tapped his connections in the military, politics, and the press in pursuit of news of his brother. ("Dear Cabot," he writes to Senator Henry Cabot Lodge Jr.) At one point, he was told that Warwick was a prisoner in a camp in Japan—"the model Japanese prison camp," someone assured him. But letters to that camp were returned. Later, word came that Warwick was in a camp in the Philippines. A series of small, regulation-style, fill-in-the-blank postcards from him trickled in, bearing the minimal news permitted. Then communication ceased again, in late 1944, as the Allied campaign to take back the Philippines, the bloodiest campaign in the Pacific War, commenced. As the Allies retook the country, news of liberated prisoners trickled home; family friends hovered near their radios, in shifts, recording names. "They have, as I expected, no news on Warwick and no suggestions how to get any," my grandfather wrote after visiting the offices of the Committee on Relief for Americans in the Philippines. "But they . . . say we can have good confidence Warwick is alive if we have not been officially notified of the contrary."

One month earlier, however, with Manila under American aerial bombardment, the Japanese had herded some sixteen hundred American and Allied prisoners onto a transport ship headed to Japan. Nearly all the prisoners were survivors of the defense of Corregidor, Bataan, and Mindanao; many were emaciated and weak. At bayonet's point, they were crammed into the airless hold. The ship, its decks studded with anti-aircraft guns, left Manila on the night of December 13, 1944. With no markings to indicate that it carried prisoners, it came under heavy fire from United States Navy planes. For a day and a half, the United States strafed and bombed it. Amid detonations and the groans of the dying, the blood of the Japanese gun crews ran in rivulets from the decks into the hold. In the blackness, men slid into madness. Crouched naked in temperatures estimated to have risen as high as one hundred thirty degrees, dozens are believed to have suffocated. On December 15, the ship burned to the waterline and began to sink in Subic Bay. More than three hundred of the sixteen hundred prisoners died. Warwick Scott, at forty-three, is thought either to have died from lack of oxygen or to have been killed when an American bomb hit the ship's stern directly above where he huddled. His body has never been recovered.

In the months after my father turned sixteen, his father and his aunts pieced together, from the recollections of survivors, an account of the final months of their brother's life. "If Warwick knew, as he must have, that the situation was hopeless, he never permitted his knowledge to affect his good cheer, consideration for others, and enthusiasm," a fellow officer wrote. During the long siege of Corregidor, Warwick had built, equipped, and staffed three machine gun outposts, then directed anti-aircraft fire against the Japanese, for which he would posthumously be awarded the Bronze Star. In the prison camps, he was said to have cut an unforgettable figure—gaunt but dignified, in epaulets till the end. He'd taught lessons in conversational French; he'd delivered a lecture on French wines. With a concealed radio assembled from stolen parts, he'd gathered news of the outside world, reporting his findings to fellow prisoners in a news conference at night. There's a story that he staged a production of *A Midsummer Night's Dream*; a nephew remembers hearing that Warwick had written home for clarification on some fine point in act two. I found no mention of such a production in survivors' letters, though perhaps it had been mounted in the months before the fall of Manila.

In Warwick's absence, the house in Maine languished. With their mother dead and their brother at war, my grandfather and his sisters had neither the heart nor the money to carry on opening Chiltern each summer. As years came and went, it sat uninhabited, its garden gone to seed. Only the black-eyed Susans and other perennials persisted. Other families put their "cottages" on the market and migrated to smaller houses in other towns, where men could arrive for the summer without having packed a tuxedo. "Bar Harbor is finished," my grandfather had declared. But he and his sisters resolved to do nothing about the fate of Chiltern until after Warwick's return. Maybe he'd dreamed of the house while he was away, they thought; maybe he'd want to recuperate there. In which case, they'd open the house one last time. They'd give their brother, back from hell, one final, heavenly summer.

In June 1945, word came that Warwick was believed dead. My grandfather forwarded the Navy's letter to relatives and friends. "Here is some sad news about Warwick," he wrote in a brief note, poignant in its restraint. "A miracle could still happen and he might come back to us, but there is nothing to do but accept the report of the Bureau of Naval Personnel. We are very proud of him." My father, at sixteen, spent part of that summer with his aunt and cousins in Maine, helping dismantle the house that his grandfather had built and that his widowed grandmother had dedicated herself to keeping. For weeks, my father assisted in the dusting of books, the sorting of furniture, and the deciding of who would take what. His father had waived any claim to the house, turning over his share to his sisters.

For himself, my father laid claim to his grandfather's favorite Morris chair, and to a French antique desk made of mahogany that gleamed like a horse chestnut fresh off the branch. The desk had a galleried marble top and a pullout writing surface inset with leather. For years it stood in a corner of my parents' library. My father's paperwork drifted there in tidy heaps. The desk, with a bowed lid that opened to reveal its fitted interior, had certain advantages. If you tugged the lid from its raised position, it would rumble down a curving track and snap shut, like a garage door, hiding behind its handsome, polished exterior whatever confusion lay unattended inside.

The family emptied the summer palace and put it up for sale. But demand for mansions in those years was not robust. The real estate market in Bar Harbor was awash in oversized "cottages" that their owners were itching to unload. Forty-five years after that first summer at Chiltern, half the family was dead, and the survivors were left to tear down their father's dream. A team of laborers embarked upon an exhausting process of demolition. My father's brother, Ed, on a boat out of Bar Harbor that summer, vowed he wouldn't look in the direction of Chiltern, according to a story one of his cousins remembers Ed telling. But Ed couldn't resist. Turning, he glimpsed the lawn sloping down toward the crescent-shaped beach. He saw the house being dismantled. For years afterward, he'd say, he regretted that final look. Not long after, the family transferred the land to a corporation, which later declared bankruptcy and eventually was able to sell the property, in pieces, and cover unpaid back taxes.

In October 1947, smoke was spotted rising near a cranberry bog on Mount Desert Island. A protracted drought had left conditions on the island the driest on record. The fire smoldered for days before the wind picked up and changed direction, herding flames toward Bar Harbor. The blaze, becoming an inferno propelled by what were said to have been gale-force winds, traversed six miles in three hours. Reaching the town, it barreled down West Street, known then as Millionaires' Row. By the time the conflagration was over, sixty-seven summer estates had burned, along with one hundred seventy year-round homes. For some, the disaster was a blessing in disguise: Many of the burned cottages, unoccupied for years, had been scheduled for demolition. "Even those who suffered extreme losses now admit that Bar Harbor cottage life was on the way out long before the fire, and that the fire was merely the *coup de grace*," Cleveland Amory wrote later. My grandfather had seen it coming. Bar Harbor—that is, his father's Bar Harbor—was finished.

Nearly sixty years later, I made an impromptu detour to the town. After five days in a cabin in the woods at the farthest reach of the Maine coast, I was driving south with my beloved when he suggested we see if we could find any trace of the house that my great-grandparents had built and their offspring had razed. Googling the name of the house some months earlier, I'd noticed the existence of a bed-and-breakfast in Bar Harbor with Chiltern in its name. Guests were shelling out upwards of two hundred dollars a night to stay in an inn said to have been "lovingly designed from the carriage house of an ambassador's estate." When we pulled into downtown Bar Harbor on a weekday morning in mid-September, flocks of senior citizens, in fall-colored fleece finery, were emerging from tour buses, flooding sidewalks, and spilling into streets. A short distance from the center of town, we parked in front of a two-and-a-half-story, gray-shingled building. One of the owners obligingly showed us around the inn. He even produced what he said were the original blueprints: twelve stalls, a carriage room, a harness room, a cleaning room, a toolroom, lockers, hay and straw chutes, and two car-wash-like "wash stands" for cleaning horses and carriages. The bed-and-breakfast had a sauna, a theater, and an indoor lap pool. In a guest bedroom, towels had been folded, origami-style, into swans, paddling on the surface of the king-size bed.

The owner pointed us up the street to the place where the putative ambassador's residence had once stood. Where there had once been a single house, we found four. Three generations of the family that had bought the land in the 1950s now had summer houses there. The original garden, greenhouses, and tennis court were gone. Trees had recolonized much of the clearing. A landscaping crew was hacking at brush that was blocking access to the crescent-shaped beach. One of the only clues to who or what had once occupied the property was a rusting street sign at the entrance to a narrow cul-de-sac, called Scotts Lane. The other lay largely buried, obscured by grass and dirt, at the foot of a house on the site of the original. If you ran the toe of your shoe back and forth, you could expose a sliver of one of those enormous, squared blocks of granite, cut from a local quarry and put in place by thirty masons, which had inspired an awestruck reporter, back when, to liken Chiltern to "a modern fort"—indestructible and destined to last far into an unimagined but no doubt glorious future.

Chapter Six

The stuffed hare dated back to my father's twenty-sixth year. He was a young lawyer then, employed in his great-uncle's firm, commuting on his great-grandfather's railroad, living next door to his parents on his grandparents' place. On the last day of 1953, my mother had given birth to their first child, my sister, the latest link in the long chain of firstborn Hopes. On a cold Sunday in January, my father drove west from the house to where one- and two-acre lots gave way to horse farms and open country. A pack of beagles was scheduled to hunt there that afternoon, and he was new to the sport. He'd met a man with a pack of hounds and a hardy band of followers devoted to passing autumn and winter afternoons traipsing around the countryside in search of some hapless cottontail rabbit or a hare. After lunch on Sundays, he'd taken to setting off, returning at nightfall, ruddy-faced, with mud pasted to his white canvas sneakers. From an account he wrote at the time, and from all the hours my sister and brother and I spent as children following him and his hounds, I can picture that January day. The wind was blowing in gusts, and the sky was a smudgy gray. A few dozen enthusiasts had turned out, parking on the grassy shoulder of the road, warming their hands with their breath. A tall man with flagpole posture stood in their midst, dressed in a green hunting coat and black velvet cap. He was the master of hounds. There was a liveried huntsman, too, and several "whippers-in," each equipped with a kennel whip with a braided thong. My father slipped in among the followers. Then, as the hounds set off, the huntsman unexpectedly tossed him a whip.

What had drawn him to beagling, I can't say for sure. It was simply this thing that he did; and, as far back as I remember, Hopie and Elliot and I were either eager or expected to go along—or some mixture of both. When I was five, the straight-backed master of hounds, who'd been hunting hare since the year my father was born, decided he'd aged out of the role. A housing development was about to swallow his kennel; access to water and cesspool had been cut off. So he transferred to my father, for one dollar, twenty-four hounds and the right to hunt in the stretch of countryside assigned, by the national beagling elders, to his pack. Each hound had its own mellifluous, bisyllabic name—Bugler, Burgess, Dainty, Dulcie, Madcap, Matchless, and so on—each new litter having been named in alphabetical order. To house them, my father envisioned a kennel in our backyard. My mother did not. So he had one built less than a mile away in a cow pasture downwind of the big house. The kennel had running water, indoor and outdoor pens, a giant drum full of dry dog food, a long wooden trough for feeding. It was more practical than lavish—a Hampton Inn for hounds. On Saturday mornings, he'd exercise his pack close to home, surfacing on lawns as family members went about their weekend routines. On Sunday afternoons in fall and winter, he'd hunt the more distant territory passed on to him by the previous master. Afterward, some hospitable beagler would invite everyone for tea, which sometimes segued seamlessly into cocktails, which sometimes segued into a handful of rosy-faced die-hards drinking into the night.

The pack had been moving only minutes, that Sunday in January, when a hare sprang up between the hounds and my father. He'd positioned himself along one flank, jogging between the beagles and the road. He called out the sighting and soon the hounds were scrambling after the hare in clamorous pursuit. It crossed the field, rounded a pond, raced uphill. The pack lost the scent, made several false starts, picked it up again, and was off in full cry. The dogs worked the line of scent alongside a stream, crossed a road, circled a dry pond. My father, reaching the pond early, watched the pack cast through high grass. A field away, someone called out a second sighting: The hare was back on the run. The hounds found the line and followed it into the next pasture, chasing the animal back across the field to a farmhouse. There, in an apple orchard, they lost their way. While they were working the ground under the apple trees, the hare jumped up in front of them. They lurched after it, following by sight. They reached a house, veered onto a road, proceeded methodically down one side. An elderly man with binoculars confirmed what the huntsman already suspected: The hare was running on only three legs.

Blood was never the attraction of beagling for my father. Not that he was opposed on principle to killing animals. He kept a shotgun behind the *Encyclopaedia Britannica* in a bookcase in the library, which he occasionally put to use picking off the grackles that roosted noisily outside his bedroom. Once, I watched him pluck a runt, with poor life prospects, from a litter of beagle puppies; cradle it in the crook of one elbow as he walked to a nearby stream; descend to the stream bank like a priest at a baptism; and hold the creature underwater until it had drowned. He did not, however, hunt with guns. Rabbits and hares rarely died at the mercy of his hounds. Once, after twenty years of beagling, he said he couldn't remember the last time they'd killed. The fact is, there weren't many rabbits left in the area. More than once, he ordered a shipment of Kansas jackrabbits by mail, intending to release them into the exurban veldt in the hope that they'd survive long enough to settle in and be chased. By the time they arrived by plane at the Philadelphia airport, incarcerated in long, wood-and-chicken-wire crates, many or most were moribund or dead. Once, carting a bag of garbage out to the trash cans in the backyard, my mother lifted a lid and found herself face-to-face with a jackrabbit, kidnapped from the Great Plains and expiring in a trash can on the Main Line.

The master made the call: The pack would carry on hunting the injured hare, probably to the kill. If his beagles didn't finish the animal off, he reasoned, the foxhounds that hunted the same territory would. So the huntsman set off down the road, the pack swirling and eddying at his feet. After crossing the road, working hard against a biting wind, the hounds found the line again. Running parallel to the pack along a steep hill, my father had the joy, as he'd later put it, of being almost on top of the hounds as they worked. They were beside the stream, following the scent. From his vantage point, he caught sight of the hare as it bolted from a spot farther down the stream, ahead of the pack, onto a dirt road. The hounds pushed on after it—across the road, up a hill, and into a cornfield. My father watched the hare, moving slowly among the fallen stalks, looking very lame. The hounds couldn't see the struggling animal until they overtook it. The huntsman reached a gloved hand into the pack, snatched the hare, and killed it with a blow from his crop. With a knife, the master of hounds sawed off the head and feet. Several children who'd arrived early at the kill were awarded the bloody feet. The head went to my father. An honor.

The next day, he took the body part to a taxidermist to have it stuffed and mounted. The hare's leg, it had been determined, had been broken for some time: It had dangled, useless, by the animal's side. Yet the hare had outrun its pursuers for an hour and a half. The spirit of the doomed beast, maimed as it was, had moved my father. For as long as I lived in my parents' house, and for years after, that animal's stuffed head hung on the library wall.

"I feel very sorry for that hare," my father wrote on the day he delivered the head to the taxidermist. "He was plucky, he gave us good sport, and he wanted to live. . . . When he hangs in my house, I think he will remind me of a lot of things. He deserves respect, that hare."

My father struck me as different from most of the fathers I'd encountered. He'd decided early on that his children should call him Popsy—a variant of the name he used for his own father, Pop, but also,

I think, one that put some distance between this father and the default, Dad. Unconventional as it was, that handle pleased him. Once, he named a small, outboard-motor boat *Seapoop.* "'Popsy' spelled sideways," he told anyone who asked (until he got tired of explaining, perhaps felt foolish, and quietly changed the name to "Popsy's"). He abstained, too, from the standard leisure uniform of men of his ethnicity and socioeconomic station; no madras sport coats, no belts embroidered with racquets or whales. His summer vacation wardrobe consisted of a half dozen identical pairs of khaki shorts and a half dozen identical navy blue polo shirts. In winter, after returning from work, he'd disappear into his "dressing room" and wrap himself in a silk smoking jacket—an article of clothing that Hugh Hefner also favored. After we moved to London, he transitioned to custom-made suits, suspenders, and striped dress shirts from the bespoke shirtmaker that had outfitted Sean Connery as James Bond in *Dr. No.*

He had no interest in football or baseball or golf. The only trace of a halfhearted stab at the country-club lifestyle was a barely touched bag of irons, wedges, and putters languishing in a coat closet under the front stairs. ("Relax!" the golf pro had barked at his student, wound tight as a watch. "Mr. Scott, relax!") Unlike my mother, who had fond memories of climbing Mount Washington as a child on skis with skins strapped to their underside, my father had never been taught to ski. On a family ski trip with us, he gamely overlooked the ridicule of strangers by attempting to master an unpromising contraption that resembled a child's tricycle on skis. Straddling the seat, he'd peer acrophobically downhill from the top of a ski slope, his thumbs rigid in an involuntary response to terror, as skiers whooshed past him, snorting in disbelief. Beneath his convincing conviviality, he had solitary inclinations. When he took up cooking, he cooked alone, the kitchen doors closed, a glass of wine at the ready, classical music blasting from speakers. Stewed things and blood and melted animal fat spattered the floor. On weekends, he'd shut himself in the library, reading biographies of British statesmen. Before it was fashionable, he was a serious cyclist, clocking as many as a hundred miles in a day. When I joined him on several cycling trips in exotic places in my twenties and early thirties, he took the lead and we rode in silence. It was parallel play.

He was, I suppose, no more or less involved in the lives of his children than were many fathers at that time. For the first decade of my life, nurses and governesses came and went, the most durable of whom was a French Canadian named Odille, who'd be remembered by her charges for, among other child-rearing strategies, her creative repurposing of old party favors—specifically, Paddle Ball paddles—into instruments for the administration of spankings. On weeknights in the Odille years, face time with our father was often limited to a ritual called "spending." It coincided with the cocktail hour, when he would return from work, settle in the library in his smoking jacket, and put away a few scotch and sodas. Hopie and Elliot and I would be delivered downstairs to *spend* time with our parents, after which we'd take our places at a Formica-topped table in a room off the kitchen to eat our supper. At a certain age, I learned to feign nonchalance when our parents stopped by to say good night before heading out for the evening. A cousin of my father's, also raised on Ardrossan, told me that his family, too, had practiced a version of spending. "You got to see your parents once a day, whether you wanted to or not," he recalled, laughing. After Odille came a succession of white-uniformed cooks. Our favorite was a small, perdurable Irish woman who, I didn't fully understand at the time, had been a beloved stand-in parent to my father during the "wintry" period of his boyhood. During her tenure, we graduated to eating in the dining room with our parents. We were to dress for dinner. (No jeans.) We'd maneuver serving dishes through the swinging door from the pantry and arrange them on the sideboard. Serve from the left. Clear from the right. Snuff the candles between thumb and forefinger, to avoid spattering wax across the gleaming surface of the mahogany table.

My family, plus Odille

Collectively, our father addressed us as his troops. Preparing to depart on some expedition, he'd stand at the foot of the front stairs and bellow, "Troops!" Or, with a call on a hunting horn plucked from the front-hall table, he'd summon us to muster. I see him now in the basement with a hand drill, a hammer, a bowl, and our first actual coconut. The three of us squat in a semicircle around him, rapt. He drills holes in the hirsute exterior, decants the milk into the bowl, clobbers the shell with the hammer, hands around fragments. I think of him, too, at the wheel of the station wagon, driving down Abraham's Lane toward the cold pool on a hot summer day, the three of us in bathing suits, balanced on the tailgate, feet dangling. I see him sitting on the end of my bed at the Bryn Mawr hospital, dealing a hand of cards on the expanse of institutional bedclothes between us. I'm recovering from peritonitis. Do I really remember this? Probably not. What I remember is how he flattered me years later, saying he'd taught me gin rummy when I was five years old, tethered to an IV pole, with a three-inch incision in my flank. He claimed I'd beaten him every time, which can't be true; he must have sensed how much I wanted his respect.

It's winter in the early 1960s. The fields, woods, stone barns, and houses on Ardrossan are blanketed in white, like a scene out of a painting by Grandma Moses. The wind has whipped the snow into drifts. In the paved yard between our house and the garage, the snow has been plowed into hills as high as the seven-foot stone wall. Two-foot-long icicles hang, glittering, from the eaves. On the front lawn, the drifts are solid enough to burrow into; we've built igloos using the drifts, the snow cold and sticky enough to be made into blocks for building. The beagles need exercise and so do we, so our father musters his troops. We haul a five- or six-seater wooden toboggan from the garage, and he arranges to meet a few beaglers. At the kennel, hounds clamor at our arrival, then tumble through the gates when we push them open. In our parkas, snow pants, and rubber galoshes, we trail our father and the hounds up the farm road, past the big house, and across a couple of windswept fields to the top of one of the steepest hills on the place. There, we arrange ourselves, zipper-style, on the toboggan—legs interlocking. Our father, positioned at the rear, inches it forward. As we begin to move, hounds lunge after us, barking, ears flapping. Gathering speed, the overloaded toboggan begins its exhilarating descent. Hounds tumble, bark, flail, some marooned in the snow. Now we're hurtling downhill, the sound of barking growing distant. The wind stings our cheeks. We're flying. Somewhere ahead, beyond the bottom of the hill, looms a post-and-rail fence and a half-hidden stream. Nearing the bottom, we throw our weight to one side in unison, as instructed. The toboggan capsizes, depositing us, facedown, in the snow. Cast adrift in the sudden silence, snow in our sleeves and our mittens, we lie on our backs, picking out the hounds on the hillside, scattered in the toboggan track. Toboggling, he called it.

Later, when we were old enough, we tagged along when he took his hounds twice a year to a five-hundred-acre farm in rural Virginia where, on a weekend every fall and one every spring, packs from all over the East would converge to compete in field trials. We'd sleep on lumpy mattresses in bunk beds in log cabins heated by potbellied stoves. We'd take our meals in a barnlike building that had once been an agricultural college—and which, it was said, the beagle club had acquired after a man intending to use it as a hunt club went down with the *Titanic* on his way home from a hound-shopping trip to England. All day, pairs of hounds from each pack competed in field trials. At night, our father caroused with other beaglers. On the long drive home, with the Sunday evening sky turning the purple of eggplant, signs advertising fireworks flashed past beside the barely lit roads. My father would steer the car and trailer into the gravelly parking area of some roadside stand where we'd squander our allowance on sparklers before crossing into our fireworks-free state.

Robert Montgomery Scott and Helen Gay Elliot, my parents, had met when they were eighteen. Though she was from Boston and he was from Villanova, their circles intersected. They met for the first time in the wedding party when my father's brother, Ed, married my mother's childhood friend. Shortly afterward, Bob and Gay were in the same class at Harvard and Radcliffe. They began seeing each other, broke up, resumed. By senior year, they were talking about marriage. By certain measures, they had a lot in common: Her father, like the Colonel, was a successful investor (who, like Edgar T. Scott, had gone to Harvard but had left before graduating). My mother had learned French at a young age, from a nurse, as had my father's parents, Helen Hope and Edgar. My mother also rode horses, as did Helen Hope; and she was a pianist, as was Helen Hope's sister Mary Binney. Yet my mother's parents had their doubts about this marriage. They thought both my parents were too young, and her father thought my father might benefit from some time in the military. He'd also heard, through the old-boy network, that his future in-laws were "café society," a quality unlikely to endear them to his intelligent, rather formidable wife—whom my father would amuse himself by calling, after she'd been widowed, "the Dowager Duchess of Boston." At the Dowager Duchess's insistence, my mother's father invited my father to lunch. They liked each other, as it turned out—though my grandfather later remarked, as perhaps only a successful investor would, that his daughter's intended, son of an heir to a Pennsylvania Railroad fortune, "didn't have two nickels to rub together." But my father was leaving Cambridge to go to law school in Philadelphia the following year; my mother would have been unable to go with him unwed. So, the month they graduated from college, they were married in Manchester, Massachusetts. The café society in-laws arrived by private plane from Pennsylvania, attended the ceremony, then offended their new relatives by skipping out on a dinner, planned in their honor, in order to fly home in time for what was assumed to have been a more desirable party.

Fortunately for my father, my mother did have nickels. In the late 1960s, they used some of her money to buy a weather-beaten, gray-shingled house on a cliff overlooking the water on Nantucket. My father had first been to the island a few years earlier with the old master of hounds, who made a practice of taking his beagles there in summers to hunt. My father had discovered both Nantucket and bicycling, which had turned out to be a pleasant way of exercising hounds. For the next four summers, my parents had rented a house on the island for a month. On the fifth summer, a real estate broker showed them the house on the cliff, with its tumbledown widow's walk and wooden steps leading through beach grass and beach plum bushes to the beach. On a wall in the front hall, near the phone jack, the owners had scratched, in ballpoint pen, the phone numbers of half-a-lifetime's worth of summer friends. At a lunch with my parents to celebrate the transfer of the property, the sellers wept. In return for my mother's having paid for the house, my father agreed to take charge of all upkeep from then on. In the years that followed, he waged war on the poison ivy choking off the beach grass that surrounded the house on three sides. He had a bulkhead built to shore up the eroding cliff. He hung the living-room walls with paintings of steam yachts rigged as topsail schooners—like the *Sagamore*, which had transported his grandfather on his grand tour. He bought a small sailboat and a canoe. On picnic days, he'd test the wind direction and accordingly select our destination. For thirty years, the deed to the house remained in my mother's name. But when the divorce came through in the midnineties, my father asked to buy half. To my mother, it seemed unnecessary; they'd been sharing it amicably since separating. But my father insisted. So my mother sold him half for a dollar.

I adored my father. I emulated his heaving laugh, which, on nights when my parents had parties in Pennsylvania, floated upstairs from the living room, through the open transom, and into my bedroom on the third floor. When we walked together, I extended my stride to try to match his, as if to prove my pace was the same. Before breakfast on school days, I'd hover in the wing chair in his dressing room, while he shaved or polished his shoes, listening to the voice of the classical station host coming from the radio on his dresser. For a time, when my sister and brother and I were young, he told us stories about the adventures of an ostensibly fictional character called Henry Huffy Puffy, and a creature, species uncertain, known as the Ant. I have little memory of the details of those stories, but I believe they centered on the personal and professional struggles of Henry Huffy Puffy and the Ant. When we were much older, we came to suspect that those characters had been surrogates for himself. Their anxieties were his. Knowing what I know now, I'm stunned by how much of his inner life he kept hidden. I'm touched, too, by his oddly oblique attempts to make himself known.

I can't say I ever understood him. I did not. Something inaccessible lurked behind all that charm. For me, he was the fifteen puzzle I never solved; the tiles refused to slide into place. Even in the intimate precincts of our family life, there was a prickliness about him. One felt from time to time the sting of his not entirely inadvertent rebuff. I'm not sure he knew what to do with the longing of his children to know him better. Perhaps it felt claustrophobic. He and my mother knew hundreds of people. I know because I sometimes lay on my stomach on the library rug and put the stamps on the stacks of Christmas cards he was addressing. Yet he had few, if any, intimate friends. "Do you have any friends who you could really go to about anything?" he once surprised a cousin of his by asking. "Yes, of course," she answered. To which he said simply, "I don't."

Another of his cousins, Mike Kennedy, told me he both knew and didn't know my father. "There was a side of him that was very closed," he said. "I wonder how many people really did know him."

He and psoriasis waged perpetual war. His elbows, chest, back, the palms of his hands were stained purple and itching. He alluded cryptically on occasion to "the black dog"—a term, I learned only too late, Winston Churchill used for his own periods of intense depression. "Like most people, I do go through vile, black depressions," my father once told a magazine writer, who shoveled the quotation into the story. More than once, he predicted he wouldn't live past fifty. Because he seemed jovial, sociable, and in good health, it was hard to know whether he meant it. Looking back, it seems an odd thing to say to your children.

His style as a parent was less pedagogical than Pied Piper. Our mother took the lead in seeing that we studied music. She organized us into a chamber music group—piano, French horn, clarinet—to accompany cousins singing carols on Christmas Eve. She read poetry to us from a book she'd been given as a child. She played tennis with us, rode with us, skied with us: The sports we learned as children were the ones her parents had made sure she knew. My father, however, wasn't of the kind that teach their children backgammon or economics in eighth grade. He was a reader but never pressed particular books on us. He knew quite a lot about art and music, but, around Christmas, he'd be alone in the library, paying bills and listening to Handel's *Messiah*. He did challenge us to walk around the house with a collegiate dictionary on our heads, as a lesson in posture. He taught me to drive, with a stick shift, in a Jeep Wagoneer. And he introduced us to *Cautionary Tales for Children* by Hilaire Belloc—most memorably, "Matilda, Who Told Lies, and Was Burned to Death." What I remember most vividly are his expeditions on which we tagged along—to sample the Double Gloucester at the cheese store in London; to the farmers' market every Saturday morning. He organized bicycle outings and boat trips. Later, he refrained from offering unsolicited career advice. He never presumed to understand our work. He might, however, let you know, after you were already married, that it would be OK to bail if you concluded you'd made a serious mistake.

My parents' own match turned out not to have been made in heaven. As children, we'd heard the story of how, on their honeymoon, they'd been mistaken for brother and sister. I probably found that comforting at the time. But, knowing what I know now, I'd say that being mistaken on your honeymoon for your spouse's sibling might be a poor predictor of marital bliss. They certainly looked like a good fit; they were a good-looking and appealing pair. And I know they'd been in love because once, in my twenties, I came across a letter written by my mother to my father sometime before they were married. The tone of the letter, which was folded in a book, was unlike the tone of any exchange between them that I'd witnessed. It was tender and filled with longing. Disconcerted by the unfamiliar intimacy, I returned the letter to the book, and the book to the shelf. Some years later, I went back to reread it, but I never found the book or the letter again. It was as though I'd dreamed it.

The truth is, my parents didn't make each other happy. Not that you'd have known it if you'd encountered them at a party. Even I, as a child, would have taken it for granted that they were as contented as anyone—if I'd bothered to think about it at all, which I didn't. Over the decades, the distance between them widened. In a low-level war of attrition, they waged their battles with muffled sniper fire and passive aggression. If they ever fought openly, they were careful to do it out of earshot, except, it seems, on very rare occasions. My sister recalls waking in her third-floor bedroom, when she was still young, to the sound of arguing in the master bedroom below. Stealing out onto the landing, she heard our father sounding angrier than she'd ever heard him. She remembers our mother interjecting, in a tone that sounded like defeat, "You're a horse's ass."

We could see, even as children, that he liked women. In his lexicon, it was high praise to describe someone, male or female, as "terribly attractive." The term covered attributes both intellectual and physical. He remarked upon it more often, and more effusively, than other qualities like, say, empathy or drive. As far as I could tell, "terribly attractive" women to whom he directed his charm and attention did not object. The way they reacted left me with the impression that he was "terribly attractive," too. He often behaved differently around those women—more playful and more wolfish at the same time. Many years later, after his death, more than one person would say confidentially to my mother, "He was very naughty." It was a word I've heard not infrequently applied to his mother, too. Whatever it meant, it's uncertain that those informants disapproved. "He was naughty," a male interior decorator once said admiringly to my mother. "But he was my ideal."

In the early 1960s, our family became close to another family. The father in the other family was bald, bespectacled, funny. A son of Lithuanian immigrants, he managed the most fashionable dress shop in Philadelphia. His wife was glamorous and flirtatious—a former debutante and model whose Main Line family had all but disowned her for marrying a West Philadelphia Jew. My father found her "terribly attractive," that was unmistakable. In 1963, the two couples traveled together through Egypt, Turkey, Lebanon, Austria, France, and England. After that, a photograph of the four of them, on camels in front of the pyramids of Giza, hung among our family photos on my mother's bathroom wall. Because the other couple had children roughly the same ages as Hopie and me, we all became friends, too. We formed a secret club, which convened in a dusty garret above my parents' garage. We called it the Bobcat Club—an homage to our father. We considered what life might be like if our families merged. Years later, we'd remember the atmosphere in that period as electrified in ways we didn't understand. We were like warblers, sensing the advent of a storm, days in advance. The children in the other family looked back on that period, half jokingly, as their Camelot—a bright, shining moment that ended abruptly, a week after the Kennedy assassination, when their father, the dress shop manager, overweight and under stress, died of a heart attack at forty-five. By then, we'd begun to sense, from the presence of stray voltage, that something was up between our father and our friends' terribly attractive mother.

☙

My father's return to his family's place with his bride after college had coincided with his mother's ascent to the throne left vacant by her father's death. The family's cash flow was no longer what it had once been, though that wasn't necessarily evident to outsiders. In the late thirties, with war brewing in Europe, the Colonel had considered shutting off parts of the big house to save money (then had decided against it after concluding that even a pared-down household would require at least a dozen staff). By the late forties, he was bedridden and barely able to speak—from the stroke his doctor had hoped to avert; and, in January 1949, he'd expired in South Carolina at the age of sixty-nine. The man who'd taught the Colonel to fly headed for Georgetown, collected the body, and flew it home to Pennsylvania. There, the Colonel was buried in the cemetery of that small, stone church where his grandson would be buried nearly sixty years later. On sheets of lined paper that would remain in her desk in the library of the big house for sixty-five years, Muz recorded the names of the hundreds of people who sent telegrams and condolence notes—a group that ranged from Strom Thurmond, the segregationist governor of South Carolina, fresh from his campaign as the States' Rights Party candidate for president, to Sara Grant, a former Mansfield employee identified in the list as a "Negro cook." The Colonel's will was thirty-eight words long. An obituary writer, effusing about how the deceased "had the foresight to build for the future," noted, with what reads like approval, that the Colonel had set up his country estate in such a way "that his death imposed no confiscatory taxes."

The corpse of Colonel Montgomery was barely cold when a visiting dairyman, casting an eye over the Ardrossan Ayrshires, was overheard to remark that he'd never seen such a neglected herd. Upon learning of the comment, the Colonel's adoring eldest, Helen Hope, my father's mother, resolved that someone needed to take charge—and promptly accepted the assignment.

"Within a month," she'd recall cheerily later, "we'd doubled the losses."

Helen Hope knew little or nothing about dairy farming when she took command, just short of age fifty. Didn't know a laxative from lactation, as she put it. For the first three years of the fifties, the dairy bled money: According to one profit-and-loss statement, which somehow survived, the monthly losses in that period soared as high as twenty thousand dollars. In the rare months when the dairy wasn't operating at a loss, the amount of profit was counted in two or three digits. Helen Hope's mother, Muz, shelled out loans to the farm in amounts as high as one hundred thousand dollars. In 1952, Helen Hope consulted an Ayrshire breeder from Connecticut, who, after finding the herd "very much above average," concluded that years of "indifferent management" had taken a toll on milk production. He suggested changes in breeding practices and feeding, pasture improvements, and culling to remove the herd's least productive cows. To raise cash, he recommended selling the services of the highest producers as purebred stock for breeding. In less than a decade, the farm's average annual milk production tripled. By the late 1970s, the herd was the highest-producing Ayrshire herd of its size in the country. With a professional operations manager and herdsman, Ardrossan Farms was shipping three and a half tons of milk a day. How often the business broke even in those years is unclear. But its proprietor was famous.

Helen Hope Montgomery Scott, glamorous dairy farmer, made good copy. She was Tracy Lord with a Rabelaisian wit, three hundred cows, and a meticulously organized closet full of designer clothes. Unlike others of her class, she did not disdain publicity. She understood what "the ladies from the social columns," as my uncle called them, were after; and since what they were after often coincided with what she wanted, she served it up. "We chatted, she laughed, she told my wife she looked 'simply divine' and chided me for not warning her my wife was 'such a beauty,'" a reporter wrote after her death, recalling their first meeting. "Soon she had us supposing the whole party would have been a flop if we hadn't come." Returning the favor, feature writers rolled out her repertoire of stories. *Once, I got locked in the rumble seat of a car—with a British trainer, no less! I won a Charleston contest at a Paris nightclub, and Josephine Baker gave me a big pot of flowers as a surprise!* Even her departure to London for a hip replacement made news. "I saw your picture in the paper *again*," her brother-in-law needled her. She laughed. "I just jump in front of any camera that's in the room!"

Photographers tracked her to the milk house, where she often sat with the herdsman at milking time, inspecting each cow as it sauntered into the barn. Every morning at 8:00 A.M., she'd be on the phone with the general manager. At haying time, she'd pull up in the fields in her gray Humber with a wicker basket of cold beer or ginger ale for the men. She sent the manager's son to sleepaway camp, covered expenses when income from the trusts was short, and spent her own income on capital improvements. Her legend was such that people in Wayne were surprised to encounter her, with her dogs in the back of her car, in the parking lot of the Acme supermarket. At Angelo D'Amicantonio's shoe repair store, she'd drop off shoes, free horse-show tickets, and her latest collection of off-color jokes. On Ardrossan, nothing happened without Helen Hope knowing. If a newly arrived family member asked the manager for salt for her driveway, she might get a call back from Helen Hope informing her that she'd be using sand, not salt. If you were foolish enough to cross a field with cows in it, figuring no one would see you, a stern phone message from Helen Hope would await you upon your return. When the residents of a subdivision on the far side of the northwest frontier committed some border violation, she invited them for cocktails and maneuvered them into submission. The sting of her reproach more than once left a family member in tears. "There was an underlying clarity that it was going to be exactly the way she wanted it," one grandchild recalled. "And, if it wasn't that way, then you'd be needing to fix it."

By the time I was a child, four generations of my father's family were living in the houses the Colonel had bought or built. My great-grandmother was the lone family member in the big house. A half mile away, my grandparents were in the house where my father had grown up. My great-uncle Aleck was in a house halfway between. Aleck's son, Bob, lived for a time in a house across Abraham's Lane from my grandparents. Bob's sister, Alix, alighted for a time in a house behind her father's. My parents were in our house, in the northeast corner. My uncle and aunt were two fields away (until they took wing). Another cousin of my father's, one of Mary Binney's daughters, lived with her husband in one of the Colonel's cottages—until she became pregnant with her first child and was reassigned to a six-bedroom house, near the main dairy barn, being vacated by my father's godmother, who was heading off into a third marriage.

My great-grandmother, Muz, passed much of her time with needlepoint work in her lap, perpetually stitching colored woolen yarn through a hand-painted canvas. She'd covered an entire eight-foot-long sofa in the ballroom, plus pillows, in floral needlepoint. All thirty dining-room chairs had needlepoint-covered seats. On the living-room walls, there were framed pictures of the big house, interiors and exterior—all done by Muz in needlepoint. You could idle in the living room, staring at a needlepoint image of the room in which you were standing. In the image, you could make out clearly the miniature portraits of the Colonel and Muz herself over the fireplaces. It was a needlepoint hall of mirrors. On beautiful days, she could be spotted outdoors, making her way beneath the sycamores along the driveway toward her son's house for a cup of coffee with the cook. Those who came to call on her in the late afternoon knew not to show up until after her favorite soaps. For a time, there'd been only one television in the house. It had been in the servants' dining room off the kitchen. It was there, I'm told, that she joined her heavily Irish household staff to watch the coronation of Queen Elizabeth II. Anyone who spotted "cousin Archie," one of the Scottish Montgomerys and a descendant of the thirteenth earl, in the crowd at Westminster Abbey was to alert her immediately.

My father's uncle Aleck, his mother's next-door neighbor, often dressed in khaki, a preference dating from his days as a lieutenant on a Navy troop carrier during World War II. After graduating from Harvard, he'd gone to work in the brokerage house founded by the father he couldn't please, but he was eventually sidelined, apparently for misbehaving with money from his mother's account. In the basement of his house, he kept his liquor supply in a walk-in safe. On a map, he'd shaded in blue every country he'd ever visited or flown over. On the second floor, he'd turned a bedroom into a display case for his pistols, which numbered in the hundreds. "I hope Aleck never goes a little crazy," the husband of a onetime maid remarked, "because he could wipe out the state." In the root cellar in the pasture beside his house, his gun club had once stored ammunition for shooting live pigeons. Wounded birds had sometimes crash-landed in the garage, where, as a child, Aleck's daughter would find them dying. Later, he sold the pistols and took out a multimillion-dollar bank loan to buy a collection of medals—which, when he decided it was time to sell, he discovered were fake. In the bankruptcy that followed, the bank took much of his personal property. Crushed, he repaired to his bed, where he spent his final years on his back, in the care of a maid and a cook, lubricated with sloshings of wine dispensed from a cooler nearby.

A feature of life on Ardrossan in those days was Sunday night supper at the big house. Adult family members were assumed to be attending unless they called to say they weren't. They were encouraged to bring friends, not least to keep the family members on good behavior. The seating was at card tables, with place cards cut from old invitations; if you flipped one over, you might find details of some wedding still two weeks away. The menu was predictable—very often, cold roast beef and a hodgepodge my parents called, no judgment implied, vomit salad. For dessert: mint chocolate chip ice cream with a dusting of Nestle's chocolate powder. Ed's rebellious wife, Linny, called the event the "Sunday Night Ghastlies." Others felt the suppers captured the spirit of what Ardrossan was intended to be. "You weren't missing Downton Abbey," Aleck's son, Bob, told me. "You *were* Downton Abbey."

In my father's generation, there were powerful inducements to settle on Ardrossan. It was a full-service, cradle-to-grave operation. In return for living there, a descendant of the Colonel would have not only a house but a place in a web of colorful clansmen and retainers. He might even end up with a job in a family firm. For small household emergencies, there was a plumber and a painter on call. A laundress would accept your linens and send them back starched, and smelling of cigarette smoke, in a woven, split-wood basket. There was a tree surgeon nearby whom we called Uncle Sidney; he was the youngest half sibling of the Colonel. My grandmother worked hard to maximize the number of family members in residence. They were assumed to share her feelings about ensuring the enterprise's survival. The family would keep the place intact—and the place might do the same for the family. On Christmas Eve, when the generations sat down together, in black tie, in the big-house dining room for dinner, after a frenzy of gifting and re-gifting, a member of the older generation would rap his or her wineglass with a knife and invite everyone to bow their heads for a moment of silence to remember those no longer living. In those fleeting seconds, a few fractious, fourth-generation, undergraduate cousins might be thinking dark thoughts about cultural hegemony, Thorstein Veblen, and social stratification. But most of those in attendance believed down deep that they were the beneficiaries of something rare and worth pre-serving. They were willing to stick around and do their bit to see that it endured.

Strange to say, I'm not sure they thought of themselves as rich. Or should I say that "rich" isn't the word they'd have used? Rich was people with income cascading in from more immediately identifiable sources—television stations, supermarkets, vodka. In the case of my father's family, the financial picture was, at least to me, more opaque. Decades had passed since the money that built and sustained Ardrossan had been amassed. Maybe my grandfather could have said exactly how that money had been made, and by whom, but I doubt I was the only fourth- or even third-generation descendant with no real clue. By the second half of the twentieth century, the men in the family be-haved like lots of others on the commuter trains in and out of the city: They went off to jobs in which they did well, but didn't appear to be making a killing. The income from the trusts went to the oldest gen-eration; or it went to maintaining the property and paying the taxes. The cost of all that upkeep added up; money for major expenses was downright tight. On at least one occasion, the trustees borrowed fifty thousand dollars from my grandmother to cover something unavoid-able, like an exterior paint job for the big house—then paid her back by slashing her rent. My mother's father, the Bostonian who'd made his own money, had shrewdly sussed out the situation: After telling my mother that he'd found her mother-in-law ravishingly beautiful and spoiled rotten, he'd tacked on, "and land-poor."

They did, however, think of themselves as fortunate. Ed, my fa-ther's brother and the eldest of that generation, had been the first to settle on the place. He'd come back from World War II and college with his new wife at age twenty-three. If anyone had asked him then, he told me, he'd have said he never wanted to leave his family's place again. As long as he lived in an Ardrossan house, his father had told him, his parents would pay his rent. So Helen Hope ejected the tenants from a small house in an outpost of the place known as Banjo Town, said once to have been a racially mixed neighborhood before the Colonel annexed it. When Ed's wife, Linny, became pregnant, Helen Hope ousted a second set of tenants from a bigger house about a mile away. "That will be the third generation to live there," her newly widowed mother, Muz, wrote with satisfaction to Helen Hope. "I think your father would be so pleased."

But Linny, like her mother-in-law, was spirited and strong-willed. She'd moved willingly from Massachusetts, where she'd grown up, but she felt like an outsider on the place. When the butler answered the door on her first visit to the big house, and Ed said, "Linny, this is Hugo," she'd answered, gamely, "Good afternoon, Uncle Hugo." Linny also happened to be in her mother-in-law's line of work—that is, horses. She rode with Helen Hope, hunted with Helen Hope, kept a horse in Helen Hope's stable. But she disliked being under her mother-in-law's thumb. When I asked my uncle why they'd left, he said bluntly, "Oh, my wife couldn't stand her. They couldn't share six hundred acres or whatever it was." Helen Hope's unsolicited memo on the proper handling of servants was the last straw. Ed and Linny moved an hour away, to a farm of their own. Helen Hope wasn't pleased, but she was practical; she didn't want a fight. Her mother, Muz, invited Linny to visit her at the big house before departing. Muz told her she understood why Linny was leaving. But to Helen Hope, Muz said something quite different: "Poor dear Ed—if she told him to jump off the roof, he'd do it to please her."

Ed and Linny weren't the only members of their generation to leave. Aleck's son, Bob, had moved into a house on the place after college, but he left for business school and then a job in California. His decision displeased his father, who seems to have subscribed to the idea there was a family obligation to live on the place. Bob, like Linny, wasn't eager to take marching orders from Helen Hope. He had no desire, he told me, to be one more descendant on Ardrossan with, as he put it, its "fairly well-developed power structure" in which he'd be "the junior guy." If an underlying principle of democracy is that agreement is not essential but participation is, Ed told me, that principle was reversed in the bailiwick overseen by Helen Hope. Participation wasn't essential; agreement was.

My father accepted those terms.

I never thought to ask him if he'd ever had doubts about settling on the place. He'd married a woman not only able but willing to fit into its table of organization. He'd launched himself smoothly, I assumed, in the profession of one great-grandfather and several uncles. He'd slipped comfortably onto the boards of schools, hospitals, banks, cultural institutions. He'd even involved himself, like his grandfather, in the local Republican Party, for a time. He'd toyed with running for office, then had decided against it, telling at least one person that he didn't have the money. In short, my father gave every appearance of having embraced the role written for him. He seemed to be playing it to the hilt. When I was younger, it would never have occurred to me to even wonder if he'd ever dreamed of a different life.

But shortly before his fortieth birthday, a door was unexpectedly thrown open. At a dinner party at his parents' house, he found himself seated two seats away from his parents' friend Walter Annenberg, then the nominee to be the American ambassador to the Court of St. James. As the meal was winding down, the woman seated between the two of them turned and murmured to my father, "He's going to offer you a job." At least on the surface, Annenberg was unlike my father: An immigrant's son, he'd built his father's debt-ridden business into a communications giant whose holdings included *TV Guide*, which had a circulation of twenty-three million. He was a philanthropist and a collector of important Impressionist art. The job offer, which came several weeks later, was the position of special assistant, which my father liked later to describe as "somewhere between his deputy and his dog."

(In private, he called himself "Walter Annenberg's nanny"—the smooth, Anglophile aide-de-camp to the sometimes ponderous billionaire who'd gotten off to a regrettable start with the British press when, presenting his credentials, he answered the queen's question about where he was living with a thicket of verbiage—"at the Residence, subject to certain discomfiture owing to elements of refurbishment.") The job offer filled my father, I now know, with panic. He worried about his career, his law firm, his "position" in Philadelphia. Friends encouraged him to go. "Your duty to yourself calls," a civic elder told him. But several family members had doubts. SECOND THOUGHTS INCREASINGLY UNCERTAIN, his father telegrammed from Barbados. Ed said he'd turn the job down if the offer were his: If my father didn't, he said, he might find himself rethinking everything, including his choice to go into the law. Ed would eventually be proven right about that. But a radical rethinking, it turns out, was what my father was after. "I have a theory about lawyers' minds," he'd say later. "Like pencils they get sharper and sharper and smaller and smaller. I wanted to stretch my mind."

My parents rented a corner house on a garden square in Belgravia. The Russian-born violinist Nathan Milstein and his wife lived a few doors down. In the window of a house across the street from ours, we'd catch sight of an elderly man, whom we knew of only as Dr. Winnicott, gazing in our direction. Years later, I discovered that the man had been D. W. Winnicott, the British pediatrician and psychoanalyst (who developed the concept of the "false self," the social manner that children exposed to inattentive mothering construct in order to comply with the expectations of others). My father became a member of several exclusive men's clubs on St. James's Street—cushy redoubts populated with marquesses, viscounts, and earls. His job brought him and my mother in contact with MPs, visiting bigwigs, the occasional royal. Sometimes, when a double-barreled name with aristocratic overtones might be advantageous, my father startled us by identifying himself as Mr. Montgomery-Scott. He insisted the British liked it. Sotto voce, my mother rechristened him Mr. Montague-Splotch.

I was dispatched to a girls' boarding school on a piece of land in Kent said to have a mention in the Domesday Book, William the Conqueror's eleventh-century survey of England and Wales. There'd once been an Elizabethan house, with a moat, on the site. By the time I got there, the main building was a nineteenth-century mansion, remodeled in a Tudor and Jacobean style, with leaded windows and crenellations. Girls from London arrived, in uniform, by train from Charing Cross Station, hauling trunks stuffed with regulation neckties, twenty-four linen handkerchiefs, and a floor-length cape. We battened on a diet of batter-fried Spam, toad in the hole, and dead man's leg. The longer we stayed, the plumper we became. Our intellectual intake included Virgil, Homer, Shakespeare, Molière, Racine, Jane Austen, George Eliot, and the Metaphysical poets. But our consuming preoccupation was food. We pilfered cheese from the staff kitchen, and hoarded iced buns, known as greased rats, served as a snack. We raided nearby orchards, filling book bags with stolen apples that we stored in our lockers until the study rooms reeked of fermentation. The gray-eyed headmistress, who bestrode the school's landscaped grounds with a matched set of dachshunds in her wake, occasionally sent us into mass hysteria by announcing, in morning assembly, a surprise day off—which we'd spend lolling among the gorse bushes, swilling hard cider until we could have sworn we were drunk. Once, returning from a weekend lacrosse match at another school, I found that my father had ridden the train out from London, biked to the school, found the music wing, stuffed my French horn case with fruit and chocolate, then slipped away, unnoticed, back to London.

My mother, unable to study music seriously while raising children on the Main Line, seized the opportunity presented by the move to London. She found a piano teacher and a college of music that accepted older students; and, after a next-door neighbor objected to her finger exercises, she rented a piano studio in Mayfair, where she took to spending her days. Her musical education was one of many reasons she loved the years in London. For both my parents, those years may have been their happiest together—not because they managed to shrink the distance between them, which they didn't, but because the distance now worked for both. My mother had wanted a piece of her life that would be hers alone: Music wasn't merely a passion, it was a foundation on which to begin rebuilding if the marriage fell apart. Before taking the job, my father had written a list of his and my mother's concerns. On that list, he noted that my mother's greatest fear was "my over drinking."

He moved first, ahead of the rest of us, to start work and move into the house. He was swept immediately into his new life. By the time my mother arrived a few weeks later, he'd been to the races at Ascot, seen *Così Fan Tutte* at Glyndebourne, watched Knights of the Garter take the oath at Windsor Castle, and been a guest at country-house weekends. When she landed at Heathrow, exhausted from the red-eye, my father met her, smelling of alcohol. At dinner that night, he was so drunk she considered flying home. Later that evening, in the handsome house on the square, which my father had stocked with flowers for the occasion, my mild-mannered mother reached for a leather-framed wedding photograph in their bedroom, wheeled around, and, in a moment of anger I find hard to imagine, smashed the frame on what may or may not have been my father's head. Glass rained in shards on the twin beds.

"Not a good evening," my father wrote, without elaboration.

The years in England were a turning point in my father's drinking. Until then, he'd drunk only at night—or so he'd say in a confession a quarter century later. But in England, there was sherry before lunch, wine with lunch, port after lunch. If there were fewer cocktails before dinner than back in the United States, there was more drinking during and after. My father was a diplomat in demand, good company, and a food and wine connoisseur. Those attributes conspired to multiply his opportunities to drink. "My overall consumption rose dramatically," he'd admit years later. He tried never to appear drunk, for the sake of his job; but back in the United States on his summer vacations, he abandoned restraint. "There the lid came off," he'd say. "High every night, beginning about 6:00." Returning home to Pennsylvania after four years in London, he added his British drinking habits to his American ones. Once, withdrawing from cigarettes, he stopped drinking for three weeks because alcohol made him crave tobacco. He never smoked again. But he resumed drinking, with his momentum redoubled. In retrospect, he'd concede later, it was too bad he didn't stop both.

"I never considered it," he'd say. "I liked to drink."

Chapter Seven

The ritual objects of my father's devotion had long held for me a special fascination. There was the industrial-strength corkscrew, like a man-operated grenade launcher, bolted to the pantry wall. There was a brushed stainless steel martini shaker, and a tool called a Tap-Icer with a leaden head capable of detonating an ice cube in your bare hand. On my periodic assignments as wine steward, I road tested every gizmo in his collection—the twist corkscrew, the winged corkscrew, the cork puller with two prongs. "The waiter's friend," with its folding blade, was my favorite; it never let you down. Outside his wine cellar, he'd hung an illuminated manuscript certifying that he was a member of a fraternal order of burgundy enthusiasts called La Confrérie des Chevaliers du Tastevin. He had their official wine-tasting cup—a sterling silver, miniature Jell-O mold sort of thing you could dangle on a ribbon around your neck. All those accoutrements seemed to me to have meaning for my father. Perhaps they possessed supernatural powers. Perhaps clues to the elusive chevalier resided in the gloomy recesses of the liquor cabinet, where, he used to tell us, the missing hindquarters of the stuffed hare might be found extruding from the back side of the wall—like the other half of the magician's assistant, after the magician saws her in two.

For a long time, I saw nothing ominous in my father's drinking. Pretty much every adult I'd ever encountered drank. If anyone had told me there were people who didn't, it would have been like learning there were people who'd sworn off, say, soap. At the annual Easter egg hunt on the lawn at the house of my great-aunt and -uncle, grown-ups swilled vodka and Dubonnet while their offspring rampaged across the greensward, Easter baskets flying. My grandfather, admired for the Meursault he served with shad roe at dinner parties in spring, and for the champagne that came out with dessert, kept a sharp eye peeled, during cocktails in his living room, for a drained glass. "How about a dividend?" he'd ask, like FDR mixing martinis for Harry Hopkins and Missy LeHand. After a bibulous dinner around my parents' dining-room table one night, one of my aunts went missing, only to be found, sometime later, nodding off on the downstairs john.

But the acceleration in my father's drinking collided with my belated adolescent rebellion. The year my parents returned from England, I set off for college and a wider world. The Senate Watergate Committee was holding televised hearings that summer. Nixon resigned the following year. South Vietnam surrendered, Saigon fell, and, during a summer job on a newspaper in Arizona, someone loaned me a copy of *The Second Sex*. A few years earlier, I'd been flattered by my father's gift of a subscription to *The Economist*. Now, during my visits home, our conversations burst into flames. The war, capital punishment, elitism, public education: Any topic could turn combustible after 7:00 P.M. My father's rhetorical style, when he'd been drinking, was maddening—all short-angle volley and backhand slice. Arguments, loaded with spin, bounced backward after clearing the net. To me, he seemed patronizing and dismissive. No doubt I was ill-informed and thin-skinned. But at least I was sober. Stung by my disrespect, he'd stalk off to the pantry. I'd stay behind, holding back tears. I'd hear the refrigerator door open, the splashing of wine into glass. Had the ambush of his children's adolescence caught him off guard? "Distant" was how he described his own parents later. Was he unprepared for intergenerational hand-to-hand combat?

My mother, frozen in the crossfire, dreaded my visits.

Once, during a year I took off from college, a British writer named Enid Bagnold stayed in my parents' house for a few nights. She had a play opening in Philadelphia, at age eighty-six. From a failed hip operation, she was addicted to morphine; my father had been asked to tap his sprawling connections and find a doctor to arrange for sixty milligrams, four times a day. On the evening of this august personage's arrival, I happened to be at home between jobs. My father had drunk more than on previous nights. Over dinner, he directed me to tell the jet-lagged octogenarian why I'd chosen to take a break from college. I'd once turned in a "good performance" on the subject, he told his guest. This time, apparently, I bombed. He cut me off. "Isn't it funny?" he observed to her, half laughing. I'd spoken "the King's English" perfectly upon leaving school in England, he said, referring to me; now I was um-ing and ah-ing "like an ordinary American." The playwright, napping over her roast lamb, came to. She'd missed most of my speech, she said, but "the last page and a half" had made sense. "That doesn't say much for the previous four pages," my father remarked, grinning in my direction.

Like him, I kept journals, too. I'd been flitting from spiral to loose-leaf to bound notebook in pursuit of the most congenial medium. Now I took refuge in scribbling and venting. I vowed repeatedly to myself to steer clear of debates with my father—a strategy that met with mixed success. The semblance of harmony seemed to give rise to a whole new problem. "We have so little to say to each other anymore," I reported. "I sense this huge mass of mutual distrust." I couldn't raise this issue, I told myself, "since the lesson I have learned all along from him is we must maintain this appearance of everything is fine, just fine." But my silence was no better. "This really is a quite serious problem," I told myself. "Will things become more and more forced, less and less genuine, generally worse and worse, for the rest of our life together?" I scrapped my plan to become a lawyer, like him. On visits home, I became Bronislaw Malinowski in the field. I was the participant observer, master of a newfound detachment. "One big battle," I boasted to myself, after a weekend at home. ". . . I was great— totally (almost . . .) calm."

In a forgotten journal entry from one Memorial Day weekend, I'm struck by my measured, ethnographer's tone. I was living in Cambridge, in the final days of my senior year in college, and I'd called home for clearance for a spur-of-the-moment visit to the Nantucket house. My mother had said sure, of course, why not. My father, she said, had flown up with some man, whose name I didn't know. They'd be thrilled to see me, she was certain. So, with a college boyfriend named Jim, I took the bus to Woods Hole and the ferry to the island on Sunday morning. Upon arrival on the island, I found a pay phone and dialed the number for the house. I'd been suppressing a nagging suspicion.

"Where are you?" my father asked briskly, after the initial exchange.

Just off the ferry, I answered.

A second or three elapsed.

"I'm not alone," he ventured.

I neglected to ask the obvious question.

He elected not to volunteer the answer.

The habit of apology, culturally overdetermined, was triggered— like the patellar reflex at the tap of a rubber-tipped hammer.

No problem! I reassured him. We'll stay in a motel!

He would have none of it. We must come ahead.

"We won't bother you," he added, "if you won't bother us."

Jim and I repaired to a doughnut shop for a breakfast of wild speculation. Jim was just fleshing out a scenario in which my father's companion was a nine-year-old Puerto Rican boy when the swinging door to the doughnut shop flew open and suddenly the man I called Popsy was standing above us, redder in the face than usual and breathing heavily. He'd checked every restaurant, he told us, in the couple of blocks between the ferry terminal and where he'd finally found us. Sliding into the booth, he apologized for the state of alarm that my call had set off. "Her name is Linda," he said, with a degree of directness that, I can say in retrospect, I admire. In a moment of panic, he said, she'd accused him of staging the encounter. She'd even threatened to leave. He reached for our bill and paid it. Then he drove us to the house.

Linda was making her way down the creaky wooden staircase, barefoot, as we entered. Diminutive and blond, she was closer to my age than to my father's. After his hasty departure from the house, she'd gone into the kitchen and cleaned up the remains of their lunch. Then, to spare herself the weirdness of being found bent over the sink, she'd gone outside onto the porch, then back into the living room, then upstairs. She'd studied herself in a mirror. She'd changed out of a shirt that had the initials of my father's law firm emblazoned across the chest. She'd knotted her long hair into a not quite matronly bun. As Jim and I stood in the hallway shaking her hand and idiotically smiling, I watched from somewhere up near the ceiling. Who knew, back when Odille was teaching my sister and brother and me the importance of manners, in what unexpected circumstances they'd come in handy? It's a miracle I didn't curtsy. Once that hurdle was behind us, Jim and I drifted into the kitchen and finished off the uneaten dessert. Surveying the contents of the fridge, I noticed two bottles of champagne and a box of vaginal suppositories, for treating a yeast infection, the prescription label made out in our hostess's name.

Should I have been angry? There's no evidence in the journal that I was. Should I have caught the next ferry back to the mainland? That might have made me a better person. Instead, I slid into the role of the reporter I was on the cusp of becoming. I watched closely, took mental notes, and, upon returning to Cambridge, filled a half dozen single-spaced pages with the story. My dispatch shows promise. There's

Linda's age, occupation, and marital status. I took note of the line of work of the man she was divorcing. I remarked on her first-name-basis references to "Virginia" and "Lytton": Having shaken off my own adolescent Bloomsbury infatuation, I appear to have found hers sophomoric. From scattered clues, I determined that this was not Linda's first, or even second, visit to the house. She was well acquainted, she let it be known, with my father's swashbuckling culinary style. When the conversation turned to movies, she reminded him, in my presence, that he'd seen *The Last Tango in Paris* with my mother and another couple, and that my mother had fallen asleep.

I wondered if that was true.

My father's demeanor didn't escape my attention. He'd gone to some lengths to import Linda, I learned. When his chartered plane had been unable to land at the little airport where they'd agreed to meet, he'd covered the cost of a taxi to drive her forty-five minutes to Newark Airport. At one point during the weekend, he let me know that my mother had called while I was out. She'd asked about the sleeping arrangements. In his account of the conversation, he made a point of telling me that he'd answered, "We won't be taking up many rooms." Did he expect from me a conspiratorial chuckle? After dinner, when Jim and I were loading the dishwasher, he wandered in from the dining room where he and Linda had been finishing off a bottle of wine. "We think you're great," he said, kissing me on the top of my head. Even now, I can't think of the appropriate response. The obvious one, I suppose, is, "We think you're both great, too."

My father and I never discussed that weekend in the months and years that followed. Maybe he figured no explanation was needed, or that the situation spoke for itself. Nor did he ever ask me, even indirectly, not to mention my holiday with Linda to my mother. Once, years later, he said he'd always assumed that I had. But how could I? By the time Jim and I left on the ferry the following day, I was complicit in the betrayal. I'd spent the night in my parents' house with my father and Linda in the next room. I hadn't even been shocked. What had struck me, in fact, was that my father had seemed more at ease with Linda than he often seemed at home with us. There's just one reference in my journal to what I was feeling when the weekend was over. I thought it had made me more able to be myself in my father's presence. The experience left me, I told myself, with a new feeling of autonomy—though perhaps what I really meant was that stumbling upon that particular secret had left me with a feeling of power.

In the years after the return from London, Philadelphia was changing. Its population, having peaked in 1950, was in a downward spiral. Industries that had churned out money that had built the Main Line were dying or departing, taking jobs and tax revenue with them. As African Americans and Puerto Ricans flowed into city neighborhoods, white residents pulled out. They sprinted to the suburbs on brand-new highways and bridges. Indoor shopping malls sprang up in places like King of Prussia, undermining the retail strength of Philadelphia. As Ivy League universities dropped admissions quotas, the city's business executives became more racially and ethnically diverse. On boards of trustees, the old Philadelphia establishment gave way to the more recently moneyed. After the first Irish American mayor came the first Italian American, the first African American, the first Jewish mayor. In nearly every sphere of city life, the influence of Philadelphia's Protestant ruling class was ebbing.

The life of a Philadelphia lawyer excited my father less than ever. His mind having been stretched by his years abroad, he had no interest in resuming its pencil-ization. He'd been attracted to public service since his twenties; he'd served on many boards and had been asked to join others. Now he devoted more and more of his time and energy to the city's civic and cultural institutions. For the better part of a decade, he was president of the Academy of Music, the one-hundred-twenty-year-old concert and opera hall where, as a boy, he'd first gone with his talented, artistic aunt to hear the orchestra perform under her adored Stokowski. Then he became the president and chief executive of the Philadelphia Museum of Art. Every morning, he delivered himself to the museum's classically inspired temple overlooking the Schuylkill River. He could be spotted riding his 1952 Raleigh Standard up the Benjamin Franklin Parkway in the rain, poncho flapping over his blue pin-striped suit, or in city hall, wrangling with the mayor's men over the shrinking city subsidy for the museum. "The job is tremendously exciting and awesomely loaded with problems, most of which are called money," he wrote to a former colleague on his first day on the job. "Please come and see me. As a child, I had dreamed of living in a palace and the only palace I knew was the Philadelphia Museum of Art. Here I am."

He was an admired figure—the civic-minded, public-spirited, socially alert patrician. At a time when the finances of many families like his were dwindling, he could lead the city's cultural institutions by contributing, if not piles of money, his lively and energetic service. He enjoyed the role and was undeniably good at it. He might choose to present himself, with amusing self-deprecation, as simply "a somewhat overweight man with a red face and a slightly English accent who seems to do a number of things," but he was proud of his contribution to the life of the city. Magazines crowned him "the quintessential Philadelphian." Reporters found him more interesting and fun than the stereotype suggested. Photographers sometimes shot him from below, his arms crossed imperatorially across his chest. In his sixteen years' tenure as CEO of the museum, its attendance climbed to an all-time high. Its endowment increased fivefold. At the hundreds of parties, receptions, and openings all over the city that the museum president might be expected to attend each year, you could find him—face flushed, eyes twinkling, drink in hand.

Bicycling had supplanted beagling as his extracurricular passion; he'd passed on his beagling duties to a younger man. On vacations, he'd check his bicycle on a flight, often but not always to some compact, English-speaking place. He'd set off with little more than a tin of tea, a set of Allen wrenches, a change of clothes. On a three-week biking trip we did in China, he congratulated himself privately on having "purposefully shed" the strongest younger cyclists on the trip—"largely to show that fat old men can do it, too." On that trip, it rained so hard and so long, hundreds of Chinese in the province where we were biking drowned. My father wore a single pair of biking shorts, his saddlebags having been lost en route. Defying our Chinese minders, he woke me at dawn for an unauthorized spin through the backstreets of Guangzhou. In a restaurant, confronted with a dreary "Western lunch," he charmed a young Chinese guide into sharing her pigs' intestines with him. For a man who'd planted himself in a single corner of southeastern Pennsylvania for nearly all of his life, my father sometimes seemed happiest on an unknown road in an undiscovered country, with his bicycling companions, if any, a half mile behind.

Once, when I was in my twenties, my brother and I joined him on a trip through East Anglia. He led us through ancient churchyards, spectacular gardens, country estates. We lingered at dusk in the silence of the Ely Cathedral close. On a trip through Ireland, I trailed him, against a mercurial headwind, through the Derryveagh Mountains in Donegal to a place called the Poisoned Glen. The ride was breathtaking and grueling, and it put me in a rage. Out of earshot, I cursed my stupidity. "I was wondering for the millionth time what it was about self-flagellation that appealed to him," I wrote that night. "But couldn't I wonder the same about myself?" If you'd asked me what I was doing, biking with my father, I might have said those father-financed trips were what I could afford. I was a reporter on a suburban daily, pulling down the pay of a garage mechanic and living in a one-bedroom apartment in Hudson County, New Jersey, next door to a philosophizing, disabled Vietnam vet who worked as a toll collector at Exit 16W. Years later, I came to see those trips with my father more clearly as an attempt at communication in a vernacular he preferred. He was "easier to do things with than to talk to," he once said. In my twenties, it occurs to me now, I was still playing gin rummy on the hospital bed.

In Hong Kong, at the end of the China trip, he threw a birthday party for himself. Three weeks earlier, after a fitful first night in a windowless room in a YMCA, he'd dodged an invitation to bond with our group and had taken me to lunch at the Peninsula Hotel. It was my father's first trip to Asia. Yet he seemed to know instinctively how to find the oldest colonial hotel in Kowloon. The grand buffet, he'd assured me, would be "good for morale." Now, five hundred miles of cycling and many pit toilets later, my father, turning fifty-three, resumed his acquaintance with the Peninsula's maître d'. By the time we returned for dinner, a table had been set for eighteen. Everyone on the cycling trip came—the British economist from the Solomon Islands;

the cider maker from Princeton; the teacher from Moose Jaw. The menu included quail with avocado, roast sirloin of beef, a 1978 Château Lagrange. Out the window, the lights of Hong Kong Harbor shimmered. To my father's left, he'd seated the guide who'd shared her pigs' intestines with him. To his right, he sat a dowdy Canadian who'd gotten on his nerves from day one by committing various misdemeanors including wearing a reflective vest and, as he put it, "doing up her hair to resemble a water buffalo." A good host, he'd told me, always seats the worst "club dumper" next to himself.

The last bike trip he and Elliot and I took together was the best. We rode down the west coast of the South Island of New Zealand at the dazzling peak of summer. The roads were empty, the mountains towering, the landscape constantly changing. Turning inland, we pedaled through a rain forest, up into foothills, and then mountains, where a helicopter eventually airlifted our group onto a glacier. Other days, we sailed past meadows blanketed in wildflowers and leaped off a bridge into a rushing river. On our final day, the three of us paid a call on a couple of charming, at-risk throwbacks. In a palatial terrarium in Queenstown, we gaped at a pair of kiwi, a remnant of one of the many species of flightless birds that once had the run of the North and South Islands. Before the arrival of competition, the birds' forebears had roamed their territory unchallenged. But, spared rival species, they'd gradually lost the ability to fly. Now they were in grave trouble: On the South Island, they'd disappeared from the wild. Here were just two, the size of small chickens, teetering on spindly legs, poking the damp soil with long, curved bills. They looked vulnerable, like humans with their hands tied behind their backs. Because kiwis are nocturnal, the terrarium was dimly lit, designed to simulate kiwi habitat at night. Someone had put out a plate of what looked like take-out lo mein. My father peered curiously into the semidarkness, silently studying the birds. In their luxuriantly landscaped prison, the kiwi couple probed for insects, passing time before death and extinction.

You might be wondering how a man in his fifties and sixties could drink heavily every night, bicycle up to a hundred miles a day, and repeat that regimen for weeks. In China, on nights when he and I found ourselves assigned by our tour leaders to the same room, I'd sometimes return late to find him beached on his bed, sheets damp with sweat, a vaguely medicinal smell radiating from his body. The only alcohol offered to us, in the places we went in China in the early 1980s, was beer. But I learned years later that my father had acquired a drinking buddy on that trip—a humorous, redheaded antitrust lawyer from Kentucky who'd made certain not to enter the People's Republic without Johnnie Walker Black. After dinner, the two of them got together and drank. When the whiskey ran out, they switched to Chinese brandy, then Chinese vodka, then more brandy, then beer. In New Zealand, my father was drinking double vodkas when a man in our group introduced himself to me and got straight to the point: "I'm worried about your father." One of the tour leaders took me aside a few days later: Why hadn't anyone gotten him help? he wanted to know. Lamely, I told him we'd tried and failed. Before the sentence was out of my mouth, I felt like a fool.

A night or two earlier, an argument about the British Empire had erupted over dinner. My father was at one end of the table, slouched in his chair, and flanked by a man from Aspen who was a designer of expensive homes. The man had the tanned, chiseled looks you might expect in a designer of expensive Aspen homes. A few seats away was a blowhard named Fred, advancing the view that the British had sent other countries into battle first so their soldiers could do most of the dying. My father, gazing balefully at him, snarled, not exactly under his breath, "Fred, you're an asshole." He was just lifting his hand to give Fred the finger when Fred happened to turn away. My father was looking unwell. Food had spilled on his shirt, and his eyes were glazed. After he weaved across the dining room on his way to bed, stopping to kiss Elliot and me on the tops of our heads, we wondered what might happen if we had a videotape of that evening to play back to him the following day. Instead, our father turned up at our room the following morning with cups of tea and an endearing expression of befuddlement on his face. Was he, consciously or subconsciously, after forgiveness? I suspect not. I've since learned that he woke up regularly with a great blank in his head where, under other circumstances, there might have been some memory of what had gone down the night before.

We'd broached the subject of his drinking with him more than once. But we'd done it so ineptly, we might as well not have tried at all. Deferentially, apologetically, we'd raised it around the kitchen table at dinner. He'd listen patiently, an expression of mild curiosity arranged on his face. When our speeches had petered out, as they inevitably did, he'd step in, like the pilot with hundreds of thousands of miles under his belt, expertly taking the controls. He was touched by our concern, he'd assure us. He was sorry to have caused us worry. But our fears were unwarranted. His doctor had just given him a clean bill of health. Et cetera, et cetera. "And now, lovely people . . ." he'd say, pushing his chair back from the table, signaling that he'd put up with enough. As the muffled thudding of his feet on the carpeted front stairs faded out, we'd sit in stung silence, marveling at how swiftly we'd been disarmed. Occasionally, we'd stay on in angry tears. It had seemed futile. But in New Zealand, Elliot and I wondered how we'd feel if something catastrophic happened. Would we feel we'd tried?

Elliot took up the matter again, in a letter sent a few weeks after returning from New Zealand. My father wrote back to him, "You are right about the drink. It did, of evenings, tend to take over." He said he was saddened by the distress it seemed he'd caused; he'd try to do better. But he blamed a new blood-pressure medication and the pain of long-distance cycling at his age. Then he added, trying a new tack, man to man, "There is also the fact, which is not an excuse, that I enjoy being drunk. Like the classic Irish figure in literature, or Churchill or Pitt (not that I put myself in their class) . . . intoxication is a release, particularly after a strenuous day. A lady sitting at dinner next to Winston Churchill said to him, 'Mr. Churchill, you are drunk.' He replied, 'And you, madam, are ugly; but in the morning I will be sober.'"

If he was Churchill, then I was that tight-ass lady at dinner. He'd never have spoken so frankly to me about his drinking. I couldn't be reasoned with on the subject because I'd decided sometime in my late teens or early twenties that I was never drinking again. When people would ask me, for years afterward, why I'd stopped—the way drinkers invariably do—I'd say that I'd stopped after waking up drunk one afternoon after a party. I thought I remembered the whole thing clearly. It was the summer after my freshman year in college. There'd been a vat of innocuous-tasting punch; and when I'd gotten out of bed the next afternoon, my room was spinning on its axis. But, many years later, I discovered that wasn't exactly true. The party had taken place two years earlier than I remembered, and I'd gone on drinking into sophomore year. I had to concede I didn't remember exactly when I'd stopped or what had precipitated the decision. Which is strange since I now suspect that that single, unaccountable, impetuous, un-articulated, possibly angry resolution may well have spared me a heap of grief.

I'd like to be told that I'd intuited that moderate drinking was not in the cards. But the fact is, I knew almost nothing back then about my family's history. What I did know was that I'd spent more time than I'd have chosen in the company of heavy drinkers. I was tired of trying to talk to people who'd stopped making sense. I think it's safe to say that my abstinence was a mode of resistance, unspoken and perhaps not even entirely conscious. I think it's safe to say, too, that it was a judgment. If my father took it personally, he never said so to me. But I could tell that my testimony on the subject of his drinking never carried any weight. I was willfully ignorant of what he felt was one of life's great pleasures. In an airport bar, I thought I saw a sneer flicker across his lip when, ordering a drink, he turned to me and asked, "Fizzy water?"

I wrote to him anyway. "I fear you are killing yourself," I said, after the reflexive preamble of apologia and obeisance. The response I received reminded me of constituent letters I'd written as a congressional intern, in which the trick was piling up enough agreeable-sounding verbiage to disguise the underlying message, which was no. He *thanked* me for my *thoughtful letter*, he *appreciated* my having written. He knew that his drinking *has long been a legitimate concern to you*. But not to worry. His doctor had just concluded that his health was good. The beta-blocker he'd been prescribed by the doctor for high blood pressure had been a mistake. The pain he'd experienced on the New Zealand trip had come from arthritis in his knee. "Do not . . . decide that I am going soon to self-destruct," he assured me. "I am much too interested in you to shuffle off until I know more of the next chapters."

By the time the rest of us got serious, he was drinking close to a gallon of wine a day. Members of his staff were no longer giving him work to do after lunch. An anonymous letter sent to the museum trustees included this ominous coda: "Does the President's drinking affect the museum?" Galvanized by the possibility that others were finally catching on to what we alone seemed to have noticed, my mother slipped away from her fortieth college reunion to scout out McLean, a psychiatric hospital in Belmont, Massachusetts, known for treating "these thoroughbred mental cases," in the words of Robert Lowell, who was one. She had two options, the head social worker in the alcohol and drug treatment program told her: Let him drink himself to death, or try an intervention. ("Is this the reason I can't stop crying?" she told me she was intending to ask a psychiatrist who specialized in alcoholism. When I gasped, she said, "No, it's not that I'm in pain. I just keep weeping. I wake up with tears streaming down my face.") Soon she'd hired a recovering alcoholic named Frank who'd built a second career advising people on how to apply emotional duress to maneuver alcoholics into treatment. Even when an intervention fails, the platitudinous Frank assured her, there's something to be gained from the family members putting their arms around the alcoholic and telling him they love him. My mother allowed as how that wasn't exactly the way our family worked.

We decided to ambush him on vacation in order to minimize the embarrassment of a sudden disappearance from work into thirty-day rehab. My parents went off to the house on Nantucket; then, one after another, Hopie and Elliot and I turned up. We rehearsed in a neighbor's garage apartment. The night before the intervention, Frank and a museum trustee who was an old friend of my father's arrived and checked into a hotel. The family alone, my mother had been told, wouldn't have a chance at succeeding. We had a long letter from my father's assistant at the museum, who'd had to back out of the intervention at the last minute because of a family emergency. On the morning of the confrontation, we waited in the living room for our target to return from a bike ride. At the sound of tires on gravel, Elliot and I stepped outside the front door to intercept him. Touchingly quotidian details remain lodged in my mind even now. The chin strap of his bicycle helmet was unsnapped. He was carrying a carton of eggs for Elliot's breakfast.

"We want to talk about your drinking," Elliot told him.

One after another, each of us made our case. My mother recalled how he'd brought her a bouquet of flowers on their fortieth anniversary, then had to hold on to the furniture to cross the room. Elliot said he'd long ago gotten used to the fact that his father was usually drunk whenever they talked, but he took it as a slap in the face that Popsy had chosen a moment when he'd been drinking not only to question Elliot's choice of a wife but do it in a loud voice within earshot of her. Hopie spoke of how inaccessible and withdrawn he'd become. I stumbled through my statement, intermittently sobbing. The trustee spoke admiringly of my father's work as president, then got to the point:

"You know as well as I do that any bank CEO with such a problem would be given two choices: Get treatment or take a walk."

It was an unsettling business, not cathartic in the least. It was hard to tell if we were doing the right thing. Shot full of adrenaline, I felt a burning sensation in my body. Our prey sat motionless in a rocking chair, his face an unreadable mask. When we'd finished our statements, he said he wanted five minutes alone. He rose briskly from his chair, exited the room, and tramped upstairs. We could hear the floorboards creak as he moved around. Suddenly, Frank, the veteran interventionist, snapped to attention. Was there a gun in the house? he wanted to know. My mother looked startled. Frank hastily dispatched Elliot and me to see that everything was all right upstairs. We found our father in the bedroom he'd been using, door closed. When we knocked and went in, he was looking at us, from across the room, his eyebrows raised as if in question. Just making sure he wasn't going to hurt himself, we explained. He shook his head. He said he wanted to pray.

We idled downstairs while our victim conferred with his God. If you'd asked me then what was going to happen, I'd have had to say I had no idea. We'd left the capsule and were floating untethered in space. Then my father appeared in the living room and said he'd go to McLean. "Why not go now?" he asked. He telephoned his mother. "I'm going into the hospital for thirty days to take care of my drinking," we heard him say. He called his colleague, the museum director, and said the same thing to her. Soon, he was back in charge, joking with Frank and offering the trustee a ride to Boston. When Hopie and Elliot and I stepped forward to hug him, he shrugged us off, half humorously, half not. "You'll drive me to drink," he said gruffly.

We set off in an entourage—like an FBI escort delivering a white-collar felon to prison but without handcuffs and shackles. A chartered plane was waiting at the airport to fly us to Boston. With a roar of propellers, we flew out over the ribbon of sand that forms the wilder, south shore of the island, where my father had often taken us in a Jeep Wagoneer with beach towels and Coppertone stuffed in a faded purple canvas bag. High above the breaking surf and the boogie boarders in the waves, the plane banked sharply and headed northwest toward the mainland. Sitting alone, my father exuded more than his usual air of preoccupied self-containment. He gave every appearance of working his way systematically through all four sections of the *New York Times*. Upon landing at Logan Airport, we parted company with Frank. Instead of delivering our hostage straightway to Belmont, we stopped in an airport restaurant for lunch. Food dreary, conversation desultory.

"You OK?" I asked my father.

"Me? Yes."

"How are you feeling?" I asked.

Bad idea.

"I'd prefer not to comment on that right now," he answered. Then he added, "You're not going to get that for your newspaper."

Not grinning.

McLean, with its red and yellow brick dormitories dotting the landscaped grounds, had the look of a New England boarding school on a languid summer day. A flag hung limp against its pole. A balding psychiatrist with a green binder took us to a conference room decorated with an Edward Hopper print. "How do you come to be here?" the psychiatrist asked. There'd been an intervention, my father told him, prompted by what he called his "compulsive drinking." The psychiatrist asked him a lot of questions about his health, then about his family. Were you ever separated from your parents as a baby? *Well, they had an apartment in New York and I lived in Pennsylvania with my brother.* How old were you when they died? *They're still alive.* What can you do to please your mother? *Well, she has a fierce temper, so—avoiding that.*

It occurred to me that he was, by habit if not enthusiastically, charming the shrink. The psychiatrist, though pleasant, was not disarmed. Fixing my father with a look of detached interest, he pressed on with his questions, occasionally glancing at the pages in his binder.

"What are you like when you're drunk?"

"Withdrawn," my father answered. "When pushed, abusive."

Not violent, the rest of us chimed in.

A bow-tied psychiatrist with a shiny face peered around the door. The patient would be unable to leave his residence hall, the man said, for the first twenty-four hours. Was he feeling violent or suicidal? the man inquired. Destructive toward himself or others?

"Not toward myself," the patient answered.

The rest of us, led upstairs, were introduced to a social worker. We'd been given a list of so-called enabling behaviors, which included "keeping feelings inside" and "allowing him/her to ignore or avoid dealing with the problem." How are you feeling? the social worker asked. Guilty, I confessed. Now that I think of it, apprehensive might have been the better word. It had begun to dawn on me that there was going to be fallout from our rescue mission.

My mother volunteered how cooperative the patient had been.

"Isn't that kind," the social worker said wryly. She seemed to be suggesting the opposite.

Could he have a single room? my mother asked.

"A single room sometimes reinforces a patient's sense of himself as special," the social worker said simply. The answer, it seemed, was no.

"He's really a very bright, charming, kind man," my mother offered.

The social worker nodded.

"The first two will be a hindrance here," she said.

We found him sitting downstairs in a cluttered lounge with a paper cup of chipped ice next to him on a table. His hair was uncharacteristically mussed, as it had been all morning. A counselor took him away for a "body search." When he returned to say good-bye, he kissed my mother on both cheeks.

"Thanks for trying," he said, with an enigmatic chuckle.

Two weeks later, we returned for family therapy. My mother had warned Hopie and Elliot and me that our father was angry at the prospect of more than another week. We climbed a staircase framed with high bars to discourage potential jumpers. In an office, we talked to the social worker my mother had met during her college reunion. What did we hope would come out of the patient's treatment? he asked. Elliot hoped for better communication and some insight into who our father was. I said I wasn't sure what I wanted: maybe just to get through dinner with him coherent.

Our mother looked distressed.

After fifty minutes, Popsy was ushered in. He'd lost weight and his hair looked whiter than I remembered. When the social worker asked him to tell us what he'd been doing, he began by delivering a rather formal expression of gratitude that seemed to border on grudging. Then he launched into what felt like a prepared speech. He'd come to see, he said, that his drinking was far worse than any of us had known: It had pervaded everything he did. But he'd taken to Alcoholics Anonymous, he assured us. He was committed to staying sober; he'd be working hard at not drinking. We were not to expect a personality change. Bob Scott, as he put it tightly, would not become Bob Hope.

Why didn't you look at anyone when you spoke? the social worker asked him.

"Just a matter of style," he said, sounding defensive. He'd do the same thing at a board meeting or a bank meeting, he said, or at any time he was "in his head."

The social worker had suggested earlier that my mother ask my father if he had any idea how hard his drinking had been on the rest of us. When my mother did, he bristled. Making an alcoholic feel guilty, he countered, is a bad idea. He chided her, too, for any implication that there'd been a halcyon period in their marriage, with all its passive aggression and muffled warfare waged under cover of darkness. Not all their problems, he said, stemmed from his drinking.

"Well, most," she answered, almost under her breath.

Someone raised the possibility of psychotherapy. Would he be willing to try it? He said he wasn't opposed but had no intention of beginning it immediately upon returning home. Before agreeing to undertake it, he added, he'd want to know the purpose.

I said I was struck by what appeared to be his anger. I said we'd gone way out on a limb to try to help him, out of what I believed was love and desperation. Now he seemed to be suggesting that we wanted to make him someone he was not. He countered by insisting that he was neither angry nor resentful. A little defensive, maybe. He'd thanked us, hadn't he?

The following morning, back in the social worker's office without the patient, we said we were troubled by the previous afternoon's session. The social worker said it might be unrealistic to expect anything better. Growing up with limited access to one's mother leaves a hole in one's heart, he said—channeling, I now see, our old London neighbor, Dr. Winnicott, with his concept of the "false self." In such cases, the social worker told us, interactions with others may be "more style than substance." Those were things that might be worth exploring in therapy, the social worker agreed, but our parents' marriage was the first item on the agenda. How would we react if it ended in six months? he wanted to know. If our parents entered couples' therapy, the status quo would not remain. Was my mother willing to run the risk that the marriage would end?

Good question. That's what she said.

We adjourned to a cluster of picnic tables and chairs on the lawn. My father was waiting at one of the tables. As part of his treatment, he'd been required to write a history of his drinking, a kind of autobiography of his addiction. He'd filled fifteen single-spaced pages in longhand. He'd made a presentation to his fellow patients. Now he was to read it to us.

His account began with the landscape of his early life. The dominating figure—that's the adjective he used—was his mother, whom he described as "equally at home in the loftier social life of Long Island and Park Avenue and in the fields with her horses or her father's cows." The writing was evocative, sometimes funny in a dry, muted way. His voice was mellifluous, his cadences lilting. In the damp heat of August, I remembered a moment from childhood, sitting cross-legged on the living-room rug, listening to him read from *The Wind in the Willows*.

He was speaking of his parents' absences, when he was a boy, in a degree of detail I'd never heard. The familiar and the unfamiliar mingled. Some details were startling. But he read on. There was no opportunity to interrupt, to ask him to go back.

"Toilet training was particularly rigorous, my mother treating the process like housebreaking dogs, rubbing one's nose in it and administering a beating," he was saying. "Most of the beating, however, was done by my father at my mother's request."

He pressed on.

"At the age of thirteen, I was sent to boarding school," he said, "which, like after the first few days here, I came thoroughly to enjoy, in part because it was an atmosphere more just to young people than my home had been."

College, marriage, law school, children. He steered his narrative back into known waters. Then came the years in London, his return to Philadelphia, his job at the museum. The chronology and groundwork laid, he looped back to his childhood, focusing now on his drinking.

He'd had a recurring dream as a small boy, between the ages of four and ten. At its center, he said, was "an extraordinary drink, red, not sweet, with euphoric and restorative qualities." From early adolescence, alcohol was a part of his life—"always in the context of the home." His grandfather, he said, drank from lunchtime on. There was hot buttered rum served on cold winter nights, and champagne, left over from before Prohibition, at Sunday night suppers. He'd had his first taste of a superior burgundy at nineteen. He could still remember the grower, the vineyard, the year—just the way his aunt, I now know, would say she could remember every piece of music performed the first time she heard the Philadelphia orchestra play under Stokowski.

At college, drinking was encouraged in the circles in which he moved, my father continued. "My first loss of equilibrium was by age twenty, and if a blackout is loss of memory, I do not remember when I did not have them thereafter," he said. By twenty-two, an evening rarely passed without "significant consumption." It never occurred to him to stop—only, occasionally, to try to drink less.

The decades rolled on. His drinking waxed, his tolerance waned. As the museum president, his presence was appreciated at well over one hundred cocktail parties, receptions, and other evening events each year. The absurdity of the situation didn't escape his notice. He began, he said, "having wine to prepare for the wine served before the wine served at the press lunch before the wine served before the opening dinner of a major exhibition."

The museum's financial challenges were formidable. The director, he believed, wouldn't confront them directly. His frustration with her, he said, triggered more drinking—"to the point where sometimes I would have a glass of wine in midmeeting to quell my anger."

At home, he said, "I was generally out of it by 9:00 . . . drunk, ready for bed." He'd wonder what had happened between sitting down to dinner and waking the next morning. For major parties, he'd try to stay just sober enough. But, among friends, he said, "my desire was to reach a certain level of oblivion as soon as possible. To my wife's sadness, our friends included us less in their activities because of my drinking."

Then came New Zealand.

"It was glorious and great fun, but almost destroyed for my children by my being hopelessly intoxicated by the end of dinner," he continued. "They viewed it as a miracle that I was always up in the morning and prepared to ride 100 miles. They viewed the evenings as a nightmare."

The intervention on Nantucket had convinced him, he said, "that the disease was ruining my family relationships and threatened my personal relationships with destruction." He recognized "in my heart the truth of what they were saying." Since entering McLean, he'd come to believe that his illness was worse than he'd thought: "Alcohol had come to pervade every aspect of my life, my decision making, my planning." He'd become isolated, his energies dissipated. He'd arrived at McLean determined to make a recovery. Now, he said, "I am convinced I can."

There was one more thing.

His aunt Anna, his father's sister and the athletic clubman's eldest daughter, had written to my father at McLean. She was in her eighth year of sobriety. She'd made a practice in recent years of mapping the march of alcoholism through the Scott side of the family. Now my father added what he knew of the Montgomerys to what his aunt had laid out.

His mother, my father began, was one of four children. One, he said, had "died of alcohol," another was "terminally ill with it." His father, too, was one of four. He'd had "a severe drinking problem"; his sister was a recovering alcoholic; his other sister, now dead, had been an alcoholic; and their brother, my father said, had been a heavy drinker before he was killed in World War II.

As for his grandparents, he continued, the Colonel had "shortened his life with drinking." And Edgar Thomson Scott, his other grandfather, had "committed suicide in World War I while drinking."

My father read on.

"Under the circumstances," he said, wrapping up, "it is folly that neither I nor we recognized the problem for so long."

The folly, I've learned since, went back at least to the death of the railroad man's son. His survivors buried the circumstances of his suicide, hiding the facts from even their children. I learned the details only because an account survived in the basement of a house near Boston, which had once belonged to Hugh Scott, Edgar's nephew and friend. During the war, Hugh had been in France, working for the Red Cross, when the two Edgars, father and son, arrived on their fateful mission to become ambulance drivers. Hugh's letters home to his wife, dating from that period, came to rest eventually in a battered, black suitcase in that basement. Two generations later, Hugh's grandson, by then a denizen of the house, came upon the letters—the sole surviving record, it seems, of the final self-destruction of my father's paternal grandfather.

The facts don't quite add up to the selfless sacrifice celebrated by Harvard. It's true that Edgar the elder had become ill in France while working for the inspector general of the American Expeditionary Forces: He'd come down with dysentery in 1918 and had been ordered to report to a facility in Deauville to recover. But he'd headed for Paris instead, on what's said to have been a bender involving a woman and booze. When he returned, his commanding officer "spoke sharply to him and said he had no business to spend his sick leave in that way when men were dying and fighting at the front where he was needed," Hugh wrote to his wife. Edgar, fearing scandal and public humiliation, panicked. "I'm afraid Edgar must have brooded over this during the night," Hugh wrote. ". . . He imagined everything worse than it was and made up his mind during the night that it was the only way out."

In a note to his superiors, Edgar wrote, "This all comes from drink." Or so Hugh reported. A military inquiry concluded, "Gunshot wound self-inflicted. . . . Not line of duty. Result of own misconduct."

The cover-up fell to Hugh.

"Am trying my best to keep stories from circulating to effect that he was to be court martialed—had been on a disgraceful drunk etc. etc.," he wrote home. "Have had a busy time. Some of the actual details were very disagreeable."

Hugh prevailed upon a friend at the Associated Press to report only that Edgar had died suddenly and had been buried with full military honors. This was the party line: Edgar had suffered from dysentery, couldn't stand the strain, was emaciated when he expired. Back in the United States, dysentery morphed into a less distasteful diagnosis: "Prominent Philadelphian, Acting Inspector General in France, is thought to have been a victim of pneumonia," the *Boston Transcript* reported, citing relatives, unnamed. Newspaper obituaries lingered over the deceased's mansions, his hobbies, his eighteen club memberships. The *Social Register*, the *Burke's Peerage* of the American Protestant upper crust, updated Edgar's entry with tact: "Died in service in France."

I can't help but wonder what effect all this had on Edgar's eldest son, my grandfather. He was the one who'd pressed his father to accompany him to France. It was he, too, who'd written ecstatically, three months before the suicide, "He's the peach of peaches now; wide awake, and in the game heart and soul, for the best motives."

The job of breaking the truth to his mother fell to the son.

What, I wonder, did he tell her?

More than a half century later, on the day of his youngest sister's funeral, I was surprised to hear him allude briefly to his experiences in World War I. I knew almost nothing, at that time, about his year in France, but the way he referred to it left me with an impression of an ineradicable grief. Another war had just ended, not long before my great-aunt's funeral. So the conversation at the reception turned to war. My

grandfather recalled having seen troops turn on their commanding officers and shoot them. He mentioned, too, having been back at Harvard
on November 11, 1919, the first Armistice Day. He'd traveled that day
from Cambridge into Boston, where entire families had poured into the
streets for the first remembrance. Alone in the crowd, my grandfather
had wept.

The account of his father's death, in Hugh's letters, had surfaced
before. Hugh's grandson, who now lives in the house, had come upon
the suitcase in the 1980s. He'd shown the letters to my father's cousin
Mike, who'd telephoned his mother, Anna, offering to have them sent
to her. He thought the descendants of Edgar T. Scott, Anna's father,
might benefit by knowing how and why he'd died. Perhaps a better
understanding, he thought, would help someone someday. There had
already been a suicide in Mike's generation in the family—that of his
youngest sister.

"It's all here," he'd told his mother, amazed by what he'd read.

But Anna and her brother, Edgar, my father's father, had no interest
in the letters.

"Let the dead bury the dead," she told Mike. She told him to return
the letters to the basement.

My father, I now know, had known enough of his grandfather's
story to want to know more. Some years after Helen Hope, his mother,
had let the cat out of the bag, my father had, in his twenties, let slip the
secret of the suicide to a younger Scott cousin. "Who would you most
like to have known?" he'd asked her one evening after dinner, where
they'd been swapping family stories. Our grandfather, she'd answered
gamely. My father, she remembered years afterward, had lit up. "Yes!"
he'd agreed. "Anyone who could take a gun and put it to their head
must have been quite something."

Years later, he came into possession of a cache of papers and mementos linked to his grandfather's abbreviated life. I found them in a
steel box after my father died. I imagine he'd claimed them after the

death of his own father, though I can't be sure. The collection had been curated by the elder Edgar's widow for her children. They included the passport their father had used when he traveled to France in 1917 and the military identification bracelet he was wearing when he died. In all the papers, there was no hint of suicide. But there was a letter from a brigadier general, who professed to believe that Edgar, severely ill and under psychological stress, had suffered a breakdown shortly before his death.

"I am convinced that Scott laid the foundation for the trouble which carried him off in the hard work he did for me just prior to and during the San Mihiel offensive," the brigadier general, Malin Craig, wrote to Edgar's commanding officer. "I am not certain that you know how hard that fellow worked regardless of hours or weather conditions which were particularly vile. I found him in what I thought particularly bad shape while attending to some work in connection with the handling of some German prisoners and it almost took an order before I could persuade him to go to bed and keep quiet for twenty-four hours while I sent a doctor to look him up. He had a rather severe attack of bowel trouble which was prevalent at the time though his attack was more severe than in most cases. Knowing how fond Scott was of you and you of him, I thought I would like to tell you, although you already know it, of the great assistance he gave me, and to express my personal as well as official regret that a man who worked as hard as Scott did for the Government, without consideration whatever for his own convenience or comfort, should have been taken."

My father, I now know, had a theory about his grandfather. He told his cousin Mike that he believed their grandfather suffered from a mild form of bipolar disorder. Mike mentioned my father's idea to me, though he said my father hadn't elaborated. The term, bipolar disorder, is more recent than the life and death of Edgar T. Scott; but the idea that a cyclical pattern of depression and manic excitement might run in families had been around since the nineteenth century. My father's theory, and it was just a theory, seemed potentially to put the puzzling trajectory of the railroad heir's life in a different light. I was left wondering what my father, who hadn't told Mike on what evidence he based his diagnosis, knew about manic depression.

So "the problem" of alcoholism, as my father was calling it that day at McLean, had been passed down on both sides of his family. There was little evidence it was stopping: A cousin of his had preceded him into treatment; members of my generation would follow. Yet my father's recounting of that history marked the first time I'd heard anyone take stock of the destruction. Disregarding the pattern had been a perpetual exercise in turning a blind eye. When my father had called his mother to tell her he was off to McLean, she'd said, "I didn't know it was a problem." Had she forgotten how her husband had sent the kettle soaring across her kitchen? Had she forgotten the plantation in South Carolina where, as she'd put it, "people went down there and drank themselves to death"? Long afterward, members of my father's generation would tell me their stories—of being confronted by offspring, of delivering themselves to AA, of swearing off even the Communion wine. My uncle Ed told me he, too, could have become an alcoholic—except for the fact that he had a habit of throwing up after the fourth drink.

Would my father have made different choices if he'd stared down the history early on? I wondered. Would he have gravitated toward a different life? Would he have stayed away from jobs that placed a high value on being unfailingly sociable and charming at parties? By the time I had children, the toll of alcoholism in the family was out in the open. Make sure your children understand that they're in danger, I was told by the cousin who'd transitioned from banking into alcoholism and drug-abuse counseling. Tell them early, he said, though my kids were young at the time. Tell them again and again and again.

The air that afternoon at McLean was loud with the din of cicadas. The five of us embarked awkwardly on a stroll along a path that wound through a wood on the hospital grounds. We fell into the old order of march—my father in the lead, my mother scurrying to keep pace, the three of us dawdling at the rear. At one point, I caught up with my father. To break the silence, I asked what he'd been reading. I'd sent him a package of magazines and books the morning after we'd dropped him off. A guilt offering.

He'd been reading material put out by AA, he said.

Had he learned things about alcoholism that he hadn't known? I asked.

"Oh, yes," he said.

Like what?

He was quiet. I glanced at him sideways, thinking he might be weighing the choice between degrees of self-revelation.

"The duplicitousness and deception involved," he answered, looking straight ahead.

He left it at that.

Chapter Eight

My father kept diaries nearly all of his adult life. His medium of choice was college-ruled filler paper in a black three-ring binder. He loaded sheaves of it, I now know, into a slim, vinyl-covered book that traveled in his brown leather briefcase. He wrote on station platforms, in his office, at men's clubs after work. From time to time, he transferred his finished pages into extra-large binders. Each one was big enough to hold hundreds of pages on its bangle-size rings. The binders he chose were nondescript, and he stored them out of sight. He wrote in black ink, using a black Sheaffer fountain pen he'd bought the day after he and my mother were married. He occasionally thought that, if he were to lose that pen, their marriage would come to an end. His penmanship was steady and even, like waves in an etching of the ocean. If he fell behind, he relied on the scribblings in his pocket calendar to catch up. Once, he destroyed several years' worth of diary entries, to make sure they'd never be discovered. On another occasion, he locked what remained of the 1960s in a steel box, then forgot where he'd stashed the key. Fifteen years later, a flat key surfaced in a stud box he'd taken to England. He tried it, and the strongbox sprang open.

That my father was keeping diaries had never been a secret. If we happened upon him writing, he made no move to disguise what he was doing. But I now see he went to some trouble to avoid leaving his pages lying around. If he hadn't, I, for one, would have read them. As it was, I'd never wondered why he was keeping diaries. I'd never asked what kept him at it, year after year. He was a reader, a letter writer, a denizen of a world of words on paper. So it seemed unremarkable that he kept a journal, too. If I'd bothered to think about it, though, I'd have assumed I understood the impulse. A diary was a bottomless box into which to toss unsorted experience for future contemplation. It was an illusionist's trick, a means toward making order from chaos. It was fire insurance against forgetting. But when he told me in my twenties that he intended to leave me his diaries, I sensed I'd come into a complex inheritance. When no volumes surfaced after his death, I had no trouble coming up with reasons he might have changed his mind. More interesting was the riddle on the flip side: Why had he offered them in the first place?

By the winter of 2014, I'd given up hope of finding the missing volumes. My father had been dead for nine years. It had been three years since his girlfriend, Margaret, had handed over a few short diaries she told me she'd found in his top drawer. I'd asked her to let me know if anything else turned up. She'd never mentioned the subject again. On the day after Christmas, I was in the house my father had left twenty-one years earlier. My mother and I and my children were poking around in the basement. In a small room past the furnace and the boiler, she pointed to a tall wooden box—the kind moving companies use for packing dishes. The box was filled, she said, with what appeared to be love letters from long-dead men to that great-aunt who'd died around the time of the end of the Vietnam War. They'd been entrusted to my father after her death. Maybe there's something in there of interest, my mother suggested, with nothing particular in mind. Unlikely, I figured. But why not check. Soon, my daughter, Mia, and I were bent over the box, pawing through drifts of love letters, digging to China.

Up from the bottom floated a black, bound notebook—like a boot on a fishing pole in an old cartoon. It had a faux-leather cover. It belonged on the desk of a small-town bank officer in one of those movies admired for getting every period detail just right. Inside, the pages were lined. The first one was dated two days before the birth of Hopie, my parents' first child. The handwriting, in black fountain-pen ink, was my father's. The book was an early journal from his midtwenties. Its contents were unlike anything about my father that I'd ever read.

I won't soon forget reading those pages for the first time. They exposed, no doubt, just one of many facets of my father. But it was a facet few of us had seen, despite his dropping of the occasional inscrutable clue. In those pages, it was as if he were performing exploratory surgery on his spirit—operating without the anesthetic of self-pity. His self-diagnosis was eloquent and damning. To me, it suggested a band of darkness verging on despair.

Bear with me. I want him to speak for himself.

I take my diary down from the shelf and I begin to write when I am in moods of reappraisal and reform. Judging from the dates of the entries in this volume, the moods are becoming less frequent. But their sensible intensity does not seem to have diminished. Formerly the moods were short, a day or two of depression or elation and the episode soon forgotten. This time it has been much longer. For almost three weeks now the mood and I have been cohabiting rather regularly. Perhaps it is the influence of vacation. The urge to create, create for the satisfaction of creating runs strong during these moods. I would try to write a novel, perhaps built on a projection of my grandfather Montgomery's life. Since I have never tried to write and never had any reason to believe I had any ability to do so, I read instead. The reading slowly stimulates the urge to write. . . .

Tonight, my first preoccupation is that I feel enormously dull. Aiming to please, I am first upset by the fact that I am and have for a long time been unable to dredge up topics of conversation, am unable to amuse. I am also dull to myself. I do not bore myself, as I do not sigh and wish myself away when I am alone, but I know within myself that I am not only uninteresting but uninterested. I am dull to other people and to myself because there is very little other than myself that I care about. There is nothing which I find exciting, stimulating, except the things which I do alone, unanalyzed and unspoken. Work (perhaps), beagling, reading, drinking (perhaps). I am cold, in the sense of being dead to so much. Short in values and interests, my horizon is illumined by the glow of human admiration. Without that glow, I am undirected.

Presumably the way to sustain my egotistic satisfaction would be to build better mouse traps, have people come knocking to my door. Write great novels. Become a great trial lawyer. But is that really what I want.

I am now twenty-six years old. I live in a beautiful formal house with grounds which I cannot afford to keep on a decaying quasi-baronial demesne of great beauty in an encroaching suburb. I am a graduate of a law school, am paid to practice law by a rather good stuffy law firm, and I am quite mediocre about it. My life is now what many inner suburbanites strive for endlessly. But I am still a virgin. Is that what I want? My mental virginity is probably greater now than seven years ago. I'll bet there are plenty of girls who'd like to learn that trick. I am married to a charming spoiled wife with whom I have little in common but background. My failure at the tennis court eliminated what she felt to be the sphere in which we would have experiences together, and the result is that we have no common experiences, except our background. We live our background. Our house is our two generations of money flowing into more of culture. This is no way to live.

But the fault is all in me and not in the environment. There is nothing else I want to do, nowhere else I want to live, no other woman I want to marry, no other background I want to accumulate. No, I must attack my own spirit to find and cure. I cause my own sterility. I make myself into a pompous ass. My own horizons I must expand myself. My garden is smaller than Emily Dickinson's, although I am not a recluse. Perhaps I should retire to the porch until I no longer shyly shrink from contact, obstinately refuse diversion, stupidly seek escape from what and into what I don't know. More likely I should practice each day going forth to live.

For most of my life, my father had seemed at some level unknowable. His final years had made that fact only clearer. Now, after being entombed for decades in the drifts of his late aunt's love letters, this single, overlooked volume had presented itself to me as a key to use in the decryption. There was nothing tentative about the conclusions my father had drawn about himself. The final entry in the book offered a glimpse of the malaise he'd been treating. The journal seemed to shed a light, albeit a sliver, on something I'd sensed. Was there more?

It had never occurred to me that my father would have left diaries in the house that now belonged to my mother. He'd walked out, in the thick of an argument. He'd returned six weeks later, with movers, to collect his desk and the contents of his "dressing room," as we still called it and would go on calling it forever. My mother had stayed on, alone in the cool stillness of the "nine-bathroom house." Several times a week, a housekeeper came to vacuum the carpets, mop the linoleum floor, water the orchids on the windowsills in the kitchen. The house was silent, immaculate, free of clutter. My mother was the opposite of a pack rat: There were walk-in closets containing nothing more than a perfectly folded blanket and a spare pillow. If my father had left his diaries in the house, I'd always assumed, surely my mother would have known. Now, the single diary fished from the dish box made it clear that I needed to search the entire place. My mother was pretty certain that she'd seen nothing—though it was possible, she said, that there were items in the basement or on the third floor that she'd overlooked.

I returned three weeks later. I bypassed the first and second floors because I knew them well. I started in the basement, a warren of low-ceilinged rooms that included a onetime laundry with a Ping-Pong table and some industrial-style sinks dating from the 1930s. I searched every room and found nothing.

The third floor was divided into two autonomous regions. In the front were a large guest room, a bathroom, and a music studio where my mother, then in her late eighties, still practiced and taught, climbing two flights of stairs every day. The back portion, designed as a "service wing," had a long corridor, two bedrooms, a sitting room, a half dozen closets, and a bathroom with a dormer window and a claw-foot tub. It had been thirty years since the last childhood cook had departed. The rooms in the apartment were mostly empty and unfurnished. In the bedrooms, all I found were cardboard boxes and framed pictures propped against walls. In the sitting room, I found my father's antique desk. In one closet, a pair of women's fringed pants, dating from the era of the Twist, dangled, in a dry-cleaning bag, from a wire hanger. I was on the verge of giving up and heading downstairs when I remembered a large walk-in closet that had captivated me as a child. It had been designed as a linen closet when that wing of the house had been built. Once, in the weeks leading up to Christmas, my mother had warned us to stay away from that closet. She must have been using it, we figured, as a staging area for presents. For years afterward, whenever I was passing by, I'd make a point of opening the door and poking around. The closet had never lost its intoxicating whiff of unused stationery and things left untouched for years.

I flipped the light switch inside the door. Shelves lined three of the four walls. There were boxes of stationery, Christmas decorations, some books, including an early edition of *Winnie the Pooh*. Along the back wall there were pewter trophies won by my father's beagles. The stuffed hare's head was there, too, long since retired from its station outside the downstairs bathroom. As I was turning to scan the shelves to the right, something unfamiliar caught my eye. Beneath the bottom shelves, a large wooden chest had been pushed into the corner. There were a few cardboard boxes in front of it, obstructing my view. But I could see a combination lock with a steel shackle dangling from the metal latch.

I moved toward the chest, shoving boxes out of the way. When I reached the lock and gave it a tug, the shackle didn't budge. Inverting the lock, I could see it had a four-digit combination. In my parents' households, the combinations were the last four digits of the phone number. For years, the phone number to the house had ended in 4317. But we'd lost that number when we'd moved to London. When my parents moved back into the house four years later, the new phone number ended in 7010. Squatting on the floor, I peered at the dial. It read 8010.

I ran my right thumb over the bottom of the lock and nudged the first wheel one notch on its rotation, turning the 8 to 7. The shackle popped open. It was impossible, the way the chest was lodged under the shelf, to lift the lid. So I grabbed the handle on one end, hauled the chest into the open, and raised the top. Inside were four extra-large black binders, each four inches thick with loose-leaf pages. They'd been arranged on a bed of white packing paper. In a plastic pocket on each binder's spine, a white card identified the dates of the entries inside: 1973–1983, 1983–1990, and so on. There was a gray steel strongbox in the chest, too, containing hundreds more pages dating from the 1960s. Manila file dividers separated those pages by year. Whoever had hauled the chest into the closet, lined the bottom with paper, arranged the binders with the strongbox beside them in the chest, closed the lid, maneuvered the chest into the corner, and set the combination lock at 8010 must have known that, sooner or later, one of us would chance upon them or come looking. Surely anyone who'd go to that trouble must have imagined that, one day, the contents would be read.

I took the binders and the strongbox back to New York.

Beginning with the earliest entries in the black book from the box in the basement, it seemed that my father believed he suffered from some sort of recurrent depression. Sometimes he used language like "in the doldrums" or "gloomy" or "dark and vacant"; other times he referred matter-of-factly to "my spring depressions." He believed his moods were seasonal; he traced them back to the year he'd turned fourteen. Like an amateur meteorologist tracking shifts in atmospheric pressure, he mapped their comings and goings. Sometimes, he described symptoms now often associated with anxiety: he felt tense, irritable, wound up. "I was in the doldrums all day, as I had been to some extent for a couple of weeks," he wrote before his thirtieth birthday. ". . . Most of the day I spent in full introversion, bringing this diary to date and tasting without analyzing a sense of general malaise, distress, nervousness, and displaying barely restrained bad humor." That evening, he turned in early, "either to sleep it off or to think about it in bed, guilty."

His self-investigations occur frequently during his twenties and early thirties. He finds himself pompous, stuffy, unamusing, self-absorbed, deficient at his work. "Ordinary, busy days at the office marked by recurring realizations of inadequacy and incompetence," he writes at twenty-eight. At a hospital trustees' meeting, he reports, he embarrassed himself "by shooting off my ignorant mouth"—an episode that left him "miserable with myself." He faults himself for what he sees as a hunger for approval: "Commentators and critics frequently point out the Americans' almost pathetic desire to be liked by foreigners, to be attractive. I have my own private case of the same." Another young lawyer's account of having built an addition onto his own house leaves my father criticizing himself for lacking "development and drive." He finds himself "wanting to be one of the gang (which I am not)." Yet the company of friends sometimes leaves him ill at ease. "I was tired and had terrible complexes, making myself quite unbearable to myself, and, I assume, to everyone else," he reports. He's often uncomfortable in the perpetual whirl of cocktail parties, dinner parties, and dances in which he and my mother are swept up. Encountering a man with a taste for solitude, he senses a kindred spirit: "He, too, is uneasy and ill adjusted to the social pattern we belong to," my father writes.

Few, I think, would have described him that way. They'd have said the opposite.

The summer he turns twenty-seven, he's on the ferry from Nantucket to Woods Hole, Massachusetts, sitting on deck near the rear of the boat as the island recedes into the distance. Gulls trail the ferry in a loose flock—gliding on the drafts of air, dropping into the churn to snag a scrap of tossed food from the wake, rising again to glide on the currents. His attention alights on a young gull, evidently in its first season. Its coloring is a yellowish gray; it struggles to stay aloft. "It was working hard, beating its wings much more than the other birds, never quite able to spread its wings and glide on the updraft," my father writes. Several times, the gull seems to tumble toward the water. It pumps its way back up. "For a long time and repeatedly I watched it," he writes. "And while the trip for the other gulls was a matter of ease, for the young gull it was all work—no relaxing. The parallel between that gull and me was obvious, and reassuring."

He interviews a young man for a Harvard scholarship. My father, now in his thirties, is fascinated and moved by the applicant, who's ten years younger. "He was almost without defenses, the most open and disarming young man," my father writes. "He was quite frank, obviously sensitive, interesting to look at, and in short order he had me captivated." The diarist retells the applicant's life story—fractured family, absent father, mother "a case." The young man set off for France after high school "because he found America 'dead.' By this he means emotional insensitivity, materialism." He fell in love with a beautiful German woman and bicycled with her around Brittany. He enrolled at the University of Virginia, dropped out, returned to France, nearly married the woman, then decided to complete his education first. "Sensitive, fascinating, inquiring," my father writes. "He may be a Don Quixote or a Thomas Wolfe or Winston Churchill. . . . Made me realize what a closed corporation I am."

A closed corporation, I find, comes from the language of corporate law, my father's field at the time. It's a privately held, often family-run, firm.

As I moved through the diaries, I began to see that he found an antidote to his troubles in drinking. Alcohol allowed him to override his anxieties and inhibitions. At lunch with a friend in Philadelphia, at which he downs "a very naughty vodka martini," he finds it leaves him "manic at the luncheon table, feeling very witty." He makes a habit of three or four cocktails before dinner. After a Sunday night supper at the big house, he reports that it was more pleasant than usual "largely because I had three Scotches and soda and, not having had much to eat, became very tight." Alcohol is his analgesic. At a dinner party given by his mother-in-law in the summer of 1957, he finds himself "sitting there tempted by a cigarette, and contemplating the senselessness of my life and questioning its continuing." When the guests leave, he and my mother "sat up and poured Scotches down until there was no need for more."

The regimen looks exhausting. A dinner party ends at 2:30 A.M.; a dance at 4:00 A.M.; he returns home with my mother as dawn is breaking. On a workday, he rises from bed worn out—"tired after the weekend bacchanalia" and hung over. "Armed with mints and Chiclets, I made it to town," he writes. Concentration eludes him. He takes an afternoon off work to play hooky, idling over a two-volume book on tea. "A terrible day at the office, full of regrets," he writes. Aware of the toll his drinking is taking, he finds himself "surly and aggressively disagreeable" at bedtime. He's "red-faced and swollen-eyed." His stamina flagging while beagling, he concludes that he's "paying the price of pumping so much proof into my system." His assessment of his own conduct when drunk is withering: "Mistold several drunken stories," spilled beer on a rug, "asserted myself alcoholically," baited a friend. On a trip to Los Angeles, my mother objects when he turns up at a museum-cafeteria lunch table with a carafe of white wine on his tray. "Imagine what it would have been like," my father writes, "if she knew I had drunk another one in the cafeteria line."

He knew early on, I realized, that he had a drinking problem. He understood before the rest of us did. Decades later, he'd concede just about nothing when we raised the subject; but it turns out that he was onto himself all along. He knew something, too, it turns out, about his family history. "My bloodlines show an interest in liquor which is less than healthy," he writes in his twenties. He describes his maternal

grandmother, Muz, as "for years insensible by dinner's end"; his grandfather, the Colonel, "bored sick . . . drinking himself into a daily stupor"; his uncle, "a poor miserable man who can't fill the gap he drinks to fill." At twenty-eight, he refers bluntly to his own "drinking problem," saying, "I drink more than I should, both in quantity and in duration." He regularly reports on his consumption. "Drank too

much Dubonnet and gin, and being exhausted turned green at the dinner table, had to collapse in bed for a half hour, returned feebly," he writes. Or, "I drowned my sorrows in a very large quantity of Canada Dry Bourbon and a 1957 Graves Chateau Magence. I was gone."

At thirty, he plunges into a three-part series on alcohol and alcoholism in *The New Yorker*. I call up a copy, to see what he might have learned. "All current bedrock definitions of alcoholism stress its compulsive character," the author, Berton Roueché, writes in the third installment, quoting from a medical paper. "A patient suffers from chronic alcoholism if he uses alcohol to such an extent that it interferes with a successful life (including physical, personality, and social aspects), and he is either not able to recognize this effect or is not able to control his alcohol consumption, although he knows its disastrous results." Alcoholism is "too dark and prickly" to be explained simply, Roueché writes. But it cannot develop in the absence of "some mental or emotional disability." It also requires a "suitable social climate"—a culture in which drinking to excess is tolerated. It's incurable but not hopeless, Roueché writes. Alcoholics need all the help they can get—medical and psychiatric, and "sensible encouragement."

My father never voluntarily sought medical or psychiatric help for his drinking, as far as I can tell. Once, a psychiatrist whom he'd agreed to see in connection with his marriage raised the matter of his alcohol intake. My father suggested four causes: a "social environment where much liquor flows"; a fondness for the taste of wine; "unrest at home"; and, he writes vaguely, "deeper emotional reasons—release, etc." The doctor then advised him to consider what effects he obtained from drinking. My father listed eight in his diary. High on the list is "easiness with people." Others include release, laughter, satiety, courage to speak his mind, and "distance from emotion." After the last, he writes cryptically, "Find out why."

To my surprise, I find he tried repeatedly to cut back. "Yes, it is time for a reformation," he tells himself in his late twenties. But reformation leaves him "wholly unable to concentrate and grossly irritable as to my wife, my secretary and the telephone." He tries substituting chilled burgundy for cocktails, hoping to avoid being incapacitated for the entire night. But chilled burgundy lacks the "rapid pickup effect of four cocktails before dinner." Soon he's back on martinis; then he's on the wagon; then he's off. He tries giving up smoking, only to discover that it sharpens the compulsion to drink. "I'm nervous from not smoking, and very much under-exercised, and so lie in bed like a bowstring," he writes. At a party, "my very first deed was to plunge to a Parliament, then for a Scotch and soda, and only afterwards to meet the guests." Plus, quitting cigarettes lands him in a nasty mood ("not improved by a bottle of white Beaujolais"). Tackling one vice sends him fleeing to the other. "My fine resolutions about smoking went out the window with the first taste of Bourbon," he writes. His New Year's resolutions: Avoid drinking too much, don't smoke, don't be tense, take an interest in others, read more, don't put on airs. "Not that I will have the fortitude to keep them," he writes—then goes home, downs two martinis, and smokes a cigar.

Before his fifty-fourth birthday, he flies to Nantucket for a long weekend alone in early spring. He writes out his agenda: Try out the new wood-burning stove; approve a reupholstered sofa; try a weekend of "no drink, not even wine." He was drinking mostly wine, "in large quantities," in those years, he writes. For fourteen years, he'd had wine at lunch and dinner as often as not. He can scarcely remember an evening since sophomore year in college when he didn't drink, usually a lot, "unless sick or repentant or both." The weekend of attempted sobriety isn't his first self-imposed therapeutic rustication; twice, he's retreated to Nantucket to give up smoking—an effort that left him shaking so badly he had to struggle to mount the baskets on his bike. Peering at the prospect of a sober weekend, he wonders if he'll have withdrawal symptoms. Will his face become less blotchy? Will he be able to work or think?

He assigns himself no serious tasks other than not drinking. He applies himself to the tranquilizing rituals of vacation-home ownership. He carries sand up from the beach to line the bottom of the new woodstove. He buys a half cord of firewood, gathers kindling, lights a fire in the new stove. ("What a success!") He rides his bicycle into town for the paper, takes a long walk on the beach, rides out to the far end of the island, fixes a flat. As the sun slides behind the darkening sea, he cooks: swordfish, asparagus, and fried onions; scrod and okra; an artichoke, creamed spinach, and medallions of lamb. When a neighbor invites him for a drink, he begs off. He's occupied, he explains, with "a major project."

The major project is an unqualified success: no withdrawal symptoms, no sleepless nights, no cravings. He thinks about drinking, even misses it, but isn't tempted. In the absence of what he calls "frustrations imposed by outsiders," he even finds himself able to relax. When it's time to leave, he does his laundry, closes up the house, calls a taxi, flies to Philadelphia, drives home from the airport, lets himself in the back door.

"Had drinks," he writes. "(Tasted rather good.)"

I was moving systematically through the black binders on the dining table in my apartment at night. It was difficult to tolerate more than a couple of hours at a stretch. My mood lurched from low-grade curiosity to boredom to feverish fascination to sadness. I'd flee the apartment with the dog for the diversions of the nighttime streets. There were passages of breathtaking candor, revealing things I was amazed he'd written down. There were revelations that I've chosen not to report, confessions that deserve to remain private. After a few months' immersion in the diaries, I paid another visit to Ed, my father's brother, on his farm near Delaware. I read him some passages from the journals and from the autobiographical essay my father had written at McLean. My uncle said he was dumbfounded. "Not the fellow I thought I knew," he said quietly. "Really not." When I asked him

> of pursuing *play*, and very touching; the first, for its total sensuality, and the second for its reportorial values. I had completely forgotten having written them, and yet remember well having expressed the thoughts in the third, and even in the second.
>
> Memory is a frail device. It is just as well, but as the warehouse of our wisdom, if that is what it is, it is woefully inadequate. I would like to remember so many things now, but of those, most of them I never really felt. They are experiences I never experienced thoughts I never *did[thoughts]*, impressions that never impressed me. If I were to remember the things which have truly impressed me, I suppose I would be miserab[le]

in what ways, he said, "All that inner dissatisfaction and self-doubt were not apparent to me." A day later, he sent me an email. He floated the idea that my father was "writing for a readership and projecting an image that he wanted seen, not really exposing his view of himself." I gave it some thought. Perhaps that might be said of the autobiographical essay, a command performance to appease his jailers. But the tone of the diarist in his twenties and thirties seemed too consistent to be a pose. Why would a person offer such a pitiless self-examination unless on some level he believed it?

The diaries, I began to think, were my father's sole confidant and confessor. He'd found something therapeutic in his solitary exercise of self-examination and self-expression. Ill at ease at a cocktail party, he's "delighted when the time came to go home so I could return to this diary." At a dinner party, he might let drop some private secret to an agreeable-looking woman seated next to him. But for the most part he offered only glimpses of his feelings about himself. His method was self-deprecating humor; his timing was good—he invariably got a laugh. But in the lull that followed, it had occurred to me that he believed what he'd just said.

Once, on a biking trip in Ireland, he and I encountered a woman from Texas pushing a bicycle up a mountain road outside the town of Dingle. We'd passed her the day before, bent into a headwind, twenty miles beyond Dingle in the other direction. Now, as we filled our water bottles at a spring, the three of us struck up a conversation. She asked when we'd arrived in Ireland. My father, jovial as usual, told her we'd landed the previous morning. What airport? she asked. Shannon, he said. In the silence that followed, I could see her calculating cumulative mileage in her head: one hundred miles from Shannon, forty more that afternoon, now a four-mile climb to fifteen hundred feet. Her eyes widened. "You must do a lot of cycling," she said. For whatever reason, my father had lapsed into silence. I was left to explain, belatedly: A taxi had ferried us and our bikes from the airport to Dingle. It was an admission: Neither of us was that tough (though we wouldn't have minded her thinking we were). We said good-bye to the lone cyclist and pressed on up the mountain. Once we were out of earshot, I admitted I hadn't known whether to own up.

"That's the sort of thing I expect you to tell and me not to," he said.

"So, what does it mean that I'm wondering if I should have?" I asked.

He flashed his big white incisors.

"Shades of your fraudulent father."

I wasn't surprised, reading the diaries, to find that my parents' marriage wasn't happy. But I was taken aback by the impression he left of the frequency and bitterness of their combat. Repeatedly, he describes my mother in states of anger I've never seen and can't imagine; he uses phrases like "in a towering rage" and "blue with rage." He writes, the year I turned four, "Fought all day long." On another occasion, "Long fight with Gay." Some accounts are little more than shorthand: "Gin. Fight. Tears." Whatever their underlying differences, the trigger was often his drinking. On other occasions, it was women. They drift in and out of the diary entries—women I've never heard of, a few I half remember, and one or two I eventually knew.

The love affair with the glamorous family friend is largely missing. My father makes it clear in a later entry that he threw out several years' worth of pages to destroy the evidence. After the diary resumes, however, I find he's restarted the affair after having called it off. At the gym, he finds himself face-to-face with a man who's asked the glamorous woman, now widowed, to marry him. In the man's expression, my father recognizes what he describes as a look he once saw in the face of the woman's husband before he died—"jealousy, repugnance, fear, curiosity." Surreptitiously, he shuttles between our household and hers. To avoid alerting her children, they meet at the end of her driveway. "Feeling unbelievably in love and overcome with the relief and the laughter and the warmth and the knowledge of where I must be," he writes on one such occasion. He then returns to our house. "Dinner at home, alone with Gay and the children," he writes.

I give some thought to the word "alone." I turned eleven that year.

During those months with the diaries, I came to believe it had been my father who'd made the decision to warehouse them in the closet. My mother had seemed as surprised as I was that they'd turned up. Had he kept that wooden chest jammed into the corner of that closet for years, slipping quietly up the back staircase and snapping his latest pages into one of the binders, leaving the lock set at 8010 for easy access for himself? Or maybe he'd stashed the binders somewhere else, then bought the wooden chest and carted it and the binders up to the closet around the time he moved out. The final entries in those binders dated from the end of the year before he'd decamped. In his subsequent exile, did he occasionally think about his secrets lying there unnoticed, in their pine box, waiting to be discovered? I wondered if he'd ever changed his mind about wanting me to have them. Did he fear that one of us would read them while he was still around to be questioned? Could he have wanted my mother to find them? That seemed unlikely. But why take the risk of leaving them in her house?

The fact was, I'd never have expected to read his journals. But once he'd dangled them before me, I hadn't had it in me to put them out of my mind. I'd been flattered—which, now that I think about it, he'd probably anticipated. I'd been curious, too. He'd offered a door to his unsearchable self. Now that I'd blundered through it, I realized I'd never thought about what I might find. Nor had I thought how that might change my memories of my father. Nor had I considered how it might force me to rethink the story I was telling—not to mention the role of the teller. At times, I felt like I was committing an invasion of privacy—though an invasion by invitation of the invaded. At times, it occurred to me that I might be involved in an act of aggression—though it wasn't necessarily clear which of us was the aggressor. Little of what I was reading was inconsistent with what I'd known or intuited. What was shocking was how much he'd committed to writing. There was some satisfaction in finally understanding what he'd hidden. But it was disturbing to contemplate his distress. The diaries, I began to think, were an inheritance of sorts—unanticipated, undeserved, a stroke of fortune. But, like an inheritance, they came at a cost.

Land, houses, money: Wealth had tumbled in my father's family from one generation to the next. Each new descendant arrived as an unwitting conduit for its transmission. You had a right to enjoy it, an obligation to protect it, a duty to pass it on to your own unsuspecting children. It was a stroke of good fortune, of course. But what you could never know, starting out, was how those things would influence decisions you'd make over a lifetime. You might resolve to live as though that wealth didn't exist, but sooner or later it would probably insinuate itself into your thinking about jobs, profession, marriage, children. Some beneficiaries flourished. Some didn't. For some, the impact of all that good fortune appeared to have been mixed. My father, I began to think, had sensed the conundrum early on. In that earliest diary, he'd glimpsed the snare at his feet. But by then, he'd already taken his place in his great-grandfather's profession, in his great-uncle's firm, on his grandparents' estate.

"I cause my own sterility," he'd written. "My own horizons I must expand myself."

I'd noticed long before that he'd never encouraged us to follow in his tracks. He'd never pressed us to return to Pennsylvania after college or to enter the law or to raise our children on the place. The career advice we received from our parents consisted of a single imperative: Find out what you love, then go out and do it. It made so much sense, I'd never asked how he'd arrived at that position. Once, though, I used a newspaper assignment as cover to explore his views on filial duty. The assignment was an essay, for a special section, on relationships between grown children and parents. I'd witnessed my father's loyal, late-afternoon visits to his parents. I knew he'd spent most of his life a field or two away. I, on the other hand, had moved from Cambridge to New Jersey to California to New York. He and I hadn't spoken in two months. So I took a tape recorder with me to his apartment in the old nursery in the big house. What did he expect of me? I asked.

All he wanted, he said, was that I not be unhappy. "I feel it's your game now," he said. "I want you not to have more misery than the game ordinarily implies."

The tone of the diaries shifts with the move to London, which liberated him from the practice of law. His entries become less confessional and less self-critical. Perhaps, in his forties, he was able to cut himself some slack. Or perhaps there was less time in those days for self-examination. Maybe he was being circumspect: At a State Department orientation, my parents had been warned to keep diaries minimal for security reasons. For that reason, my mother's hewed strictly to the facts. My father's were stuffed with concise accounts of trips with the ambassador, meetings, receptions, house parties, dinner parties, dishes consumed, terribly attractive women, and hundreds and hundreds of names, recorded with a diplomat's concern for retention. Children's ages were listed, friends' servants identified by name. "Butler: Cornish; Cook: Mrs. Cornish."

Back in Philadelphia, his professional life became busier and his personal life more complicated than ever. On the one hand, by the early 1980s, he was living with my mother in the house on the estate where he'd spent nearly all of his life. He commuted in and out of town by bicycle, train, and car to and from his job as president and chief executive of the museum. At the same time, the diaries make clear, he'd developed what can only be described as a parallel life. He was in love with Margaret, who ran another arts organization in Philadelphia and lived in the apartment building that had replaced the Rittenhouse Square mansion of the railroad baron. My father, who I doubt was oblivious to the Scott connection, was more than a frequent visitor to the apartment. He contributed furnishings, stocked the refrigerator with groceries, laid on bottles of champagne. At Christmas, he distributed holiday tips to the building staff.

His double life appears not to have been much of a secret. He dined with Margaret at popular Philadelphia restaurants. They spent weekends together in the house on Nantucket. They had rendezvous in New York and London and occasionally stayed together in my parents' house when my mother was out of town. Not surprisingly, wires crossed. A bill for flowers delivered to Margaret's apartment materialized in my mother's mail. An interior decorator's invoice for curtains for Margaret turned up on a table at home. The route to my mother's piano lessons took her past Rittenhouse Square, where it was hard to miss my father's dark green 1974 Chevy Nova parked in front of Margaret's building.

From the diaries, I learn that he shuttled dutifully between the house on Ardrossan, the apartment in Philadelphia, and the museum. He'd wake up in one household and spend the night in the other. He'd eat lunch on Saturday in the kitchen with my mother, say he was going to the museum, spend the afternoon with Margaret, stop in his office, then head home for dinner. One Christmas Day, when Hopie and Elliot and I had all gathered, he slipped away after the ritual exchange of presents saying he needed to replace a tire, drove into Philadelphia, spent a half hour with Margaret, and drove back out to the Main Line in time to roast a leg of lamb for all of us for dinner.

Not every transition, it appears, was seamless. Recriminations erupted on either end. Sometimes, he awoke in a state of dread.

At the museum, there were financial tensions and a perpetual need to raise money. There were struggles with the city, nearly broke, over funding. The mayor might unexpectedly announce a plan to eliminate all one hundred forty-three city-funded museum positions. There were strikes of city workers. Along with other members of the management team, my father spent a night at the museum as a substitute security guard, dozing on his office floor. Then there were all those galas and benefits and out-of-town trips to cultivate donors. There were museum conferences, groundbreakings, dedications, award ceremonies, speeches, and meetings of bank boards and foundation boards and committees and who knows what else. In light of his demanding domestic arrangements, I marvel at how well he carried off his public life.

Not surprisingly, all of this appears to have taken a physical toll. Psoriasis is not generally improved by alcohol and stress. Now he came down with hives, too, as well as an alarming condition called esophageal spasm, which caused bouts of uncontrollable gagging. It tended to come over him just as we were sitting down to a holiday meal he'd spent the day preparing. My mother would rush him to the emergency room, leaving the rest of us, and some aunts and uncles and cousins, to carry festively on. They'd return several hours later after the table had been cleared, my father pale, clutching a handkerchief, and visibly drained.

Nine months before our intervention, I discover from the journals, the glamorous family friend executed a private one of her own. She invited my father to a picnic lunch on a grassy slope beside the museum and informed him kindly that his behavior at a recent dinner had been a disgrace. She presented him with material on treatment programs and urged him to enlist before he did himself in. "Don't break my heart again," she said. In his account of the episode, which was detailed and factual, he wrote that he'd listened "much saddened, knowing, of course, that there was so much in what she said." Nevertheless, he "recognized that I was not ready to commit myself." Only he could make that decision, he assured himself. Then he thanked his old friend warmly, returned to his office, telephoned Margaret, and reported what had gone down. "She was as upset and disagreed," he writes. "I was upset and didn't disagree."

The diary contains no account of our intervention or the month in rehab. I found only a few McLean handouts, some weekly "therapeutic contract updates," and an "aftercare plan," including an ominous statement of his intention to return to "the life I have previously lived." In light of what would follow, I'm struck by how, upon returning to that life, he struggled to remain sober and shore up his resolve. Several weeks after returning home, he took out a sheet of loose-leaf paper. "This is an exercise," he wrote. Since leaving McLean, he'd come to think that his drinking hadn't been, after all, as bad as it had been painted. Wine-drinking friends, as he called them, had told him they had no idea it had been a problem. Margaret had said the condemnation of his behavior had been cruelly overdone. (In my father's file at McLean, I'd find a passing reference to the patient's "mistress," as the hospital called her: "She's never seen patient drunk.") Evidently torn, my father wrote, "This list is designed to remind me of why I reached the decision I have and why I must stick to it." He then set about listing the reasons he'd believed his drinking was a growing danger.

My father's list included admissions I'd heard during the visit to

McLean—that he'd been drunk every night for forty years; the forgotten dinners and nights, the after-dinner speeches he'd drunkenly delivered; the three liters of wine consumed daily; the urge to drink in the morning; the perpetual lining up of the supply in advance, certain that no quantity was ever enough; the knowledge that he should not have been driving at night; the effects on his blood pressure, memory, complexion, weight. But there was more—especially painful to read. He'd gone to church, year after year, "asking for help with the drink, and then forgetting the request." He'd suffered from an "almost chemical longing." He wrote of his "withdrawal into myself when drinking or looking for it," and an "estrangement from others, except at work or when drinking"—though the purpose of the drinking wasn't camaraderie, it was "taking care of a need." There was a question, too, about the effect of his drinking on my mother: "Why continue to make Gay's life so miserable with the drink and give her the cause to be so?"

I thought of the vow that his grandfather, the elder Edgar, had made to himself—to prove himself worthy. I thought of his pledge to be energetic, responsible, faithful, useful. My father's list reminded me of the resolutions his grandfather had put in writing eight months before shooting himself in the head.

For months following McLean, my father attended AA meetings daily or twice daily. He went from church to church, apparently never comfortable in any particular meeting. He kept a running total, in his diary, of meetings logged. He dropped fifteen pounds, felt his memory recovering. His doctor declared him "an improved specimen." He began staying up late reading; he found himself able for the first time to write in his diary every night before bed. His entries became longer, more detailed, often focused on the challenges of sobriety. He got through Elliot's wedding "a little sad that inebriation was no longer a way out." At my own, three months later, he was "uneasy in my drinkless situation (though not badly so)." Longing for a drink at a friend's surprise birthday party, it occurred to him that if he had one glass of wine, he'd ending up drinking three bottles. Finally, a full day came and went with "no desire to drink, no resentments, almost normal. My mind and spirit seemed free for a day of all the chains and lacerations of the week before."

He adds, "I wish it would last."

As months passed, he rethought the intervention. He began to feel it had been done less out of consideration for him than out of anger and a sense of grievance. Margaret called it "your abduction." Soon, he would be calling it "a form of battery." He began to think his drinking had become a scapegoat for other problems in his marriage. He terminated his weekly sessions with the psychiatrist recommended by the social workers at McLean. He began reading a book that made the case that alcoholism was strictly a hereditary biochemical disorder, to be treated medically, and not a product of personality defects. AA, the book argued, mistook the psychological effects of alcoholism for causes. As months passed, my father's attendance at AA meetings waned. Seven months out, the better part of a week passed without his attending a meeting. Two weeks later, I find, he writes tersely at the end of a short diary entry, "I had some sherry before dinner. Not a good idea."

Sobriety had done little to resolve the tensions in his domestic life. He took to ruminating about his marriage. He noted that the urge to drink vodka was strongest when he was writing, in his diary, about his wedding anniversary. He elaborated arguments for staying and leaving. Margaret had moved to New England by then, but she and my father remained in close contact. He decided to stay in his marriage "for the time being"—out of respect, he said, for their forty-one years together, the shared life, the houses, the children, and what the psychiatrist had called their "long investment." He was feeling better, knew he looked better, enjoyed being thinner. He was more energetic, and his memory was working well. He liked having more time in the day. But the most powerful disincentive to returning to drinking was the knowledge that he'd have to give it up again. He couldn't bear the thought of returning to McLean.

Bent over the diaries on the dining-room table, I watch him teeter on the brink of relapse. "I sneaked some vodka," he writes a month after the regretted sherry. "A senseless and unsatisfactory thing to do." A week later, more vodka. "Shame!" His crowded evening calendar, he observes, isn't ideal for a recovering alcoholic. He returns to AA. He argues with my mother. More vodka—"eased the pain but didn't help." In his eleventh month of sobriety, he's overpowered by "the urge to be full of wine." He repairs to the hammock in "a happy, sleepy daze." He attends AA meetings on six consecutive days. Then vodka, rum, gin. In Nantucket with Margaret, he blacks out. He pencils marginalia into his diary: Vodka. Dry. Vodka. Vodka. Dry. On his first anniversary, I find, I telephoned to wish him well. Why celebrate? he asks himself. "Because I haven't really 'picked up' and I remain committed to not drinking," he writes reassuringly. "At least I have widely avoided the pattern of regular drinking." Looking back, I calculate that he lasted eight months before beginning his descent into relapse.

My parents' household survived another twenty months. Then, in the throes of one last argument not long before Thanksgiving, my father walked out the back door and into the blackness of that night. From a room in a hotel in Rittenhouse Square, where he'd pitched camp, he ceded the house to my mother. He arranged to relocate to what had been his mother's nursery in the big house. In the lead-up to moving day, an ice storm encased the city and the suburbs in ice. Branches, sheathed in shimmering glass, snapped from trees. There was a forty-car collision on a bridge over the Schuylkill River. Holed up in his hotel room and unable to reach the museum, he ventured out only for dinner. Encountering a friend, he said he was too depressed to join him. Later that month, as he was stepping into the hotel lobby in white tie and tails, the tendon connecting his thigh muscles to his kneecap snapped, producing a popping sound so loud that the doorman shuddered to attention. Upstairs, as the muscle contracted into a fist, he took a tablet of Alka-Seltzer. After a surgeon repaired the tendon and reattached the muscle, my father would still be recovering six months later—though he got some mileage out of the story.

On moving day, my mother left the house early, by prior arrangement. My father arrived at nine, packed a few belongings, and waited for the movers. An age seemed to creep by. Then their work went slowly—a process he'd later say he found infinitely depressing. While he waited, he thought back on the day he'd moved in. My mother had been away then, too; her father had been ill. Now they'd lived there together for forty years. Maybe he'd anticipated the possibility that his marriage might end, but I doubt he'd thought of himself leaving and my mother staying. His presence would remain imprinted in every room of the house. While he sat there numbly in the muffled silence, the movers went about their business. They emptied his dressing room of every piece of furniture—the twin bed, a chest of drawers, a wardrobe, a bedside table, the wing chair where I'd idled in my school uniform while he dressed for work. From the library downstairs, the movers took only his grandfather's antique cylinder desk, a desk chair upholstered in green leather, and the lamp that had always sat on the galleried marble top of the desk. Other than those few items, my father left behind nearly everything else—furniture, rugs, paintings, photographs, records, CDs, books, cookware, glassware—as it had always been.

A mile away, the movers arrived in the driveway at the big house. They hauled the furniture and boxes into the broad transverse hallway; up the winding, carpeted front stairs; across the second-floor corridor; and on up the second staircase to the empty apartment on the third floor. By the end of the day, the dressing-room furniture had been rearranged in what would be my father's bedroom, which he pronounced presentable. The rest of the rooms, by contrast, looked barren. "It also felt very strange and lonely," he wrote. He left and drove to his parents' house. It was his father's ninety-fifth birthday. Helen Hope had organized a small celebration. My father found his father looking unwell. There was an awkward exchange with my mother. When the celebration was over, my father drove back to the hotel in Philadelphia—grateful for dinner alone, away from what he called "the horrors and dreariness of the day."

A week or two later, I stopped by to visit.

"Thank you for coming to visit me in my Ardrossan rooms," he wrote to me afterward. "You looked mildly skeptical as to the possibilities of their being comfortably attractive but I remain hopeful. It will however take a bit of doing."

The house my father left behind

Chapter Nine

The halcyon years of the big house were long past by the time my father dropped anchor in the nursery. His grandfather had been dead nearly fifty years. A quarter century had elapsed since his grandmother, Muz, snowy-haired and frail, had last greeted visitors in the living room at teatime. In the ballroom, a pothole had opened up in the Aubusson carpet. Mothballs, like tiny golf balls, lay scattered across rugs. Damask dangled from the library walls. Shades, yellowed to the color of parchment, were perpetually drawn. On humid afternoons in August, when the sky darkened and thunderstorms rumbled across the fields, rain water burst out of cracked copper downspouts and cascaded down the brick face of the house. Seeping into the masonry, it blistered the plaster in the old playroom on the third floor. Even the immense lawn stretching south from the terrace looked diminished in those days: Brambles, briars, and fallen branches were encroaching on either side. In a small rental apartment over the kitchen, the humming of bees, nesting between the walls, was so loud it was keeping a pair of tenants up at night.

It had never been easy keeping the big house inhabited. As far back as 1970, the death of Muz had left it flush with servants with no one to serve. In pursuit of a replacement, Helen Hope had suggested my parents move into the second floor, and share the ground floor with her and Edgar, for entertaining. After my mother demurred, the family rousted my father's aunt from her South Carolina redoubt. Charlotte

Ives traveled north with a mynah bird, a pair of whippets, a Great Dane, and a cat, in a jeweled collar, named Kitty Miss. They moved into the nursery, which Charlotte Ives remembered fondly from childhood. The second floor, left dormant, was dusted once a month. Even in a wheelchair and reliant upon round-the-clock nursing, Auntie Ives was a sociable soul. In late afternoon, a half dozen regulars would drop in for cocktails. Tea sandwiches and other delicacies arrived in the living room on a three-tiered tray. One niece, back from Europe and savoring what appeared to be a cookie, was brought up short when her aunt turned to her and inquired, eyes twinkling, "Do you like dog biscuits?"

When Charlotte Ives died, Helen Hope talked her eldest grandchild, my cousin Mary, into filling the vacancy. They'd been close since Mary was young. Growing up on her parents' farm near Delaware, Mary had looked forward to nights spent with her grandmother (whom her mother had bolted the reservation to escape). With her then husband, Mary moved into the second floor of the big house. Helen Hope introduced her to the operations of the dairy. At milking time, they'd meet outside the milk house to eyeball each cow as it sashayed past on its way to its assigned stanchion. Circumambulating cow pies in her red Belgian loafers, Helen Hope would bring refreshments for the men. Later, Mary would become a breeder and trainer of prizewinning bull terriers. She'd also operate a canine obedience school out of the big-house basement and keep a kennel of her own on the edge of the lawn. Upstairs in her apartment, bull terriers lounged on sheepskin-draped sofas. For her pet pig, there was a sty accessorized with a fine mud hole. The pig had the run of the place. Once, as he sauntered past on the front lawn, my father, who by then had moved into the third floor of the house, remarked drily to Mary, "He has such a great ass." He suggested Mary name the pig after a British friend, Sir Reresby Sitwell. Mary appended the first name.

The dairy herd was nearly three hundred strong in the last decades of the twentieth century. A half dozen farm families still lived and worked on Ardrossan, sending succeeding generations off to college and graduate school, sometimes subsidized by Helen Hope. Cathie Moran, born in Ireland, had been hired in her early twenties as a live-in maid for Charlotte Ives. Ardrossan reminded Cathie of Ireland: Anyone who owned land in Ireland paid their taxes, took care of their houses, and was otherwise broke. The Montgomerys, she figured, must be the same. Yet, in the big house, there were six people waiting on Miss Ives. In the house where Cathie's sister worked for my father's uncle Aleck, the employee-to-employer ratio was two to one. There were three maintenance men on Ardrossan, too. Cathie, who also worked the night shift at a nearby nursing home, called the maintenance men the Three Stooges: They arrived in three cars, drove to the hardware store in three cars, and returned to the house in three cars— all to repair a running toilet. "I can remember saying, 'This is the craziest place,'" she told me years later. "Because there were so many people doing nothing. They kept a culture alive when it should have been dead and gone."

My father's initial intention, it seemed, was to carve out a serviceable apartment on the third floor. A few rooms in the old nursery had been rented out before as an unprepossessing flat. There were other rooms up there, too, some filled with furniture, cast-off bathroom fixtures, and heaps of papers (including a collection of pocket-size notebooks in which Uncle Aleck had alphabetized cocktail recipes, one per page). My father took the flat and annexed most of the other rooms. He had floors refinished, casement windows milled, new doorways cut, closets lined with cedar. He had the master bathroom repiped in copper, and he installed recessed stereo speakers. Eventually, his well-appointed quarters comprised a broad front hall, a kitchen, a dining room wallpapered in deep red, a book-lined study, an informal sitting room with a fireplace, a master bedroom suite, a two-bedroom guest suite, and an enormous living room he continued to call the playroom, in deference to its origins. He had the playroom walls papered in midnight blue studded with a thousand gold stars—a decorating choice inspired by a room he'd once admired in a palace in St. Petersburg.

To restore the roof, which had been leaking for decades, he hired a carpenter self-schooled in the mysteries of slate roofs. Unimpressed by the handiwork of professional roofers, the carpenter had taught himself how to surgically replace the rotting copper linings in the valleys where the planes of a roof converge. He spent nine months up on the big-house roof, sixty feet off the ground. He custom-ordered replacement tiles from a Vermont quarry. He repointed chimney flashings, replaced downspouts, reroofed each dormer, rebuilt gutters where birds' nests had once frozen, cracking the copper. The repairs cost more than the original construction of the entire house, my father liked to say. But he didn't seem to mind. "The house thanks you," he'd say cheerfully to the carpenter whenever they met. "And I thank you."

He'd been in the apartment a year when his mother quite unexpectedly died. Despite two artificial hips, the champagne-cork injury to one eye, and other greater and lesser misfortunes, Helen Hope had appeared, at ninety, to be striding briskly toward her centennial. Seven days a week, she was up early, downing a soft-boiled egg and instant coffee at the kitchen table. She was on the phone with the herd manager at 8:30 A.M., the horse-show chairman at 9:15. She was behind the wheel of her Jeep Wagoneer by 10:00, home for lunch, at the dairy in the afternoon, then back home to dress for dinner after exercising her dog. Once a week, she still made a point of going out to dinner with friends, even after my grandfather was no longer able. Once a month, she gave dinner parties at home. "If I don't see my friends, they'll forget me," she explained to her young property manager, who thought that seemed unlikely. Eighteen months before her death, three hundred people showed up to celebrate the seventieth anniversary of her marriage to Edgar. Her ninetieth birthday party was a black-tie gala that raised ninety thousand dollars for the Bryn Mawr Hospital, her favorite cause. The weekend of the fall that killed her, she'd been at the dairy, communing with the cows. She told the property manager he needn't return to bring her donkeys in from the field late Sunday. She'd do it herself.

It was Cathie Moran who found her. Many years earlier, she'd heard Helen Hope complaining, in her brother's kitchen, about an unsatisfactory haircut. Cathie, who'd volunteered to fix it, had ended up cutting Helen Hope's hair for twenty years. During the busy ten days of the Devon Horse Show, Helen Hope would bring scissors and meet Cathie in the turf club bathroom for a trim. When Cathie became engaged, Helen Hope and Edgar hosted a party at their house for Cathie and her future husband. "Everything Hope said was surprising," Cathie said to me. "She'd have you on the floor laughing." On that balmy Sunday afternoon in January, Cathie had dropped by to do the monthly haircut, which she always did as a favor, for free, even when she no longer worked on Ardrossan. Outside on the driveway, she heard a voice calling for help. Helen Hope was on the ground, unable to get up. Cathie, who'd been trained as a nurse, noticed a swelling on the back of her head. "I said, 'You're going straight to the hospital,'" she told me years later. "She said, 'No, I'm not. I have people coming over for a drink.'" Helen Hope refused to accept any help getting up off the ground until Cathie had found the two donkeys Helen Hope had been leading back to the stable when she'd fallen. Back inside, she insisted Cathie cut her hair, as planned. Two more times, she refused to be taken to the hospital. She even forbade Cathie from alerting my father. "She was very, very strong," Cathie told me. "She knew what she wanted and how she wanted things done."

My father was one of the people his mother was expecting that evening. He stopped by regularly, checking in, bringing news, regaling her and his father with stories. If there were complicated feelings left over from the wintry period of his childhood, he'd sealed them up, decades earlier, in some impenetrable interior vault. It was clear to everyone that he adored his parents, and that the feeling was mutual. Arriving at their house that evening, he found his father in his chair in the living room, his mother not yet downstairs. Upstairs, he found her on the bathroom floor, barely conscious. Her last conscious act, he'd say later, was to reach for his hand and pull it to her lips. She was airlifted that evening to a hospital in Philadelphia, where she died the following day. Death by donkey, everyone seemed to think, had its merits: She'd gone quickly, doing what she loved. Her obituary on the front page of the *Inquirer* dwarfed the lead story, which was on the Russian leveling of the capital of Chechnya.

The task of choosing Helen Hope's burial attire fell to Mary, the eldest and closest grandchild. Mary was familiar with the filing system in her grandmother's closets: clothes for hunting, clothes for New York, clothes for dinner in town, et cetera, all hung by category. Mary settled on a stylish blue suit and the well-worn red Belgian loafers. Like an ancient Egyptian entombed with the essentials for the afterlife, Helen Hope was placed in her coffin with a purse into which Mary had slipped a few photos. One, taken in her thirties, found her flanked by her two young sons; in a couple of others—Polaroids apparently taken by Edgar—she was, in her early seventies, smiling bewitchingly at the camera while posing naked.

Outside the church where the funeral was held, television reporters prowled the parking lot, trawling for sound bites. Inside, mourners overflowed the nave, spilled into the choir loft, and jammed the entrance. Latecomers, turned away at the door, made a beeline for the first-floor windows, which were open because the day was uncommonly warm. As late arrivals leaned in to listen, people inside handed hymnals out through the windows. From the book of epigrams my grandfather had bound as a boy, my father's brother, Ed, read a quotation from the Scottish evangelist Henry Drummond: "To love abundantly is to live abundantly, and to love forever is to live forever."

In the aftermath of his mother's death, endings rained upon my father. His aunt Mary Binney died three months later, at eighty-eight, having spent much of the last third of her life traveling in India and Sri Lanka, creating nine thousand photographic images of bodhisattvas, cave monasteries, monks and mendicants, erotic sculpture, nomads, wrestling, worship, and other features of life in South Asia. The University of Pennsylvania, which later acquired the photographs, would call her "the last in a long line of 'romantic' artistic and literary travelers, true adventurers of the human spirit seeking to discover and unlock the mystique of faraway lands." On the day of her death, she'd delivered a slide lecture to a sold-out benefit at her house. When the talk was over and the audience had departed, she suffered a heart attack and died. Her life had been a remarkable run—performance as a soloist at Carnegie Hall; a love affair with Leopold Stokowski, in two installments; the founding and running of a dance company; two adoptions, as an unmarried woman; fourteen trips to South Asia. Still, the opening sentence of at least one obituary identified her as "the sister of the late Hope Montgomery Scott."

Edgar was next. He died in May, at ninety-six. His brother-in-law Aleck was now the sole surviving child of the Colonel and Muz. After the death of his third wife, he'd stayed on alone in his big stone and stucco house, in the care of his housekeeper and cook. There, the two women kept him alive by bringing meals to him in his bed and diluting his drinks, dispensed via a delivery system constructed by a man who'd become something of a surrogate son. An intervention, years earlier, had bombed for the usual reasons; its target had announced he had everything under control. Increasingly deaf, and cut off from social contact, Aleck had carried on. His collections were gone. In bankruptcy, he'd even sold his share of the portraits and other paintings in the big house to his sisters. When kidney failure finally killed him, neither of his children spoke at his funeral. The eulogizing fell to their spouses and the local police chief. Aleck's housekeeper, too distraught

to attend, sent her nephew. "You wouldn't have believed it," he's said to
have reported back. "They had professional mourners!"

With Helen Hope gone, the family moved swiftly to halt the out-
flow of cash through the dairy. Within two weeks, they announced it
would close. The jobs, health insurance, and free housing for the farmers would terminate at the end of the year. An orthopedic surgeon
with a ranch in Colorado and a herd of Ayrshires agreed to buy the
cows—along with the "semen inventory" and some storage tanks for
an extra ten thousand dollars. The arrangement looked promising.
The orthopedic surgeon viewed the Ardrossan cows, he told me later,
as "the Los Angeles Lakers of the dairy world." My uncle Ed, in a letter
sealing the deal, expressed confidence that he was "doing the right
thing by my mother's cattle."

Over the course of the summer of 1995, the cows headed west, one
truckload at a time. Every one was a lineal descendant of the Colonel's
original nine. By the time the final trucks pulled out of the main
dairy complex in September, the herd manager had decided to go
along. The milking barn fell silent; grass grew high in the pastures;
equipment idled in the sheds. It sometimes seemed as though the
barns and silos, devoid of life, had aged a half century overnight. For
the first time in eighty years, the pastures sat empty, apart from the
presence of a handful of elderly cows kept on as pets. Mary Binney's
daughter Joanie, who'd spent much of her life on Ardrossan, told me
later that the day the last cows departed was one of the most painful
of her life.

The dairy operations weren't all that Helen Hope had been keeping
afloat. She'd sent monthly checks to beloved former employees, subsidized capital improvements, even paid health-insurance premiums for
one of the last surviving employees of her parents at Mansfield. She'd
funded those activities with income she received from trusts set up by
her parents. "Regrettably, this will be the last check sent to you," read
a letter to recipients of her largesse, sent a month or two after her

death. That she'd been squandering money to keep the dairy going had been clear ever since Ed's examination of the books. My father would profess later not to have cared. "Never bothered me at all," would say the man who'd go on to do something similar himself. She was "trying to keep something so anachronistic alive because it was so beautiful. . . . She was treasuring something that was going, gone."

The pileup of losses weighed on my father. He blamed himself for the separation from my mother—"probably of my causing but certainly not of my planning," he wrote in a letter. On top of that loss and displacement, his parents were gone, too. "It is all very sad indeed," he wrote. *Vanity Fair* assigned a magazine writer, steeped in Philadelphia, to write about Helen Hope, whom the magazine called "the unofficial queen of Philadelphia's Wasp oligarchy." The article was humorous, elegiac, and tinged with melancholy—a mood that also seemed to emanate, in that period, from my father. In one of the photographs published with the article, he's decked out in a tuxedo, seated in a threadbare armchair in his grandparents' library, the damask wall covering peeling in the yellow light of a sconce. He'd served champagne to the photography crew. "I didn't realize how depressing it would be," he told the writer, speaking of his divorce, his mother's death, and reaching the age of retirement. ". . . It's the death of a portion of me. This is the portion of my life that has no promise of resurrection."

Then came the news of his impending retirement as the museum's president. Announcing his plans to the museum staff, he appeared close to tears. The standing ovation rumbled on and on until he finally cut it off. In the days that followed, the reviews of his fourteen-year tenure were admiring. Membership had soared; the endowment had ballooned; galleries had been renovated. He'd presided over a turnaround in operations. Major collections had been reinstalled. The job had been no picnic, an editorial in the *Philadelphia Inquirer* observed: It was "more like a bone-jarring ride down the Rocky steps on his treasured black bicycle." A columnist for another publication lavished

praise on the outgoing president, calling him a traitor to his class—the rare Philadelphia patrician for whom the "anti-leadership vaccine" identified by E. Digby Baltzell, the University of Pennsylvania sociologist of the once ruling elite, had failed to take.

Rather vaguely, my father attributed his upcoming retirement to feeling older and "less elastic." He'd be sixty-seven, past retirement age, by the time he stepped down at the end of that year. A few reporters speculated that testy relations with the mayor's office might have been a factor. They didn't dwell on the fact that his successor would be the strong-willed director, long thought to be eager to run the museum solo. For a decade and a half, they'd been equals: She'd run the art side; he'd overseen the operations. They'd given every outward appearance of working well as a team. But in private, he'd complained about her, even occasionally to her curator husband. At McLean, he'd claimed that his frustration with her sometimes drove him to drink.

Now the board was giving her the whole show. To Margaret, he said he'd seen it coming: The director wanted the top job, and some board members wanted him out. To my mother, he said, "I don't know how much you know about what happened at the museum at the end?" Very little, she said. All she remembered him saying was, "It was pretty grisly."

Years later, I came upon a letter sent to him a month before the news broke. It came from a man who'd known him in the law office when they were young. They'd been friends. The man, Alan McFarland, had admired him for his style, humor, and intelligence; he'd remember my father later in bow tie and suspenders, seated in an antique corner chair. In January 1996, McFarland, who'd become an investment banker in New York, had found himself at a dinner at the big house. It was in honor of a few dozen supporters of a small museum in Philadelphia, and my father had agreed to host. McFarland had been pleased to see him again. His old friend appeared to have ascended to the role for which McFarland had imagined him destined. "I find your current status as lord of the manor one for which you must have certainly been intended since your earliest hours," McFarland had written to him after the dinner. ". . . You're as good at it as even the most rigorous casting director could ever have arranged." But the letter had ended on a cloudier note. McFarland hoped my father would find that role fulfilling. "I worry, even from my position way down below the salt in your life," he'd written, "that there will be a price, harder to pay than you deserve."

Reading the letter twenty years later, I was startled by McFarland's presentiment. He'd encountered my father only rarely in later life. Yet, when I reached him, he remembered the evening and the letter. My father, he said, had done many things well; he'd ended up where McFarland had imagined he would. Yet McFarland sensed that something was amiss: His old friend didn't seem happy. McFarland knew that my father's marriage had ended; he wondered about his health.

Whatever the causes, McFarland said, he detected a certain sadness. "We make choices, all of us do," he told me. "And we're measured by our choices. But we don't always pay attention to the cost of our choices—and the devil is in there somewhere."

In the years that followed, the lord of the manor inhabited his part. He transformed his mother's nursery into his late-in-life home. In his sitting room, he hung one of the Augustus John portraits of Helen Hope. Beneath it, he positioned the antique desk he'd inherited from his paternal grandfather's vanished house in Maine. On a library table in the hallway, he arranged other artifacts—the framed photograph of his parents at the foot of the gangway to the *Île de France* in 1938 and the hooves of his mother's pony and of the Colonel's Irish stallion—stuffed, mounted, and trimmed with engraved silver. On visits to the apartment, I'd pass that table and think of all the disembodied animal parts that had hung from the walls in my great-grandparents', grandparents', and parents' homes.

My children, young then, were fascinated by their grandfather in his aerie. He kept a rocking llama, with flowing hair and big enough to carry a grown man, in his book-lined study. He'd brought it from his office at the museum, where it had been christened "the President." Above the staircase to the third floor, he'd hung a full-length portrait of himself. I'd never try to make the case that it did him justice—though you'd have to assume, since he'd hung it there, that he liked it well enough. My daughter, Mia, who would turn thirteen the year her grandfather died, would be left with an indelible memory of his presence. In his company, she once told me, she felt as though she belonged to some exclusive club. Perhaps it was the house, she said, or the portrait or the way he walked. He left her with an impression of power. She respected him, and sensed that he respected her. There was something protective in his interest, even on those occasions when he affected a certain humorous irascibility. On a visit late in his life, we found him in his wheelchair in the playroom at the far end of the long hall. My son, Owen, six or seven, hovered nearby, uncertain how to proceed. My father, at his most Churchillian, turned and growled at the curly-headed boy, "Kiss me, goddammit."

After a couple of years in the nursery, he turned his attention to other parts of the house. To the surprise of some of his cousins, he began planning to restore the first floor. That seemed odd because, as I've mentioned, the house didn't belong to him: It was held in a trust that wasn't set to expire until he was almost ninety, and he was just one of its six beneficiaries. Not long after he vacated his office at the museum, a document arrived in the big-house mail. It came from the interior decorator who'd helped him redo the apartment. Titled "Revised Preliminary Budget Estimates, Phase 1," it listed dozens of proposed purchases for the downstairs ballroom—from drapery fabric ($15,120) to armchair trim ($10) to plaster-restoration and wall-paint labor ($28,660). The estimated total price for restoring the ballroom alone was $98,357 (not including $3,643.40 for shipping the carpet to England for repairs). A year later, an updated version of the "Phase 1" plans arrived. By then, they'd expanded to include the first-floor library, living room, dining room, front hall, study, and powder room. The document was eleven pages long. The estimated cost of the project was $478,590—for decoration alone.

Once, an architect friend told me something I hadn't considered. A renovation, she said, is a difficult thing to stop. Once you restore one room, the one next to it looks shabby; so you renovate that one, too. And on and on it goes. My father's apartment wasn't, of course, next to the first floor. But he was intimately familiar with how the downstairs looked. He knew what it had been like when he was young; he'd seen it age; he'd used it for parties and charitable events. "You could put a million dollars into this place and it wouldn't even show," one guest had remarked in the presence of a reporter, who'd then tossed the line into the newspaper. My father, it began to seem in those years, had set out to test that premise.

In the library, he had sofas and armchairs dismantled down to the frames, rebuilt, and reupholstered. He had new silk damask wall covering woven to order in France. Portraits were taken away and cleaned; decorative fixtures were restored and reinstalled. In the dining room, he had his grandmother's needlepoint seat covers removed, refurbished, and reapplied to all thirty chairs. He had the oak paneling treated. He had wood carvings renewed, porcelain cleaned, silver touched up. In the ballroom, original textiles were meticulously copied, and draperies were reproduced. Furniture was reconstructed. Needlepoint sofa covers were removed, cleaned, stabilized, and returned to the sofas from which they'd come. In the long hall, the lanterns were taken down, carted away, cleaned, and rewired. For the living room, my father had a carpet custom-made, copying one that had caught his eye at the Wallace Collection in London. He'd liked it so much, he had it reproduced for three downstairs rooms.

Combing through the paper trail he left behind, I was reminded of the Colonel's rodent exterminator from the Ritz-Carlton. The extravagance of my father's undertaking was puzzling. The man who'd taken pride in driving his green Chevy Nova for twenty years was now spending $17,419.54 for a custom-made front-hall rug. He'd dropped $13,320 to clean gutters and power wash the roof, $6,853 to reupholster a chair, $3,360 for fourteen "double crisscross tassel tiebacks," $925.50 for "lampshade tassels," $400 for a monogrammed bathroom rug. I suppose some of the expenses couldn't have been avoided. But were there others he came to regret—for example, the ten thousand dollars he spent on an unsuccessful effort to clean a couple of limestone walls? Once in a while, he objected to bills for unapproved items. At least once, he scaled back his plans. "Not for now," he scribbled next to a proposal for guest room number three. But for the most part, it was as if money was no object. Had he resolved to do a museum-quality restoration of the house, regardless of the price? Or had he started off wanting a comfortable place to live, then gotten seriously carried away?

He had the exterior trim of the house scraped, scaled, sanded, caulked, primed, and painted. He had the driveways repaved and potholes filled. He had the turning circle spread with eighteen tons of decorative stone, and the mile-long wall treated with sixty gallons of silicone sealer. Damaged storm drains and broken water pipes worked again. Water flowed into the pond beside the back driveway for the first time in years. Tree crews planted zelkovas, sweet gums, oaks, locusts, sugar maples. Where the driveway turned sharply and headed uphill to the house, overgrown rhododendron bushes disappeared. White dogwoods bloomed beside the road to the pool. Tree crews came and went, racking up bills of eight to ten thousand dollars each time. Bothered by the sight of empty fields, my father made arrangements for them to be used for fattening beef cattle before they went off to be slaughtered.

I'd never thought of my father as especially cavalier about money. In fact, I'd seen him occasionally be quite frugal. Early in their marriage, he and my mother had made a point of trying to hold the cost of dinner at home to one dollar a night. Once, I'd watched him squander an hour over lunch trying to repair a cheese grater he could have replaced for $3.99. Now, I can only conclude that his attitude toward money had gradually changed. After returning from England, my parents had bought two unpretentious, reliable 1973 and 1974 Chevrolet Novas. But, in the late eighties, my father had taken my mother's Nova in for a modest overhaul, which turned into the automotive equivalent of a month-long rest cure at a medical spa in the Alps. Six weeks in, my mother began to wonder what was up with her car. Dropping by the body shop my father had chosen, she discovered it specialized in restoring antiques. On the day of her visit, all that remained of the 1973 Nova was its chassis: The body and the engine were off being rebuilt; the trim had been sent off for replating; even the upholstery was being redone. By the time the car came home a few months later, its sanded, primed, and painted body had the feel of exquisite enamel. Its chrome parts gleamed like mirrors. For years afterward, gas station attendants would sidle over to admire it whenever she went to fill up. The bill had come to twenty thousand dollars—more than the price of a new car.

Now that I think about it, my father had never disdained extravagance, even when he couldn't afford it himself. He'd admired grand houses and grand gestures by those who had the wherewithal to pay. He was generous: He took pleasure in giving other people a good time, and he gave liberally to institutions (though, truth be told, the money was sometimes my mother's). At sixty-six, the deaths of his parents had left him flusher than he'd been. Though the trust that owned the big house shared the cost of exterior repairs, he paid for the rest. His restoration project was an act of vanity, surely. You don't pour a million dollars into a rental, as my brother, Elliot, put it crisply—especially when it stands a chance of being demolished. But my father chose to think of it as a decade-long exercise in historic preservation. In the process, he came to imagine he might save the land from developers and the house from destruction.

Not everyone shared his enthusiasm. Around the time the "Revised Preliminary Budget Estimates" first landed, at least one cousin of his made clear her reservations. She lived on Ardrossan, but she chose to raise the issue in a typewritten letter. She was taken aback by the scale of his undertaking: She'd had no idea, she said, that he intended to restore the ground floor. She asked him to hold off until the other members of his generation could meet with him, since the project could limit the family's longer-term options for the house. My father, she told me years later, didn't answer her letter. Other relatives, bobbing between puzzlement and bemusement, observed the goings-on from a distance. "This was just something he chose to do and was doing," his brother, Ed, told me. "I thought it was certainly something I wouldn't have done. But it was something he wanted to do." Cathie Moran believed she'd seen that sort of thing before. "They don't want to let go," she theorized later. "They don't want to see something deteriorate. But sometimes you have to let go. It's like putting money into the fire, because you're never going to get it back. And they do it over and over again. It's craziness."

It seemed also to be making my father happy. It was surely a diversion from the gloomy contemplation of aging and loss. If he had reservations about the colossal expenditures of cash, they were outweighed by the pleasure and pride he took in seeing the place transformed. Feature writers and photographers turned up to marvel at the progress, and to profile the self-appointed steward in the usual absurdist style—"the benign lord of Ardrossan, the squire of the farm, the last defender of the realm," as one put it, casting aside all restraint. Always obliging, his lordship played along—escorting all comers around the house, discoursing wryly on the provenance of objects and the quirks of his forebears. *That's a portrait of a suit with my uncle in it. . . . Somewhere around, there's a full set of Kipling. . . . Charming, wonderful, soft-spoken, flirtatious—even with me. . . . She was a marvelous hostess. Ran a very good household—if you didn't care what you ate. . . .*

A few years into the restoration, the house became the stage set for the first of my father's Thanksgiving extravaganzas. His idea was to invite everyone to a feast on the day after. Invitations went out by word of mouth. He seemed barely interested in the head count. Cousins, nieces, nephews, children, grandchildren, great-nieces, great-nephews, and friends would turn up, from as far away as California and Maine. Minivans and station wagons would sail into the turning circle, scattering the new decorative pebbles in their wake. Elderly aunts and babies in arms would cross the threshold. Margaret would be in attendance; so would my mother. Not to mention the deposed "King of Wall Street," John Gutfreund, forced out of Salomon Brothers in a bond-trading scandal. He and his socialite wife and my father had become friends. Now the Gutfreunds had rented the stone and stucco house where my father's uncle Aleck had, not long before, whiled away his golden years in bed. Sometimes in those years, I'd encounter the Gutfreunds strolling down the driveway at Ardrossan, attired in their country-house finery and in the company of houseguests like Valentino.

Thanksgiving-dinner turnout soared into the nineties. The dining-room table at the big house, fully extended, would be draped in white linen, set with crystal, china, and silver. Smaller, round tables spilled from the dining room into the breakfast room next door. There were place cards for everyone, toddlers included. The cooking and serving fell, naturally, to the catering company whose founding father had served as bootlegger to the Colonel. Waiters would glide through the newly restored rooms, circulating cheese sticks and party dogs on silver platters. At the appointed hour, the bagpiper would herd the guests toward their tables. The menu hewed to tradition: turkey, stuffing, cranberry sauce, gravy, green beans, pureed sweet potatoes, pies, et cetera. Glasses would be raised, toasts delivered to those no longer able to be with us. Small children, their party finery rumpled, would disappear under tables. After my father's death, my children were destined to find all Thanksgivings anticlimactic. No holiday meal could compete with a cast of thousands, a kilted bagpiper, and cheese sticks on silver platters.

There had been, of course, a few casualties of my father's addiction. Among them was his relationship with Elliot's then wife. On the occasion of our father's seventy-third birthday, civil discourse between the two of them had abruptly snapped. On that evening, he'd arranged a celebratory dinner in the dining room of a starchy men's club on Fifth Avenue in Manhattan. He'd invited Margaret, the three of us, our spouses, and some of his oldest friends. He'd had plenty to drink by the time he made the fateful decision to seat my sister-in-law to his left. Sometime toward the end of the first course, an argument erupted between them. Angry fire was exchanged. Later, my father would concede to me, if not to her, that he'd lost his temper—"not entirely, but I did." He'd even admit to being ashamed of himself. But the blowup at the table took place in such muffled tones, perhaps an accommodation to club decorum, that I, sitting just two seats away, remained oblivious. By the time I turned toward my father's end of the table halfway through dinner, my sister-in-law had bailed. She was driving home to Scarsdale, vowing never to be in the same room with my father again.

She kept her promise until what would turn out to be his final day-after-Thanksgiving dinner. In the weeks leading up to it, word reached her that the host was hoping she'd attend. She polled a few of us on the question of what to do. My suggestion was that she learn to dissemble, like the rest of us, and go for the sake of her children, if not him. Which she did, to her credit. That evening, when she entered the big house through the heavy front doors, her erstwhile antagonist was in a wheelchair, becalmed amid his guests on the oceanic living-room rug. Entering the room through the milling crowd, she headed in his direction, kissed him hello, and concluded that she'd done her bit.

He'd been released from the hospital a day or two before, having gone in for treatment for a collapsed lung. A gallon of fluid had been drained from his chest. His spectral aspect that evening, with his hair mussed and his gaze uncharacteristically vacant, seemed to provoke some sotto voce speculation.

"It was his mother," one of his cousins theorized about possible root causes of his troubles. "And he believed his grandmother never liked him. You must have heard her famous line, 'Bobby never walks into a room: He makes an entrance.' She got him completely—but she could never accept him."

At dinner, I made a small toast to him, thanking him for his generosity and close-hauling between the shoals of hypocrisy and excessive obedience to fact. I couldn't tell how the salute went down: How could I put the squeeze on some distant cousin for an honest appraisal when levity was expected to be on tap? Later, I somehow landed the assignment of wheeling him out of the dining room and upstairs to his apartment. As we circumnavigated the kitchen, he snagged a fistful of cookies in the hand not occupied by a glass of red wine. On the third-floor hall, the wheelchair kept getting jammed on the edge of the carpet. In his bedroom, I helped him out of his clothes and into bed. His face on the pillow, pink and round, reminded me fleetingly of my children and, at the same time, a sadly distorted version of himself.

His health was failing, that was clear. In the summer of 2001, on the beach below the house on Nantucket, his belly was a basketball, fully inflated, belly button angrily protruding. Even he must have been alarmed. That fall, he acceded to pressure from the rest of us to ditch his longtime doctor, author of effusive testimonials to his patient's superior health, and try someone else. The new internist came highly recommended as a wise soul with charm, wit, and a certain social cred assumed to be a prerequisite to winning the confidence of the patient in question. He'd known alcoholics intimately, too. In the unsettled days after 9/11, when the conversations of stunned New Yorkers kept veering toward flight, my first trip out of the city was to meet my father and Margaret at the office of the new doctor. The diagnosis, we learned that day, was cirrhosis. The damage done to my father's liver couldn't be reversed. Continuing to drink would kill him. The doctor declined to venture a guess as to how soon. But a liver specialist, to whom he referred my father, didn't hold back. Two to four years.

The internist put him on an antidepressant to raise the level of serotonin in his brain, and a second drug to reverse the buildup of fluid in his abdomen, a complication of cirrhosis. There was talk of his seeing a psychiatrist, returning to AA, going into rehab, this time at a different sort of place, like the Betty Ford Center in California. But the patient stalled. To me, he said he was thinking. To Margaret, he said there was no way he was going. A routine colonoscopy, requiring the removal of a few polyps, landed him in the emergency room with uncontrolled bleeding, another complication of cirrhosis. On a trip to

Paris, he fell, gashing his head, and was hospitalized with bleeding from his liver. He began falling regularly—a problem attributed in part to shrinking muscle mass because of disease. He stopped drinking at breakfast. He had other problems, too—arthritis, spinal stenosis, a pinched nerve—unrelated to his illness. Then came vertebral compression fractures, from a fall, leaving him in a corset and on painkillers for weeks. He began using a walker. Fluid built up in his abdominal cavity, causing an umbilical hernia. He was back in the hospital. This time, doctors siphoned off eight to ten quarts of fluid.

I wonder now whether I honestly imagined he could be persuaded to stop. He seemed barely willing to acknowledge his diagnosis: He talked of his symptoms as though they were mysterious, unrelated to any underlying cause. In the hospital in Philadelphia, he had bottles of wine delivered to him in a padded cooler. The hospital in Paris thoughtfully served wine with meals. At home, bottles piled up in the recycling. On visits to the doctor, the patient sometimes showed up loaded. I asked for the advice of his cousin, the recovering alcoholic working as an alcohol and drug abuse counselor. "It's a low-grade suicide," he said. The most effective way of maneuvering a recalcitrant alcoholic into treatment, he told me, was to do something I couldn't imagine: tell him that if he didn't go, he'd never see his grandchildren again.

I call my father to check in. He tells me he's decided against "going to California"—a euphemism, apparently, for what I'd have called going back into treatment. He's feeling cornered by the pressure, he says. It's a nasty feeling: It leaves him unwilling to "run into the cage that's been prepared in the corner." In a couple of weeks, he'll be seventy-three. "Is that really what I want to do?" he asks. The question, evidently rhetorical, goes unanswered but silently answered. He's been thinking about how to explain all this—"why not to do it just now—or why not to do it at all"—to me and Hopie and Elliot and the doctor. It's especially difficult, he says, to make me understand why he enjoys drinking. In case I'm too obtuse to get his point, he likens the challenge to, say, my "trying to explain about fucking" to my six-year-old son.

"It doesn't mean that I'm intent on drowning," he says, by way of fatherly reassurance.

Doesn't it? I ask.

"I said, 'It doesn't mean that I'm *intent* on drowning.' That doesn't mean that I won't drown."

Eventually, I gave up playing lifeguard. The swimmer showed no interest in staying close to shore. My campaign seemed to be having the opposite of the desired effect: My quixotic incursions only annoyed my father. What's more, I'd begun to question my motives. Was I driven more by anger than kindness? Maybe I wanted to prove to him that I'd been right. Or maybe I couldn't accept that I wasn't, after all, an irresistible argument for going on living. A year or two before his death, we talked about his drinking for the last time. We were sitting in a pair of slipcovered armchairs in the sitting room of his apartment—like President Nixon and Mao Tse-tung. Except that I'd been sobbing, probably more in rage than sorrow. There was a table between us, scattered with books and newspapers. We were barely looking at each other. Appearing unmoved, he restated his position: He no longer had things he needed to get done; he had the right to decide how he wanted to live. He loved us all but he had no intention of giving up drinking. He was asking—he said this with a jocular air—that I fuck off.

It seemed the wiser course.

Meanwhile, the question of the long-term fate of the house and the land hung over his generation. The trusts that held the property would expire in the decades to come. If he and his brother and four Montgomery cousins couldn't come up with a plan for the disposition of the land and buildings, how would the next generation, with seventeen members, decide anything when the problem landed in its lap? In the late nineties, the older generation and the trustees had agreed twice to go ahead and sell some buildings and land for low-density development. A man who'd made a fortune in supply-chain software was now living in the Colonel's onetime stable. A Big Pharma heir and his family were in my grandparents' house. Rolling fields were studded with self-consciously tasteful McMansions, each with its own swimming pool and four-car garage. It wasn't easy to love what the place was becoming, though there was no denying it could have been much worse. And there were three hundred thirty more acres awaiting a decision. So when two local women put up a notice in the last independent bookstore in the area, proposing a conservancy to save open land, Bob Scott was the first to call.

He was no longer walking by the time the fledgling conservancy and two other land organizations held a four-day workshop at the big house in the spring of 2005. The objective was to come up with ideas for preserving what remained of Ardrossan. Traditional approaches were out: The land couldn't simply be donated to some nonprofit because the trustees were required, under the original terms of the trusts, to get something like fair market value. So the three organizations invited nine experts in land conservation and historic preservation to come for a visit and throw out some ideas. They arrived from as far away as London; toured the house and the farm; immersed themselves in local history, regional demographics, the economy; and sat in on panel discussions on possible cultural, agricultural, and public uses. By early June, they'd come up with a proposal. The family could form a nonprofit to serve as steward of the land and the buildings in future. The big house could be used by a research institution or become a "premium entertainment venue." The farm could be converted to community-supported agriculture. The township could buy some of the land for open space. Easements would protect much of the rest of the land. And a corner of the property could be sold, if necessary to provide the required financial return, for residential development.

It was a possible starting point, nothing more than that. It was going to take time, commitment, and money in amounts that family members may or may not have felt they had. They'd need a business consultant, a master plan, a strategic plan, a land-use plan, a house-conservation plan, an operating budget. But it wasn't impossible, the conservancies believed. How the various family members felt about the exercise was less clear. Some seemed curious. But another round of land sales with limited development—big houses, big lots—would be simpler and would generate more cash. My father, I'm told, was elated. The outsiders who took part were touched by his passion for the place. He was delighted to be showing it off to people who appreciated it in all its facets—as landscape, as architecture, as open space, as an opportunity for historic preservation. Because many of the visiting experts ran other historic properties, they knew what was possible; others, who didn't, could glimpse the potential through the experts' eyes. I don't know whether my father believed Ardrossan would be saved. But he seems to have intended to give it a shot. If he couldn't finish the job, someone else might.

I saw little of him that summer. In the years since the divorce, my parents had both continued to use the house on Nantucket. My mother would be there in July, my father in August. I'd straddle the transition, spending time with each. My children took it as unremarkable that their grandfather drank orange juice and champagne in bed first thing in the morning. Later, they'd be at his elbow in the kitchen while he concocted a dessert he'd discovered in England, made from stewed berries and slabs of bread. But after his diagnosis, his attachment to the island had seemed to wane. The house wasn't easy to get around; nearly every inside doorway involved an unexpected step up or down for no apparent reason. The place hadn't changed in the thirty-five years since my mother had bought it. Nor had the expanse of beach grass and poison ivy on which it sat—except that the value of the land, being waterfront property, was on an upward trajectory toward Pluto. Which may have had something to do with why my father proposed to my mother that they sell it—the half that still belonged to her, and the half she'd given him for a dollar. She wasn't interested, so it never happened. But, on the advice of her lawyer, she made sure her half of the house would be out of her estate when she died. My father, the former estates lawyer, did nothing. As his condition worsened, the most valuable asset in his possession had undergone a thirtyfold capital gain.

That last summer, he and Margaret relocated for several months to Vermont. She had a farmhouse on the side of a hill with a view across half of New Hampshire. They passed the weeks reading and moving between the terrace and a first-floor bedroom they'd added for when he'd no longer be able to climb stairs. At midsummer, I stopped by for lunch. My father sat at the kitchen table, his face looking ravaged, as though badly burned. Dark red blotches stained his cheeks. His eyes were watery. He was unmistakably in pain, though he never said so. It occurred to me that he'd acquired an alternate family in those final years. Margaret had become his de facto wife. Tommy Dowlin, his property manager, was a surrogate son; the two of them would sometimes have lunch together at my father's club in Philadelphia. When Margaret was out of town, Tommy would cook lamb chops in the nursery kitchen while his wife sat with my father. Then the three of them would sit down at the dining-room table to eat.

"It sometimes struck me that you and Margaret had become his family," I said to Tommy, years later.

"I think that probably is accurate," he said.

He and I had never talked much about his experiences with my father until that day, seven years after my father's death. Tommy had gone on to become the property manager for the family who owned the building that had been the Colonel's stables. We were sitting in the renovated clock tower; outside, gravel paths crisscrossed a broad green lawn. Tommy seemed to make no judgment about my father's precipitous decline—something perhaps I should have been better able to do.

He'd respected my father. He'd appreciated having the job and an employer who cared about him. "The more I got to know him, the more I liked him," he told me. "I would have liked to have seen him live a lot longer. I think he still had a lot to give and a lot to do and I just think it was unfortunate."

"Did you understand what was wrong?" I asked.

He hesitated.

"I think he had a drinking problem," he said simply.

Yes, I agreed. "He drank himself to death."

"I know," Tommy said. "I just didn't want to say that."

The end came on schedule, just like the liver specialist had predicted. By early autumn, my father was in the hospital in Pennsylvania. In a manila folder labeled "RMS Health," in a file drawer in my desk, I find pages torn from reporter's notebooks, covered in notes scribbled during phone calls with various doctors in those final weeks.

"If bowel looks viable, will put back in abdomen and sew up."

"Lung in bad shape. If not do anything, toxic fluid will kill him."

"What can do is operate on liver. Might take care of things. But 2 risks.

"1—operation kill.

"2—might → dementia.

"Should they operate or send home to die?"

I was at my desk in New York when word reached me that his doctors were out of options. By the time Hopie and Elliot and I arrived in Pennsylvania, our father was in intensive care. We sat in his curtained enclosure as people dropped in to say good-bye—his brother, Ed; the housekeeper's family; the museum director. She'd brought her husband, the curator, and a poster-size image of a painting of a woman, which the museum had just acquired. With humorous fanfare, she unfurled the poster, like a hawker displaying a pinup. My father tried to grin, chuckling weakly. Then, in an expression of love and forgiveness I wish I'd been able to match, she and her husband leaned across the bedrail, before the flashing green blips on the monitors, and softly told their old friend how much they were going to miss him.

The unwinding, I learned later, had taken him by surprise. A decade after his death, Margaret and I were in my apartment in New York. I was asking her questions that can only have made her unhappy. She seemed to be doing her best to answer.

Did you understand he was killing himself? I'd asked.

"In the hospital, when the doctor said he was dying, I didn't believe it," she said. "I didn't realize it was going to be so soon. . . . When the doctor said, 'He's dying,' I said, 'I had no idea.'"

And my father?

"Honestly, I don't think he knew," she said. Because, she said, after the doctor had broken the news, my father had turned to her and asked sadly, "How did this happen?"

The day after his death, I emailed the internist to tell him. My father had eluded him, I'd learned, in the last year or two of his life. Perhaps the patient preferred the specialists: They concerned themselves with his complications, not his underlying disease. Whatever the reason, I felt badly about my father's circumventions. The internist had gone to superhuman lengths. "We may not crack this nut," he once let me know, kindly. He must have intuited that from the start, but he hadn't given up. So I sent him an email telling him that DOD was dead. That's the name, Dear Old Dad, the internist had sometimes used. I thanked him for everything he'd done, and said I was sorry about how unsatisfactorily it had ended between them.

His answer came back a day later.

Sic transit gloria mundi, he'd typed in the subject field.

"I loved him too," the internist wrote. "And he knew it. We had a truce. It's all OK."

Epilogue

The Duke of Villanova would have been touched by the send-off. The women in his life could be spotted in pews near the front of the church. There was an impressive display of High Church pomp, a moment of silence, and a melancholy bagpipe response. In an affectionate eulogy, the museum director called her sometime antagonist "that inimitable man . . . utterly and unabashedly himself." Another eulogizer plucked a parallel from ancient Greece: Athens had Pericles, Philadelphia had Bobby. The headline on his obituary in the *Inquirer* summoned the spirit of the one woman in his life who couldn't be there, with the words, "Philadelphia Story in His Own Right." The obituary described him as one of the last true Main Line aristocrats, a civic éminence grise, "widely adored as a singularly stylish blend of wealth and brains, polish and strong opinions, pedigree and easy amity." Had His Eminence somehow managed to stick around for the tributes, a copy of that day's paper might have turned up in my mailbox, bearing a yellow Post-it: "This (page 1) was such an ego trip that I had to send it to you. Love, P."

The cause of death, I'd told the reporter when he'd asked, was "liver failure after a long illness." I knew that answer was a dodge when I served it up. Not that I was covering for my father; I wasn't in the mood. I was just trying to avoid a charge of gratuitous indiscretion. The death certificate, when it arrived later, identified the immediate cause as "end stage cirrhosis of the liver." It listed several secondary conditions, all of them complications of cirrhosis. If you were to ask me now, I'd say my father drank himself to death. But that leaves a lot unsaid. I've come to think of his disease as something more complex, shaped by the whims of economic and social history, along with the strands of the double helix. He was the beneficiary of abundant good fortune, that's a fact. But good fortune doesn't necessarily drop from the heavens unencumbered. Like the rest of us, he had his wounds. He was that hare, resolving to "practice each day going forth to live."

Recently, I found myself reading another play by Philip Barry. Like *The Philadelphia Story*, it had been made into a movie starring Katharine Hepburn and Cary Grant. The play, *Holiday*, had some details that sounded familiar, as had *The Philadelphia Story*. In *Holiday*, a bright young man named Johnny Case falls in love with the aristocratic eldest daughter of a financier. Precipitously, they decide to marry. But when Johnny wants to quit his job so they can travel abroad for a year or more, his future father-in-law tries to derail the plan with an offer of a job in finance. The play opened on Broadway in 1928, a year after my father's parents cut short their trip around the world after the Colonel offered to make my grandfather his partner in a new brokerage firm. Unlike my grandfather, however, Johnny Case turns down the job, blows up the engagement, and sets sail for Europe. The message of the play, Brendan Gill writes, is "that wealth and convention suffocate the soul" and "a man must take radical chances in order to find out who he's capable of becoming." As Johnny Case puts it, "Damn it, there's no life any good but the one you make for yourself."

The descendants of the Colonel are scattered now. They're in Los Angeles, Denver, London, Paris, and points between. They work in education, medicine, technology, consulting, music, banking, business, finance, landscape gardening, the law. They don't live in big houses. They work for a living. But they're beneficiaries, in one way or another, now and forever, for better and worse. These days, just one of the four surviving members of my father's generation lives on what was once the Colonel's place. Only one of the seventeen in my generation lives there. My grandparents, of the wondrous seventy-two-year marriage, didn't live to see all five of their grandchildren divorced. As I write this, my mother remains in the house where I grew up, which she bought in one of the early sales. At eighty-eight, she still climbs those two flights daily to the studio where she teaches and practices piano. As for the cows, last seen heading west to their new home in the foothills of the Front Range, things didn't work out quite as hoped. Unable to scale up his dairy, the orthopedic surgeon sold the young cows at a sale attended by dozens of buyers, then sold the milking cows to a farmer elsewhere in Colorado. Some of those were bred with Holstein and Jersey bulls; others, no longer considered productive, were auctioned off for slaughter. When I checked in 2014, the surgeon told me he'd heard there were no more than a handful of pure Ardrossan Ayrshires left.

The children and grandchildren of the men and women who worked on Ardrossan are scattered, too. In a single generation, those immigrant families entered the middle class, the children leaping from the farm labor and domestic service of their parents to professions like veterinary medicine, business, and finance. Molly Roddy, who left Ireland in 1928 and went to work as an upstairs maid in the big house, had grown up as the eldest daughter of cattle farmers in Roscommon. She was eighteen when she traveled alone to the United States to establish a foothold for her half dozen sisters being raised back home by their widowed mother. On a trip home, she married a prizefighter and barber named Terry Casey, who returned with her to Villanova and went to work on the farm. They raised their two children in a white house on the periphery of the place, where they and other Ardrossan children raced go-karts on Sunday afternoons on the empty road and floated in inner tubes down Darby Creek. Molly worked in the houses; Terry worked with the cows. Their children went off to college and into careers in defense contracting and teaching. The children's children, in turn, have gone from college to graduate school or jobs in environmental contracting, finance, public relations.

The relics of the Gilded Age are on the endangered list now. The colossal house built for Edgar T. Scott in Lansdowne is subsiding into ruin: After years as an orphanage and as a nursing home, it sits abandoned, ringed by barbed wire and chain-link fence. In Whitemarsh, the hundred-forty-seven-room palace built as a wedding gift for the second wife of another investment banker is history: Twenty-eight bathrooms couldn't save it from demolition. The iron and steel man with the Elizabethan manor in Lower Merion had it razed after an incinerator smokestack intruded upon his view. It lasted less than fifty years. There are freshman dorms in the castle in Glenside that Horace Trumbauer built for the sugar-refining magnate; and the former home of a Baldwin Locomotive Works president is now part of a retirement community that boasts nine dining rooms. As for the house still known as Ardrossan, its future is up in the air. Because of its full-body makeover during my father's tenure, it's in good shape for its age. But entropy has set in again.

There's no nonprofit acting as steward, as the delegates to the "visioning workshop" had envisioned. There's no community-supported agriculture farmer dispensing rutabagas from the back of a truck. There's no master plan, no strategic plan, no land-use plan: Those ideas expired with DOD. Instead, the final few hundred acres have been sold for "limited development"—more large houses on large lots. The old stone houses are being tidied up for market. The cold pool in the woods is derelict, its contents as black as the oil in the La Brea Tar Pits, from decaying branches and leaves. One proposal discussed at the workshop, and for years before, has come to fruition: The township bought the fields on either side of the intersection where the traffic paused on that now distant memorial-service afternoon. Those fields will be preserved as open space. Someday, the sole intact vestige of the Colonel's demesne will be those rolling meadows and an adjacent ninety acres, known as Skunk Hollow, which the township had bought from my father's grandmother forty years before.

Philadelphia is no longer the roaring industrial furnace it was in the years when the Pennsylvania Railroad set its sights on developing the farmland along its main line. Its suburban zip codes, however, remain some of the richest in the country. In some towns, average home values are closing in on one million dollars. Main Line denizens crop up regularly on the *Forbes* list of the four hundred wealthiest Americans. And while the white population in Philadelphia shrank by a third between the censuses of 1990 and 2010, the towns along the Main Line, though less monochrome than they once were, remain overwhelmingly Caucasian.

Somewhere in the world, a new "place" is being born. Maybe it's in the Bay Area or Mumbai or Shenzhen or Hangzhou. Maybe it's fueled by a fortune reaped in private equity or online shopping or social media or a quantitative hedge fund. The titans of the new gilded age, like their predecessors, wish to be known for their superior taste. They, too, recruit the go-to architects-to-the-plutocracy to design their homes. They adorn their houses with Abstract Expressionist paintings, cruise the high seas in custom-built yachts, own homes in Wellington, Florida, to watch their horsey daughters compete. Their net worth dwarfs anything the Colonel could have imagined. Surely even he never envisioned the twenty-seven-story house built by India's richest man. But the rules of the consumption game appear to be not all that different. The signifiers of arrival are remarkably unchanged.

Biggest remains best. There's a sixty-two-thousand-square-foot beach house in the Hamptons built by a junk bond billionaire. There's a Manhattan penthouse that sold for one hundred million to an anonymous buyer. Any self-respecting tech billionaire needs a yacht, it seems, ideally measuring somewhere north of three hundred feet in length. Things British remain enviable, one hundred years later. Today's titans hunger for the best English country garden outside

England. Wealthy Chinese want butlers schooled in England who wear white gloves and speak with the diction of Jeremy Irons.

Killing animals for sport has not lost its cachet. Nor have private aircraft: How else to get to Jackson Hole? Vacation homes, birthday blowouts—it all continues. Though today's rich want their rural and subterranean retreats to be doomsday-proof.

They are, after all, planning for the future, just as the Colonel did. They're stashing their money in irrevocable and generation-skipping trusts. They're transferring land and houses to their children and grandchildren.

Do they ever wonder how it will play out, one hundred years hence?

My father left his affairs mostly in order, as I would have expected. With one not-insignificant exception: He still owned his half of the Nantucket house when he died. Maybe the former trusts and estates lawyer had good reasons for ignoring the advice of his trusts and estates lawyer. But he omitted to give a heads-up to his executors, his children. The value of the Nantucket house had multiplied so many times over, in the years since my mother had bought it, that the half my father took from her for one dollar was the most valuable item in his estate. Because he'd spent so much of his money on the big-house restoration, he left just one simple way to pay the estate tax owed on the Nantucket property: sell it. But his co-owner loved the house. She was the only one of us who used it for a month every summer. She kept a small piano in the dining room that dangled off the west-facing side. On windless afternoons, a grandchild climbing the wooden stairs from the beach would hear Schubert's Impromptus wafting across the field of poison ivy. I've sometimes wondered why our father put us in that awkward position. Maybe he was no longer thinking clearly. Maybe he'd never intended to shell out so much in those last years. Whatever his reasons, the three of us spent the next five years jousting with the Internal Revenue Service, while the lawyer who'd let him do it logged billable hours. In the end, we and the government reached a settlement on the value of the property, making it possible for us to pay the estate tax without having to throw our mother out of her house.

There were few objects among my father's possessions that I felt driven to keep; the spirit seemed to me to have been drained from them by his death. I took the black leather wallet, its edges softened, in his pockets, like a bar of soap; and I took the umbrella he'd carried thirty-five years earlier in London, which turned up in the back of a coat closet in his apartment. It had a black silk canopy and a dark, polished, wooden crook handle with a gold-plated band engraved with his name. It had been handmade by a British company with a two-hundred-fifty-year history in umbrellas. But when I opened it in the rain on Broadway a few months later, it exploded into pieces. I couldn't bring myself to throw the carcass into the nearest trash bin. In response to an email query, the umbrella company said, yes, they could fix it. Off it went in my beloved's luggage to England, returning by mail some months later. Every part but the handle and name band had been replaced: canopy, ribs, rib tips, runner, stretchers, ferrule, et cetera. When I discovered that the company wanted nine hundred dollars for the repairs and shipping, the restoration impulse seemed idiotic. Then again, such extravagance applied to refurbishing a memory seemed in the spirit of the umbrella's original owner.

There was a photograph, too, that had enthralled me ever since I'd first seen it. It had been taken by a newspaper photographer, I think my father once said. Someone, maybe the photographer, had sent it to him later. He'd kept it, framed, on a bookshelf in his study. The photographer had been standing on the sidewalk outside the Academy of Music in Philadelphia. The brownstone and brick facade, with its original gas lanterns, was one of the most recognizable in the city. The photographer had pointed his or her camera down the sidewalk, leaving the Academy to the right. In the foreground, a disheveled man with matted hair is hunkered on the stoop. He's emptying a bottle, in a paper bag, down his gullet. His face turned from the camera, he's gazing down the block in the direction of an impeccably turned-out gentleman in a Savile Row suit, walking into the distance.

The photographer, I imagine, was taken with the juxtapositions. There's the Academy, "the grand old lady of Locust Street," symbol of old Philadelphia. There's the destitute man crouched on her doorstep. And there's the honorary consul, from a vanishing country, sailing toward the horizon.

Once, I couldn't tear my eyes from the drinking figure. He seemed to me a premonition, a sprite lurking in the corner of the artist's canvas. Now I study the man in the suit. I see the Colonel's torso, the way it thickened in midlife. I see my grandfather's long, slim legs. I see my father striding into the distance, exiting the frame.

Acknowledgments

I benefited from the generosity of several historians—John K. Brown of the University of Virginia; Susie J. Pak at St. John's University in New York City; Albert J. Churella at Kennesaw State; and Richard R. John Jr. at Columbia. Professor John also introduced me to the indefatigable Jeffrey Nichols, without whose research assistance I'd still know nothing about how the Colonel made his money. The landscape architect Patrick Chassé and the landscape historian Judith B. Tankard gave me insight into the garden at Chiltern. Caroline Rennolds Milbank, the fashion historian, enlightened me about Helen Hope's wardrobe. I'm grateful, too, for the assistance of Douglas V. D. Brown, the archivist at the Groton School; Nicole J. Milano at the Archives of the American Field Service and AFS Intercultural Programs; Frank Donahue and Michael Panzer at the *Philadelphia Inquirer*; the staff of the Urban Archives at Temple University; Richard Peuser at the National Archives in College Park, Maryland; Kevin Pratt at the National Personnel Records Center in St. Louis; and Donald R. Anderson of Marist College.

Julius E. White, the copyright holder for the estate of Augustus John, gave me permission to quote from John's sonnet to Helen Hope.

Among the many family members who patiently endured my questioning, I'm especially indebted to my father's brother, Ed Scott. Thanks, too, to their cousins Joanie Mackie, Bob Montgomery, Alix Estey, John L. Montgomery, Mike Kennedy, Maisie Adamson, Sandy

Kennedy, Rick Wheeler, and David Greenway; my siblings, Hope and Elliot Scott; my cousin Mary Remer; and several family members by marriage—Lindsay F. Scott, Gresh O'Malley, and Mollie McNickle Wheeler. My mother, Gay Scott, might not have minded if I'd settled on a different topic, I suspect, but she's much too wise to have ever let on. Instead, she allowed me to ransack her house for lost diaries and to rummage relentlessly through her enviable memory over many lunches at Whole Foods.

I'm grateful to Margaret Everitt for kindly answering every question I asked. Thanks, too, to Joe Rishel of the Philadelphia Museum of Art; Liddy Lindsay and Witney Schneidman; Nannette Robertson; Alan McFarland; Miranda Barry; Norman Wilde; Charles A. Hanson, MD; Lee G. Brockington; George King III; Paul Krautheim; Jean Miele; and Beverlee Barnes. Also to Cathie Moran for her astute reflections on her many years at Ardrossan; Maureen Gallagher, for the story of her parents, Molly and Terry Casey; and Tommy Dowlin, for his kindness to my grandparents and my father, and for everything he told me.

Andrew Wylie, my extraordinary literary agent, gave me superb advice. Sarah McGrath at Riverhead Books is the ideal editor— exacting and sympathetic. Catherine Talese did wonderful work finding and selecting photos. Steven Rattazzi kept my computer and me from the brink of crack-up. Amy Stursberg, Geraldine Baum, Dinitia Smith, John and Nina Darnton, Suzanne Spector, Allison Silver, Gay Scott, Hope Scott, Elliot Scott, and Michele Franck read drafts and gave me valuable comments.

But there's one person without whom this enterprise might well have foundered. Joe Lelyveld believed in the idea before I did and declined to be dissuaded. On sleepless nights when I whined about what could ever have possessed me, he gave no quarter. Unflappable, wise, funny, kind—Joe is the rarest gift of all.

Photograph Credits

Photographs are courtesy of the author's family unless otherwise noted.

Page 5: Ardrossan. © Jonathan Becker.

Page 14: Helen Hope Montgomery Scott. Horst P. Horst/*Vogue* © Condé Nast.

Page 35: Robert L. Montgomery.

Page 37: Charlotte Hope B. T. Montgomery.

Page 42: Early advertisement for Ardrossan Farms.

Page 50: Helen Hope Montgomery with Mary Binney and Aleck.

Page 62: Edgar T. Scott, Maisie Scott, young Edgar Scott, and Jeanne Cruchet at Chiltern.

Page 71: The Sagamore. Courtesy of H. D. S. Greenway.

Page 86: The two Edgars in France.

Page 91: Helen Hope and Edgar Scott boarding the *Ile de France*, 1938. Courtesy of the Special Collections Research Center, Temple University Libraries, Philadelphia, Pennsylvania.

Page 93: A desk at my grandparents' house. © Jonathan Becker.

Page 116: My father as a boy.

Page 133: The street at Mansfield. Courtesy of the Library of Congress Prints and Photographs Division, Washington, D.C.

Page 149: My father with beagles.

Page 151: My family with Odille Nadeau.

Page 180: My father outside the Philadelphia Museum of Art.

Page 213: My father as a young man.

Page 217: Partial page of journal.

Page 229: The house my father left behind. Photographed by Christopher Biddle.

Page 240: Robert Montgomery Scott. © Jonathan Becker.
Page 266: Outside the Academy of Music, Philadelphia.

Family Tree Photograph Credits

Thomas A. Scott. Courtesy of the Railroad Museum of Pennsylvania, PHMC.
Edgar T. Scott.
Robert L. Montgomery.
Charlotte Hope Binney Tyler Montgomery.
Edgar Scott. Courtesy of the Special Collections Research Center, Temple University Libraries, Philadelphia, Pennsylvania.
Helen Hope Montgomery Scott. Courtesy of the Special Collections Research Center, Temple University Libraries, Philadelphia, Pennsylvania.
Robert Montgomery Scott.
Gay Elliot Scott.

Notes

Page 13 **he found them interesting and therefore to be cultivated:** Brendan Gill, biographical essay in *States of Grace: Eight Plays by Philip Barry* (New York: Harcourt Brace Jovanovich, 1975), 4.

Page 36 **as though he belonged to another family:** Horace Binney Montgomery, *Return the Golden Years* (Philadelphia: Franklin, 1965).

Page 38 **expensively appointed old-world-style houses:** Michael C. Kathrens, *American Splendor: The Residential Architecture of Horace Trumbauer* (New York: Acanthus Press, 2002), 135.

Page 39 **featured in *Country Life*:** Kathrens, *American Splendor*, 183.

Page 39 **but of a quality unsurpassed:** "Palatial Home Distinctive for Lack of Ornamentation," *New York Times*, rotogravure section, January 11, 1914.

Page 42 **had its own dairy, too:** Lower Merion Historical Society, *The First 300: The Amazing and Rich History of Lower Merion* (Ardmore, PA: Lower Merion Historical Society, 2000), 258.

Page 47 **investment banking firms were underwriting new issues of industrial securities:** Thomas R. Navin and Marian V. Sears, "The Rise of a Market for Industrial Securities, 1887–1902," *Business History Review* 29, no. 2 (June 1955), 105–38.

Page 47 **The Baldwin Locomotive Works:** John K. Brown, *The Baldwin Locomotive Works, 1831–1915: A Study in American Industrial Practice* (Baltimore: Johns Hopkins University Press, 2001).

Page 48 **Baldwin's net profits:** Brown, *Baldwin Locomotive Works*.

Page 51 **Helen Hope would recall vividly eighty-some years later:** Doris Yocum Markley, "At Home Ardrossan," *Main Line Magazine*, February 1993, 17–20.

Page 52 **A liveried butler met them at the door:** Sarah Hayward Draper, *Once Upon the Main Line* (New York: Carlton Press, 1980).

Page 53 **In a book about the Bund, the waterfront quarter of Shanghai:** Peter Hibbard, *The Bund Shanghai: China Faces West* (Hong Kong: Odyssey, 2007).

Page 64 **the Pennsylvania Napoleon:** Albert J. Churella, *The Pennsylvania Railroad, Volume 1: Building an Empire, 1846–1917* (Philadelphia: University of Pennsylvania Press, 2013), 442.

Page 64 **the beginnings of the age of industrial and class warfare:** Churella, *Pennsylvania Railroad*, 480.

Page 65 **the quintessential railroad man:** Richard White, *Railroaded: The Transcontinentals and the Making of Modern America* (New York: W. W. Norton, 2011), 3.

Page 66 **the most profitable corporation in North America:** James A. Ward, "J. Edgar Thomson and Thomas A. Scott: A Symbiotic Partnership?" *Pennsylvania Magazine of History and Biography* 100, no.1 (January 1976), 37–65.

Page 66 **bending the Pennsylvania legislature to his will:** Churella, *Pennsylvania Railroad*, 210.

Page 66 **a single force so formidable:** William G. Roy, *Socializing Capital: The Rise of the Large Industrial Corporation in America* (Princeton, NJ: Princeton University Press, 1999), 89.

Page 67 **the greatest mass movement of troops by rail:** E. Digby Baltzell, *Philadelphia Gentlemen: The Making of a National Upper Class* (New Brunswick, NJ: Transaction, 2004), 113.

Page 75 **a motorized dining-room table:** Cleveland Amory, *The Last Resorts: A Portrait of American Society at Play* (New York: Harper & Brothers, 1952), 287.

Page 76 **the first American woman to break into landscape architecture:** Judith B. Tankard, *Beatrix Farrand: Private Gardens, Public Landscapes* (New York: Monacelli Press, 2009), 10.

Page 77 **drifts of summer flowers in washes of color:** Tankard, *Beatrix Farrand*, 30.

Page 77 **work out a scheme of color, absolutely by instinct:** Beatrix Farrand, in Farrand Collection, Environmental Design Archives (notes circa 1913, Box 4 III:3), University of California, Berkeley.

Page 79 **Stretched on the rack of a too easy chair:** Alexander Pope, *The Dunciad*, Book IV, line 342.

Page 81 **a photograph of fourteen men:** Photograph by O. King of men in the garden of 21 Rue Reynouard, 1916; American Field Service World War I Photographic Collection; Archives of the American Field Service and AFS Intercultural Programs, New York, NY.

Page 81 **Would Groton raise money:** Letter from Endicott Peabody, April 7, 1916; American Field Service World War I Records; Archives of the American Field Service and AFS Intercultural Programs, New York, NY.

Page 81 **called the "upper-class gentry":** George Plimpton, foreword to Arlen J. Hansen's *Gentlemen Volunteers: The Story of the American Ambulance Drivers in the Great War, August 1914–September 1918* (New York: Arcade, 1996), v.

Page 91 **an antique metal chastity belt—a gift from a congenial friend:** H. G. Bissinger, "Letter from Philadelphia: Main Line Madcap," *Vanity Fair*, October 1995, 165.

Page 102 **I don't know if that's what I look like:** Michael Holroyd, *Augustus John: The New Biography* (London: Vintage, 1997), 464.

Page 102 **John wrote in a memoir:** Augustus John, *Chiaroscuro: Fragments of Autobiography* (New York: Pellegrini & Cudahy, 1952), 101–2.

Page 110 **partial to palaces and to the people who dwelt in them:** Gill, biographical essay in *States of Grace*.

Page 112 **Make her like me but make her go all soft:** William J. Mann, *Kate: The Woman Who Was Hepburn* (New York: Henry Holt, 2006).

Page 112 **Tracy Lord was not only designed for Hepburn:** Donald R. Anderson, *Shadowed Cocktails: The Plays of Philip Barry, from* Paris Bound *to* The Philadelphia Story (Carbondale, IL: Southern Illinois University Press, 2010), 115.

Page 115 **speaking to an oral historian, a stranger:** Joel Gardner, Interview with Robert Montgomery Scott. Villanova, PA, April 29, 2005.

Page 118 **But very decent, loving people:** Mike Mallowe, "The Prince of the Main Line," *Main Line Today*, March 1996, 30–34.

Page 121 **a couple hundred observational planes:** "213 Airplanes Cost Taxpayers Billion Dollars," *New-York Tribune*, October 21, 1920.

Page 121 **an inexcusable waste of men and money:** U.S. House. Select Committee on Expenditures in the War Department. *Rep. of Subcommittee No. 1, Aviation*. Washington, Government Printing Office, 1920, 3.

Page 143 **the fire was merely the *coup de grace*:** Amory, *Last Resorts*, 265.

Page 162 **whole party would have been a flop:** David O'Reilly, "To Life, Hope Scott Added a Dash of Glamour," *Philadelphia Inquirer*, January 15, 1995.

Select Bibliography

Amory, Cleveland. *The Last Resorts: A Portrait of American Society at Play*. New York: Harper & Brothers, 1952.

Anderson, Donald R. *Shadowed Cocktails: The Plays of Philip Barry, from* Paris Bound *to* The Philadelphia Story. Carbondale, IL: Southern Illinois University Press, 2010.

Andrew, A. Piatt. Introduction to *History of the American Field Service in France, Vol. 1*, by James William Davenport Seymour. New York: Houghton Mifflin, 1920.

Baltzell, E. Digby. *Philadelphia Gentlemen: The Making of a National Upper Class*. New Brunswick, NJ: Transaction, 2004.

Barry, Philip. Papers. Yale University Library, Beineke Rare Book and Manuscript Library, Yale Collection of American Literature, New Haven, CT.

Bissinger, H. G. "Letter from Philadelphia: Main Line Madcap." *Vanity Fair*, October 1995: 158–82.

Brown, John K. *The Baldwin Locomotive Works, 1831–1915: A Study in American Industrial Practice*. Baltimore: Johns Hopkins University Press, 2001.

Bruccoli, Matthew J. *The O'Hara Concern: A Biography of John O'Hara*. Pittsburgh: University of Pittsburgh Press, 1975.

Burgess, George H., and Miles C. Kennedy. *Centennial History of the Pennsylvania Railroad Company, 1846–1946*. Philadelphia: Pennsylvania Railroad Co., 1949.

Burke, Bobbye, Otto Sperr, Hugh J. McCauley, and Trina Vaux. *Historic Rittenhouse: A Philadelphia Neighborhood*. Philadelphia: University of Pennsylvania Press, 1985.

Chassé, Patrick. "Beatrix Jones: Design-Build in Maine." PowerPoint presentation, 2013.

Churella, Albert J. *The Pennsylvania Railroad, Volume 1: Building an Empire, 1846–1917*. Philadelphia: University of Pennsylvania Press, 2013.

Draper, Sarah Hayward. *Once Upon the Main Line*. New York: Carlton Press, 1980.

Farrand, Beatrix. Notes on garden for Edgar T. Scott. Farrand Collection, Environmental Design Archives, Box 4 III:3, University of California, Berkeley.

Floyd, Margaret Henderson. *Architecture after Richardson: Regionalism before Modernism—Longfellow, Alden and Harlow in Boston and Pittsburgh*. Chicago: University of Chicago Press, 1994.

Gardner, Joel. Interview with Robert Montgomery Scott. Villanova, PA, April 29, 2005.

Gill, Brendan. Biographical essay in *States of Grace: Eight Plays by Philip Barry*. New York: Harcourt Brace Jovanovich, 1975.

Hansen, Arlen J. *Gentlemen Volunteers: The Story of the American Ambulance Drivers in the Great War, August 1914–September 1918*. New York: Arcade, 1996.

Heinzen, Nancy M. *The Perfect Square: A History of Rittenhouse Square*. Philadelphia: Temple University Press, 2009.

Helfrich, G. W., and Gladys O'Neil. *Lost Bar Harbor*. Camden, ME: Down East Books, 1982.

Hibbard, Peter. *The Bund Shanghai: China Faces West*. Hong Kong: Odyssey Books, 2007.

Holroyd, Michael. *Augustus John: The New Biography*. London: Vintage, 1997.

Jansen, Axel. *The Incorporation of Sacrifice: The American Ambulance Field Service and the American Volunteer Motor Ambulance Corps, 1914–17*. Thesis. University of Oregon, 1995.

John, Augustus. *Chiaroscuro: Fragments of Autobiography*. New York: Pellegrini & Cudahy, 1952.

Kamm, Samuel Richey. *The Civil War Career of Thomas A. Scott*. Unpublished dissertation. University of Pennsylvania, 1940.

Kathrens, Michael C. *American Splendor: The Residential Architecture of Horace Trumbauer*. New York: Acanthus Press, 2002.

Kennedy, Moorhead. "Please Roll Over, Mrs. Potter, or Six Generations on Mount Desert Island." *Mount Desert Islander*, January 17, 2002.

Lachicotte, Alberta Morel. *Georgetown Rice Plantations.* Columbia, SC: State Commercial, 1955.

Leaming, Barbara. *Katharine Hepburn.* New York: Crown, 1995.

Lower Merion Historical Society. *The First 300: The Amazing and Rich History of Lower Merion.* Ardmore, PA: Lower Merion Historical Society, 2000.

Mallowe, Mike. "The Prince of the Main Line." *Main Line Today,* March 1996: 30–34.

Mann, William J. *Kate: The Woman Who Was Hepburn.* New York: Henry Holt, 2006.

Montgomery, Horace Binney. *How Dear to My Heart.* Philadelphia: Franklin, 1975.

———. *Return the Golden Years.* Philadelphia: Franklin, 1965.

Morse, Edwin W. *The Vanguard of American Volunteers in the Fighting Lines and in Humanitarian Service, August, 1914–April, 1917.* New York: Charles Scribner's Sons, 1919.

Nanda, Ashish, Thomas Delong, and Lynn Villadolid Roy. "History of Investment Banking." Harvard Business School Background Note, 902–168, 2002.

Navin, Thomas R., and Marian V. Sears. "The Rise of a Market for Industrial Securities, 1887–1902." *Business History Review* 29, no. 2 (June 1955): 105–38.

Pak, Susie J. *Gentlemen Bankers: The World of J. P. Morgan.* Cambridge, MA: Harvard University Press, 2013.

Reeve, J. Stanley. *Radnor Reminiscences: A Foxhunting Journal.* New York: Houghton Mifflin, 1921.

Roppolo, Joseph Patrick. *Philip Barry.* New York: Twayne, 1965.

Roy, William G. *Socializing Capital: The Rise of the Large Industrial Corporation in America.* Princeton, NJ: Princeton University Press, 1997.

Tankard, Judith B. *Beatrix Farrand: Private Gardens, Public Landscapes.* New York: Monacelli Press, 2009.

Toner, James E. "Thomas Alexander Scott Residence, 1830–34 Rittenhouse Square, Philadelphia, PA." Unpublished paper. Historic Preservation Program, University of Pennsylvania, 1993. On file at the Athenaeum of Philadelphia.

Trumbauer, Horace. Account books, volumes C, D, E, and F. On file at the Athenaeum of Philadelphia.

Vincent, Brooke E. "Thomas Alexander Scott Residence 1832–34 South Rittenhouse Square." Unpublished paper. Historic Preservation Program, University of Pennsylvania, 1989. On file at the Athenaeum of Philadelphia.

Ward, James A. "J. Edgar Thomson and Thomas A. Scott: A Symbiotic Partnership?" *Pennsylvania Magazine of History and Biography* 100, no. 1 (January 1976), 37–65.

White, Richard. *Railroaded: The Transcontinentals and the Making of Modern America.* New York: W. W. Norton, 2011.

Archival Resources

American Field Service World War I Records and Photographic Collection; American Field Service and AFS Intercultural Programs, New York, NY.